A
Ministry Resources Library
Book

RAY S. ANDERSON

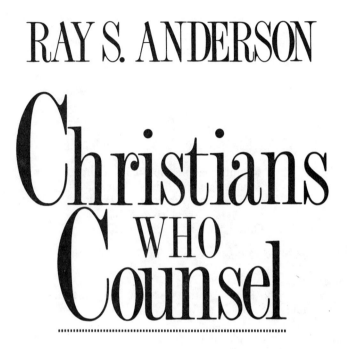

Christians
WHO
Counsel

*The
Vocation
of Wholistic
Therapy*

Zondervan*PublishingHouse*
Academic andProfessionalBooks
Grand Rapids, Michigan

A Division of HarperCollins*Publishers*

Christians Who Counsel
Copyright © 1990 by Ray S. Anderson

Requests for information should be addressed to:
Zondervan Publishing House
Academic and Professional Books
1415 Lake Drive, S.E.
Grand Rapids, Michigan 49506

Library of Congress Cataloging in Publication Data

Anderson, Ray Sherman.
    Christians who counsel : the vocation of wholistic therapy /
Ray S. Anderson.
        p.   cm.
    Includes bibliographical references.
    ISBN 0-310-52231-5
    1. Pastoral counseling. 2. Peer counseling in the church.
3. Psychotherapy—Religious aspects—Christianity. 4. Christianity—
Psychology. I. Title.
BV4012.2.A63   1990   90-42532
253.5—dc20   CIP

Edited by Lori Walburg

Printed in the United States of America

90 91 92 93 94 95 / AK / 10 9 8 7 6 5 4 3 2 1

Contents

Introduction   7

PART ONE: FOUNDATIONS FOR CHRISTIAN COUNSELING

1. *Integrative Counseling*   13
2. *Counseling the Whole Person*   30
3. *The Counselor as Growth Promoter*   56

PART TWO: SPIRITUAL DYNAMICS IN COUNSELING

4. *The Kingdom of God as Therapeutic Context*   81
5. *The Grace of God as Therapeutic Intervention*   103
6. *The Word of God as Empowerment for Change*   121
7. *The Healing Praxis of Prayer*   136

PART THREE: COUNSELING IN A CHRISTIAN MODE

8. *Counseling as a Christian Calling*   157
9. *Counseling as Christian Ministry*   176
10. *Counseling as a Professional Practice*   195
11. *The Counselor as Moral Advocate*   214
12. *Dynamics of Pastoral Care in Counseling Praxis*   232

Bibliography   248

Index   254

Introduction

Learning comes by listening, while listening is a skill acquired through acknowledged ignorance. For twelve years I have listened to and learned from students enrolled in doctoral programs in clinical psychology at a theological seminary. As a theologian with no formal training in psychology, but with eleven years experience in pastoral counseling, I am keenly interested in the role of the counselor and/or therapist from the perspective of Christian theology and ministry.

Unlike many who write in this field, I will not attempt to integrate of psychology and theology, though I am deeply interested in such integrative approaches. I write primarily as a theologian and offer this work as a contribution toward a theological approach to wholistic therapy. My approach is from the perspective of the person who is growing toward a meaningful and effective life with the self, others, and God.

Although my approach leaves me open to criticism from both psychologists and pastors, I nonetheless advance a basic thesis in this work. An effective therapeutic intervention is one in which the client's motive power to grow is facilitated by the counselor's perceived presence as a partner in the growth process. This thesis is stated and developed in chapter 3. The fundamental assumption underlying this thesis is that a theological anthropology, or concept of the person, is the key to a theological basis for integrative work as a Christian counselor and therapist. My focus is therefore on the role of the person who counsels, whether it be as a pastor, lay counselor, psychotherapist, or family therapist.

Next to the word *therapy* itself, perhaps the word *counseling* is the most ambiguous in this entire discussion. I like the definition of counseling provided by Roger Hurding in his marvelous book, *The Tree of Healing*. Counseling, says Hurding, is "that activity which aims to help others in any or all

7

aspects of their being within a caring relationship."[1] Those who counsel may be placed on a continuum with some form of pastoral care on one end and the most intensive level of psychotherapy at the other. Christians who counsel will be found at every point on this continuum. It is for them that this book is written.

Nothing makes theologians more suspicious than the threat of "psychologizing" the gospel. Many talk of the "psychological captivity" of pastoral care and even theological approaches to therapy. "The theologians sat at the feet of the psychiatric Gamaliels and seemed to like it," writes Paul Pruyser.[2] Eugene Peterson is more dramatic but no less critical when he writes concerning the effect of psychology on the parish minister: "Pastors have been herded into the temple shrines of psychiatry . . . and return to their parishes thoroughly convinced of their inferiority."[3]

As both a theologian and a parish minister, I believe that if there has been seduction by psychology, it was caused by the lack of a compelling theology. Note that most of the books written on the integration of theology and psychology have come from the psychologists and therapists who sense this need. Theologians have not been quick to respond, perhaps out of fear of being enchanted by the wicked witch *Psyche*. I hope in this book to calm the fears of pastors and theologians as well as propose a basis for theological integration to those trained in the behavioral sciences and therapy.[4]

The book is divided into three parts. Part 1 establishes a theory of counseling based on a model of personhood that is integrative and wholistic. Part 2 examines the spiritual dynamics in counseling, beginning with the nature of the kingdom of God as therapeutic context, followed by chapters on the grace of God, the Word of God, and prayer. Finally, part 3 explores the nature of counseling as a calling, a ministry, and a profession and concludes with two chapters on the moral advocacy of counseling and the dynamics of pastoral care in counseling praxis.

I offer this book more as a case statement for Christians who counsel than as a final word on the task of integrating theology and psychology. In testing these concepts, I have been encouraged by a great many students and counselors that this is, at least, a viable approach. I believe that it is a Christian approach. And I trust that, in its own way, this book will inspire those who have chosen to exercise their Christians calling by living within the circle of other people's pain and perplexity. They will find the Lord already there.

Notes

1. Roger Hurding, *The Tree of Healing: Psychological and Biblical Foundations for Counseling and Pastoral Care* (Grand Rapids: Zondervan, 1988), 26.

2. Paul Pruyser, *The Minister as Diagnostician* (Philadelphia: Westminster, 1976), 23.

3. Eugene Peterson, *Five Smooth Stones for Pastoral Work* (Atlanta: John Knox, 1980), 112–13.

4. From a growing list of books on integration, I mention just a few:

David G. Benner, ed., *Christian Counseling and Psychotherapy* (Grand Rapids: Baker, 1987); *Psychotherapy in Christian Perspective* (Grand Rapids: Baker, 1987); and *Psychotherapy and the Spiritual Quest* (Grand Rapids: Baker, 1988).

John D. Carter and Bruce Narramore, *The Integration of Psychology and Theology: An Introduction* (Grand Rapids: Zondervan, 1979).

Gary R. Collins, *The Rebuilding of Psychology: An Integration of Psychology and Christianity* (Wheaton, Ill.: Tyndale House, 1977); *Christian Counseling—A Comprehensive Guide* (Dallas: Word Books, 1988); and *Psychology and Theology: Prospects for Integration* (Nashville: Abingdon, 1981).

C. Stephen Evans, *Wisdom and Humanness in Psychology—Prospects for a Christian Approach* (Grand Rapids: Baker, 1989).

Kirk Farnsworth, *Wholehearted Integration: Harmonizing Psychology and Christianity Through Word and Deed* (Grand Rapids: Baker, 1985).

J. R. Fleck and John D. Carter, eds., *Psychology and Christianity: Integration Readings* (Nashville: Abingdon, 1981).

Stanton L. Jones, editor, *Psychology and the Christian Faith—An Introductory Reader* (Grand Rapids: Baker, 1986).

Ronald L. Koteskey, *Psychology from a Christian Perspective* (Nashville: Abingdon, 1980).

R. E. Larzelere, "The Task Ahead: Six Levels of Integration of Christianity and Psychology," *Journal of Psychology and Theology* 8 (1980): 3–11.

Ronald P. Philipchalk, *Psychology and Christianity: An Introduction to Controversial Issues* (Lanham, Md.: University Press of America, 1988).

Mary S. Van Leeuwen, *The Sorcerer's Apprentice: A Christian Look at the Changing Face of Psychology* (Downers Grove, Ill.: InterVarsity Press, 1982).

PART ONE

FOUNDATIONS FOR CHRISTIAN COUNSELING

1

Integrative Counseling

Dr. Johnson, I must say that you have helped me overcome my
compulsive behavior and ungodly temper in a way that I would
never have thought possible. I feel better about myself—I think
that I am a changed person! Even my husband says that I am so
much easier to live with. You have probably saved my marriage.
But tell me, doctor, I know that you are Christian and so am I. I
tried to change by reading the Bible and praying, but it never
worked. And one thing I noticed during our counseling times, you
never prayed with me or used the Bible to tell me how I should try
to be more like Christ. How is that you could help me when God
couldn't?

Sue Johnson, a successful Christian psychologist in private
practice, remembered this conversation with an uneasy conscience. It didn't help her to think back on the cheerful
platitude she left with her client: "Well, Martha, God works in
mysterious ways, his wonders to perform!" At the time, she only
wanted to cover herself and dodge the issue. Later she had to
ask herself a troublesome and nagging question: Could she in
good conscience leave out God and still be doing God's work in
helping people?

The Uneasy Conscience of the Christian Therapist

The uneasy conscience! What Christian psychologists—or, for
that matter, pastors as well—don't have a twinge of conscience
when they find that a little transactional analysis once a week

works better than a "month of Sundays" in curing the souls of troubled parishioners? How is it that psychology comforts some while prayer only seems to compound the pain? Why is it that for some, faith falters when most needed and being "born again" is more like "thirsting in a barren land" than having a "river of life flowing through me"?

Being a Christian as well as a psychologist, Sue Johnson feels assured of her salvation through Christ. She would say that her life was transformed through coming to know God as Savior and Lord of her life. She would insist that she believes in the efficacy of both prayer and the Bible for her own life of faith and growth as a Christian. And when pressed, she would say that she believes that the Bible and Christian faith are resources for emotional healing for others as well.

Being a trained and licensed psychologist as well as a Christian, Sue enjoys a life vocation that offers a high degree of fulfillment. She facilitates emotional healing, helps her clients restore shattered self-worth, and mends broken relationships. And she is good at it. Her clinical skills are professional and personal. She is especially helpful to those who come to her from the churches in the community, for they know of her Christian faith and seem to feel more secure spilling out their pain and confusion to one who shares their own ultimate spiritual values. But she also knows that the real reason why many come to her is that she is an *effective* counselor. She has helped people change from being ineffective and emotionally crippled persons into persons who can be reasonably happy again, who can leave the past behind and begin to live life in a fuller and richer way.

So why the uneasy conscience, Sue Johnson? Is it because, behind the mask of professional competence, you yourself have whispered your client's question, "How is it that I can help people when God cannot?" Or, given your penchant for clinical insight, is your question a more practical one, "Am I really helping people in their faith life, or do I only provide psychological healing so that they feel that they don't really need God?"

Suddenly the idea of Christian counseling can all fall apart. Being a Christian and a psychologist seems a natural blend. Both have the goal of helping persons. Both bring resources to bear upon the total life of the person. One can be good at both! But can one blend the two so as to encourage spiritual growth through therapeutic techniques? Or, to put it the other way around, can one facilitate emotional and mental health through spiritual exercises of prayer, Bible reading, and faith? Either way, the counselor may suffer an uneasy conscience!

Do some Christian psychologists, in an attempt to preserve the integrity of a therapeutic relation and methodology, leave "God talk" outside the clinical session and focus too narrowly on psychological dynamics and therapeutic goals, ignoring spiritual dynamics such as sin, forgiveness, grace, and prayer? Many counselors believe that such spiritual concepts and exercises should be left to pastoral care and not intrude into the therapeutic hour. Others may assimilate spiritual practices into the counseling relation in order to make their counseling Christian, but then feel uneasy for practicing beyond the bounds of their clinical training. The license to practice psychotherapy is ordinarily issued by the secular state, not the church. Moreover, the discipline of psychology tends to dislike theories and practices that include phenomena beyond direct observation and control.

For the Christian who counsels, God may be thought of as the great healer, especially in matters of the soul. Accordingly, one ought to suppose that God and his grace are sufficient without the aid of "secular" devices such as clinical psychology.

Pastor Ken Jones once thought that way, but is no longer so sure. While comparing notes with Sue Johnson, he confessed, "I have a similar problem, but from the other side. My professor of pastoral care warned me against the danger of 'psychologizing' the emotional problems of Christians who come to me for counseling. As a result, I offered biblical precepts and spiritual counsel, only to find that people who came to me for help began to feel guilty for not being able to manage their emotions more effectively. Since attending a seminar led by a Christian psychologist and reading some recent books that suggest more effective ways of helping troubled persons manage their emotions, I see people healed and helped more effectively. But I have an uneasy conscience about using all of this psychology!"

Do some pastors who counsel, anxious to relieve distress which their preaching and spiritual counsel fail to alleviate, turn too quickly to psychological means and so betray spiritual ends? Many are unsure and so exclude these means in order to do "biblical" or "spiritual" counseling. Others may assimilate psychological theories and methods into pastoral care with good results, but with uneasy consciences. They struggle with the nagging feeling that they have had to resort to secular means in order to produce therapeutic results.

What are counselors who wish to integrate psychology and Christian faith to do? Can feelings and faith be touched with the same therapeutic insight? Does a Christian counselor need two sets of lenses, one through which to view the sinful heart and another to peer into the sickness of the soul? Or is there, as some suggest, a Christian psychology that understands the mystery of the human psyche better than ordinary psychologists and facilitates personal spiritual growth more effectively than the average pastoral counselor? Where are we to look for answers?

Sue Johnson says that she is a Christian *and* a psychologist. She knows nothing of a "Christian psychology," yet she is sure that in facilitating emotional healing and growth she is helping people experience more fully and effectively what the Bible calls the "fruit of the Spirit." But she has an uneasy conscience. She would like to have a better sense of integration as she practices therapy as a fulfillment of her calling as a Christian. She would like to understand her role as a therapist as one providing integrated counseling. She desires more than anything to take off the "bifocal" lens when she looks into the faces of her clients. She wants to believe that her clients are whole persons by nature before they become fractured persons through patterns of pathology. She wants a model of personhood that integrates faith and psychology and that realizes the full potential of each person. She needs help.

Ken Jones feels responsible for the spiritual well-being of all who come under his pastoral care. He knows well the pervasive power of sin and believes strongly in the healing power of grace, the Word of God, and prayer. He also knows that Sue Johnson and many Christian psychologists like her provide effective therapeutic intervention and become catalysts for personal growth and wholeness for their patients beyond that which a pastor can do. But he is not happy with the dichotomy that he senses between the psychological and the spiritual. He wants to feel that those who seek God's grace can find relief from psychological pain and emotional trauma as well as assurance of divine forgiveness. He too needs a model of personhood that integrates the spiritual and the psychological, a model that respects the role of Christian therapists who also help persons to experience wholeness. He needs help.

And so this book is written for both Sue and Ken and for all Christians who counsel. We all need a better, more integrated vision of what it is to be human, of how to live more effectively in relationships, and above all, of what it is to be open to the spiritual resources of God's grace and love.

Integrative Competence

The core of this chapter can be stated as a thesis: *Before there can be competence in counseling, we must understand competence in being human, in living humanly, openly, and lovingly with others and with God.* This competence in being human involves more than "getting our own act together," to use a contemporary expression. The self, when alone, eventually aches with solitariness, even when God is present! Adam moved from solitariness to society when he cried out, "This at last is bone of my bones and flesh of my flesh" (Gen. 2:23). He could not say this of God or of the animals. In the differences of bone with bone and flesh with flesh lies the mystery of the human form.

This was the primal movement of integration. Adam and Eve recognized themselves as humans in this grace-filled and loving encounter. In their differences, each experienced a wholeness and unity of being. God was present, and they experienced him in the joy of their own unity of being. In this way the human self was integrated as personal, social, and spiritual being.

When disintegration occurred, these differences became divisions, sown in mistrust and unbelief. The self withdraws instinctively from God and from the other, though a pretense of relation with both is maintained, one in the form of religious or anti-religious armor, and the other in the form of social or anti-social sanity and safety. The way back to authentic humanity is through a personal encounter in which the grace of God is experienced as an integrative core, opening the emotional, social, and spiritual aspects of the self to new dimensions of life. This "rebirth" is itself a return to our core humanity and is essentially a therapeutic recovery of personhood as a personal, social, and spiritual "gestalt."

This "gestalt" may be defined as the total configuration or

pattern of a life. A person's gestalt emerges in the historical process by which a person forms his or her own life pattern in relation to the environment. This environment is social and spiritual as well as physical. I am using the term *gestalt* in the broadest sense, not in the technical sense as used by some psychological theorists.[1] It is to become, as it were, a "child" again and so placed upon the very threshold of the kingdom of God. This is one way of understanding the language of Jesus, who spoke of being born "from above" or "a second time" (John 3:3) and who also placed a child in the midst of his disciples saying, "unless you turn and become like children, you will never enter the kingdom of heaven" (Matt. 18:3). Here we have the beginning of a core paradigm for personhood as a model for integrated competence.

Humans instinctively reach out for a transcendent reality—a reality that they can experience and a reality that integrates the self. But those who receive the gift of faith, who are spiritually reborn and become children of God, must also come to terms with the reality of human existence. Those who claim the gift of faith but deny their humanity or fail to experience it fully cannot experience their human wholeness, despite fanatical excesses of spirituality. Human life demands integrative living. It requires integrative competence. Let us examine this more closely.

The integration of the self as a healthy human believer is a goal worthy of the deepest aspirations of the spirit. Integration requires change and growth as we learn to hear, respond to, and believe the divine Word, *wherever* it encounters us.

For us to develop into the image of God we must be persons in families, communities, and culture. Adam as the solitary human creature received the divine verdict "not good" (Gen. 2:18). This original "dysfunction" preceded any concept of sin or pathology. The first human did not have the competence to begin, much less complete, the task of being human. Only when Adam could relate to himself through the other, Eve, was he "good" and on his way to becoming a complete human being. The original dysfunction and despair of solitariness were healed by the fellow human, not by God alone!

The astonishing and astounding fact is this: Humanity is by its very nature therapeutic. Healing is grounded in humanity, not in the removal of pathology. To put it another way, being human requires openness to the other and permission for the other to touch the core of our being. Adam expressed it in amazingly concrete terms as "bone of my bones and flesh of my flesh." This "helping and healing" encounter integrates the self with itself as well as with the other as necessary to one's selfhood. All subsequent therapy, whether physical, psychical, social, or spiritual, is grounded in this core therapy of being human.

My concern in this chapter is to lay a foundation for the rest of the book. The focal point for integration is not the counselor, whether pastor or professional therapist, nor is it merely a concept or theory. The integration of our personal, social, and spiritual beings lies at the very core of personhood itself.

People are by nature integrative, for we are composite and not simple in nature. As persons we are "composed" in the sense of having a gestalt, or "structure," that includes but entails more than the mere assemblage of components. As an artist or a photographer might "compose" a painting or a picture, so persons are composite in the same dynamic and creative sense.

Being human is itself a creative tension that relates the self to its embodied state and the embodied self to others. The self must be integrative in order to be a human self. That is, the self must exist with and for others intentionally, openly, and therapeutically—for the good of the other. In addition, human persons are by nature integrative because growth forces the gestalt of the embodied self to be open to change as significant others, including God, impinge upon the self. Human selfhood must continually "recompose" itself through a process of change. This process is called growth.

Growth also is a fundamental therapeutic process in which therapy means growth rather than removal of pain or the overcoming of dysfunction. In this sense, "conversion" in a spiritual or theological sense is not only a one-time thing, but also an ongoing process of change and growth. We need the ongoing conversion process of development and growth because we are becoming integrative humans through our relationships with others and God. When something disrupts this process, it can be called sin, because it produces spiritual blockage as well as personal and social alienation.

All dysfunction or even disorder of personhood is disintegrative, destroying the fundamental competence of the human to function integratively. The integrative core of the person can thus be depicted as threefold:

1. There is integration as embodied soul, where the self forms a "gestalt" in which the physical and mental aspects of personhood are connected as a living whole. Dysfunction and disorder at this level of integration may take on psychosomatic forms as well as loss of self-esteem and a sense of despair and doom.

2. There is integration as related self, where the self and others are differentiated within a unity of being—so as to be spoken of as being "one flesh" (Gen 2:24). Dysfunction and disorder at this level may reflect problems both with interpersonal relationships and with self-defeating anxieties and fears.

3. There is integration as spiritual self, where God is the source of the human spirit. Dysfunction and disorder at this level may take the form of preoccupation with guilt and depression, with symptoms manifest through each of the other two areas.

This threefold integrative task can be seen as a developmental trajectory of the life of the self experienced as the image of God. On this trajectory of personal growth, competence is relative to the stage of development. A psychosomatic competence (first level) enables the self and the embodied self to form a healthy gestalt very early in life. A person who experiences integration at this level will express a healthy and realistic sense of his or her body: "I feel good about my body. I am comfortable with being male/female and with my sexual feelings. I'm glad to be alive and living in this world, even with all its limitations and frustrations."

A psychosocial competence (second level) is learned later. Love becomes integrated with the gestalt of the self in the form of promise, trust, fidelity, and community. Such a person will express feelings and actions of openness toward others while retaining a strong sense of personal identity: "My friends (family) like me for who I am. We sometimes disagree and even fight, but the bond between us grows even stronger. I look forward to forming new relationships while I discover the value of present and former relationships to my life."

The competence of the psychospiritual (third) level of the self as orientation toward God, others, and the self indicates maturity. Persons who have developed this competence will often be unable to account for their deep faith in God, despite challenges, losses, and even tragedy: "I feel that God is faithful and that he understands, even when I fail or do not understand.

I experience the love and reality of God through others, even as I am sometimes the source of God's love and grace for them."

This brief sketch of the nature of human personhood as personal, social, and spiritual will be developed more fully in the next chapter. It is set forth here as a core paradigm, or model, to show the basis for an integrative approach to counseling.

This integrative structure of human life demands a competence that must be acquired through growth. It is on this trajectory of growth that competence can be measured in the threefold sense presented above. Competence in any of the three areas—personal, social, or spiritual—at the expense of the other two destroys the self.

Sometimes a person can mask his or her failure in one area through developing particular skills in another area. For example, an extreme extrovert may relate competently at the interpersonal level, but be an utter failure at the intrapersonal level. Søren Kierkegaard once wrote in his journals, "I just returned from a party of which I was the life and soul; wit poured from my lips, everyone laughed and admired me—but I went away— and the dash should be as long as the earth's orbit——and wanted to shoot myself."[2] On the other hand, Adam before the creation of Eve could well have developed skills in private meditation and worship of God, as well as competence in husbandry of the soil and the animals. Yet God decreed that he was incomplete at the level of co-humanity, and no degree of competence in the other areas could compensate for this deficiency.

Being a person is a matter of growing into this integrative competence. It is essentially a therapeutic process in which the best form of therapy is being and becoming human in this threefold sense. But we often need help, for the way of growth is precarious, if not treacherous. The patterns of pathology are woven into the fabric of the very humanity that gives us the vision and hope of our own selfhood. And the ones with whom we most often relate are often the ones most caught up in our own patterns of pathology and dysfunction. Adam and Eve had each other, even in their state of mistrust, betrayal, and unbelief. They remained human, but the therapeutic bond had been broken, and so their humanity needed healing. Enter God the therapist! And if metaphors mean anything, we can read a depth of comfort and hope in the statement, "The LORD God made for Adam and for his wife garments of skins, and clothed them" (Gen. 3:21).

But as Sue Johnson would put it, seeing that God doesn't make house calls any more, I am supposed to be the next best! But who is really "competent to counsel" in this integrative way?[3]

Counseling on the Therapeutic Continuum

The trajectory of being and becoming human as described above suggests a therapeutic continuum on which various levels of therapeutic enablement with appropriate skills can be plotted. The very nature of our humanity is therapeutic in that we give access to each other and provide care for one another in the simplest and most routine experiences of living together. All Christians can and do counsel in their own way. Within every Christian fellowship there are many who can gain additional expertise in counseling and serve as "lay counselors" alongside of and in support of "pastor counselors" and professional psychologists and therapists.

The therapeutic continuum includes those who are open and relatively healthy persons ministering care and providing a context of growth for each other. Certain levels of competence come from experience and are passed on from generation to generation through the rituals and traditions of family and community. Often persons assume particular roles in this therapeutic context, being parents, teachers, or significant others. Some persons are healed through the pastoral or priestly role of creating and ministering the symbols that enable the ordinary to be touched and inspired by the extraordinary. But in all these ways and roles, the integrative life and power of God are mediated and experienced. The pastors and priests may use symbols and metaphors, while the professional caregivers use therapeutic means and methods. Nonprofessional caregivers use wisdom, develop listening skills, and provide supportive presence and encouragement. Domestic caregivers use human hands and perform personal actions. But all alike touch the life of persons in such a way that God becomes real.

While the concept of "counseling" seems a relatively modern phenomenon, with its own theoretical and professional discipline and practice, the practice of caregiving is as old as humanity itself. Roger Hurding suggests in *The Tree of Healing* that the "tree of pastoral care" is sunk deep into the soil of human experience where God's ministry and calling of extending mercy, love, and forgiveness are as ancient as the story of humanity itself.[4] Indeed, the concept of pastoral care, though construed as the ministry of the pastoral leaders of the church to its members, is the Christian church's way of recognizing the basic needs of humanity as foundational to the ministry of God's grace and love. In *Pastoral Care in Historical Perspective,* Clebsch and Jaekle define this ministry broadly in this way:

> The ministry of the cure of souls, or pastoral care, consists of helping acts, done by *representative* Christian *persons,* directed toward the *healing, sustaining, guiding,* and *reconciling* of *troubled persons* whose troubles arise *in the context of ultimate meanings and concerns.*[5]

With this concept of pastoral care, we are clearly moving along the therapeutic continuum to the place where caregiving goes beyond the ordinary therapy of encouraging growth through the structures, rituals, and traditions of family and community. Many who are reading this book will find themselves in this category of therapy, whether as ordained clergy or as layperson. As Christians who counsel, we will be expected to have a level of competence that goes beyond the ordinary. However, we will be participating in and assisting others in the same integrative task as described above.

The task of integration does not emerge with the degree of therapeutic competence required or with the presentation of "troubled persons" for special forms of therapy. As we have seen, integration is grounded in the very nature of personhood. A Christian who provides counseling, either through pastoral care in the church or through professional therapy in a clinic or private practice, ought to be competent in the integrative task of being and becoming human. "Troubled persons" are the primary texts for integration to be read and interpreted by the counselor, who will then design methods and strategies for caregiving. The clinical therapeutic method they will use is an intentional form of caregiving designed to help the client become competent in the integrative task of being and becoming human.

Integration as a task for Christians who counsel demands a multilevel competence of the counselor. Counselors must help their clients find therapeutic relief and enable their growth by working competently in the three integrational levels: integration as embodied self in a total "gestalt" of the lived life; integration as related self in "grace-filled" encounters with others; and integration as competence in living openly before God, with others, and with self in a wholistic and realistic life of faith.

When Sue Johnson feels uneasy and ambivalent about having helped her client recover a sense of her self-worth without direct use of spiritual resources such as prayer and the Bible, she is expressing some lack of multilevel competence. For her, integration remains stuck at the level of theory. She is competent in using clinical strategies to promote personal growth and healing for her client. But "God talk" has not been integrated into her therapeutic strategy at the conceptual level. She feels that this is where she needs integration in order to satisfy her conscience as to being a *Christian* psychologist.

But if she feels uneasy, it is probably because she feels that she might have "failed" to integrate her own Christian faith into her therapeutic practice. Her client expresses significant integrative growth at the level of her humanity, but she does not perceive it as an effect produced by the Spirit of God. What Dr. Johnson may need more than a conceptual scheme of integration between psychology and Christian faith is a biblical paradigm of the person as an integrative gestalt. She has accepted the theological dogma that human persons are created in the image of God and that saving grace through Jesus Christ restores that image. She believes that one becomes a child of God through grace alone, by faith. However, her church has not helped her to see that the image of God is actually a gestalt of selfhood experienced in healthy relationships. In addition, her psychological training in personality theory and therapeutic techniques did not provide a paradigm of the person as an integrative process in which the spiritual and the emotional constitute the gestalt of selfhood.

For Pastor Ken Jones, the theological training received at seminary probably covered the area of human nature under the category of sin, with little attention given to the psychological and social aspects of the divine image as constitutive of personhood. His recent appropriation of psychological perspectives and therapeutic skills lacks theoretical grounding in a biblical anthropology.

It is to meet the needs of people like Sue and Ken that this book was written. From a theological perspective, a biblical anthropology will be developed as a core paradigm for integrative counseling as a ministry for Christians, a ministry that may be pursued through a variety of modes.

Counseling as a Form of Christian Ministry

Christians who counsel minister human hope as well as psychic healing. Some of us will counsel as laypersons, some as a form of pastoral care, others in a more specialized role as psychologists or family therapists. While we will devote a later chapter to the professional role of a counselor, we need to state here that certification as a therapist should be the minimal kind of qualification, not the maximum.

The professional practice of therapy, as with any other profession, can be done in a way that is less than human and not necessarily Christian. Psychologists are human, of course, and many have deep religious commitments. Yet Christians who counsel as psychologists or psychotherapists can bring a special expertise. The psychologists who bring about a healing and growing encounter that is fully human and that releases faith are practicing a form of ministry—they are being Christian where it really counts.

Christians who counsel have a ministry that goes beyond the demand that theology be integrated with psychology, or that psychology be integrated with theology. While that is a valuable task, it is not my primary concern in this book. My concern is to show that integration is focused most acutely on the role of the person as well as the competence of the person who counsels as a Christian. This means having a special expertise in helping persons grow more effectively in the life of faith, and spiritual persons more effectively into whole persons. Treating the integration of theology and psychology merely as a theory can lead to an approach that confuses and compromises the disciplines of each. Even when the theory seems to succeed, it tends to produce a mythical creature that never becomes real outside of academia, where integration is the avant-garde of the new curriculum. Our concern is more for "embodied integration," as Kirk Farnsworth presents it in his book *Wholehearted Integration: Harmonizing Psychology and Christianity Through Word and Deed.*[6]

The real subject of integration, then, is not a synthetic product offered as an academic exercise. The subject of integration is the Christian who helps others to heal and believe. Such a person applies psychological and therapeutic techniques as a form of Christian ministry.

For those who commonly associate the word *minister* only with those ordained in the church, I beg their indulgence in using the word in a much more general and less clerical way. I use the word *ministry* in this context to speak of that role which belongs to every Christian person—that of representing Jesus Christ through word or act. It is into this "ministry" that the particular skills and competencies of a psychologist can be integrated. The concept of ministry is discussed at greater length in chapter 9.

My assumption is that every Christian is a kind of minister of growth and healing to other persons. This is a ministry of sharing that empowers persons to experience the reality of the kingdom of God as a community of hope and promise. It is a calling inherent in the gift of faith. It is the ministry of growing in faith as whole persons, and thus faith development is itself a ministry that reaches out to others.

Some undertake this calling as nonprofessionals through a variety of forms of lay counseling. Others find their calling in professional roles. For some of us, integrating therapeutic skills with Christian ministry demands a special sort of curriculum. This curriculum will study the nature of the person and God's revelation in Scripture. It will emphasize personal growth as a psycho-spiritual individual so that the student will develop as a healthy person and a believing Christian. And it will enable the student to produce therapeutic gain and personal growth in the lives of others. The person who has this knowledge, along with continued personal development and clinical skills, will have integrated faith and psychology.

This book attempts to define and demonstrate this particular kind of integration. This integration has a fundamental assumption: the goals and techniques of psychological counseling are critically determined and effectively applied when the counseling practice is understood to be directed toward the lived life of the *whole* person and as a function of the ministry of a Christian. I will not judge any psychotherapeutic technique to be inappropriate or unusable merely because it is a therapeutic technique or a theory of human behavior. No therapeutic technique is inherently more or less Christian; techniques that seek to move persons toward more authentic experience of their humanity are to be judged by that criterion. No technique that relates essentially to the human psyche alone can satisfy the need of a person for wholeness as a psycho-spiritual reality. The Christian counselor can freely select appropriate techniques from the wide range available, even as a Christian doctor can make appropriate use of the expanding range of techniques and medical treatments now available.

Summary

In this chapter we have probed the uneasy conscience of the Christian therapist, discovering that the integration of Christian faith as a resource for counseling tends to fall apart in practice. Attempts at integration for the sake of the conscience of the Christian counselor create ambivalence and frustration. What is lacking is a model of personhood that provides an integrative "gestalt" toward which the counselor can direct therapeutic strategies.

We proceeded to develop a model for integrative competence that includes a threefold "composite" of personhood for understanding the image of God in a developmental way. Each human being seeks integration as embodied soul, as related self, and as spirit-directed life toward God. This model describes a trajectory of growth that passes through the context of social, family, and community life for each person.

A therapeutic continuum was described based on this integrative process of human growth and development, in which the core human relationship of self to embodied self, related self, and spirit-directed self constitutes a therapeutic bond. Specific therapeutic strategies seeking to overcome dysfunction and facilitate growth were shown to be related to this core therapeutic human process, with appropriate competence required at each level.

Finally, we suggested that counseling is a ministry to persons with whom God is working to complete the divine image and likeness. Integrative counseling is counseling the whole person. Every person is a text to be understood and interpreted in accordance with God's purpose and design. To this we give our attention in the next chapter.

Notes

1. Gestalt psychology, pioneered by Frederick (Fritz) and Laura Perls, is based on the German word *gestalt*, which is difficult to translate into English. It has the connotation of configuration, structure, theme, or organized whole. See their *Gestalt Approach and Eye Witness to Therapy* (New York: Bantam, 1976). My use of the term in this context is not based on gestalt psychology as such. I am using it more in the sense used by the theologian Jürgen Moltmann, who describes the gestalt of a person as "the whole human organism—that historical Gestalt which people, body and soul, develop in their environment. . . . In acquiring Gestalt, the person acquires both individuality and sociality; for the Gestalt binds him and his environment into a living unity, and at the same time distinguishes him from that environment as this particular living thing. Gestalt is the form of exchange with the various environments in which a person is identifiable, and with which he can identify himself. . . . Consequently, in the lived Gestalt of a human being, body and soul, the conscious and the unconscious, what is voluntary and what is involuntary, interpenetrate" (*God in Creation: A New Theology of Creation and the Spirit of God* [San Francisco: Harper & Row, 1985], 159–61).

2. Søren Kierkegaard, *The Journal of Kierkegaard,* trans. and ed. Alexander Dru (New York: Harper Torchbooks, 1958), 50–51.

3. This is a sly reference to the title of the book by Jay Adams, *Competent to Counsel* (Grand Rapids: Baker, 1970). I shall have more to say about Adams's approach in the next chapter.

4. Roger Hurding, *The Tree of Healing: Psychological and Biblical Foundations for Counseling and Pastoral Care* (Grand Rapids: Zondervan, 1988), 15–16.

5. William A. Clebsch and Charles R. Jaekle, *Pastoral Care in Historical Perspective* (Englewood Cliffs, N.J.: Prentice-Hall, 1964), 4. Emphasis is in the original.

6. Kirk E. Farnsworth, *Wholehearted Integration* (Grand Rapids: Baker, 1986). Farnsworth distinguishes embodied integration from critical integration as follows. Critical integration focuses on the assumptions that underlie research methodologies, which makes it a more philosophical orientation. Critical integration looks for specific psychological conclusions that are incompatible with a more general Christian worldview. Embodied integration, by contrast, looks for

specific psychological and theological conclusions that are comparable with each other. Embodied integration focuses as much on the concreteness of psychological and Christian *living* as on Christian *thinking;* it connects both psychology *and* theology with the real world (91–93). My own focus, as will become clear in the next chapter, is not so much on the project of integration between psychology and theology itself as on a foundational anthropology that is developed theologically as the basis for an approach to counseling from a Christian perspective. I expect that those who do not share this view of a Christian anthropology will not feel that there is much integration.

2

Counseling the Whole Person

"I am *not* dying of AIDS; I am living with AIDS," protested Andrew, who was being interviewed for a news feature on the effects of the disease. Statistically his distinction was not very significant. Of twenty acquaintances who were diagnosed with the disease one year ago, only six were still living.

Why did Andrew cling stubbornly to a perspective of living with an incurable disease as opposed to dying from it? Is he permitted this illusion simply for the sake of preserving his personal dignity and emotional stability? Will his attitude affect the inevitable outcome of the sickness? Will he buy more time through this "therapeutic" redefinition of his situation?

He was unable to answer these questions. Nor can anyone else, for no one has yet explicated the mysterious connection between the mental and the physical so as to predict or manipulate the outcome with any degree of certainty. Will he succeed in defying the statistics of this fatal disease? Maybe. Some do, most do not. But this did not seem to be his point. He had, as we suggested, therapeutically redefined his situation, not in defiance of the facts, but in defiance of a logic that made him merely a victim.

The fact of his disease did not in his view make him a mere statistic. He saw his life as a structure of reality over which he retained control by integrating one factor—his sickness—into the whole. He refused to think of himself as a diseased person. He was a person with a disease, perhaps even a life-threatening disease. But he retained "script rights" over the story of his life!

From a medical perspective, there may well be therapeutic gains resulting from his positive attitude. Again, there may be none. But the potential therapeutic gains grew out of the goals that he set out to define and reach as a living and value-creating person.

Andrew can use support and counseling as he struggles to keep his life integrative and whole. Instinctively he maintains that he is still an intact, whole person. He does not deny that he has the dread disease, but he chooses to think of himself as a living person rather than a dying patient. Yet he will also be tormented by terror, and he will live with the demons of doubt and despair. It will require tremendous resources of psychic energy and sustained hope to fuel his faith and provide the power that holds body and soul together. He may face loss of body functions, feelings of shame and guilt, and rejection from others who fear to touch or even be with him. He will need to redefine these experiences therapeutically in order to maintain this wholistic view of life. If he seeks a counselor, he will need one as "whole" as he is, one who will tap his resources and continue his integrative process even as his body deteriorates.

Unlike Andrew, those who have not succeeded in reinterpreting their lives will need more than supportive counseling. They will require extraordinary therapeutic insight and skill. How does one enable another to overcome that sense of shame and outrage resulting from senseless attacks upon the core of self? Surely those who counsel need encouragement and empowerment in order to lead troubled persons to a wholistic and healthy view of their lives.

Such understanding and insight is what we hope to provide in this chapter. Christians who counsel must counsel the whole person, especially when that person experiences dysfunction in any aspect of life. In the previous chapter we stressed the point that healing is grounded in the integrative powers of our personal humanity, not in the removal of pathology. Andrew has little chance of recovering from AIDS as a physical disease. But the integrative powers of his core humanity are responding to an internal drive toward wholeness as well as to the love and support of others. The purpose of this chapter is to look more closely at components that comprise the integrative core of personal humanity. There is a mental and physical aspect to each person's life, but the integrative core lies between them as a development of the self in its total "gestalt," or form of life as personal, social, and spiritual being.

The development of this integrative model will take three stages. We will look first of all at the dynamics of the self as an *integrative task*, showing how the various aspects of the self are related to each other, to other persons, and to God. Second, we will look at the *ecology of the self*, showing how the core of the self is integrated in three spheres, or environments, each interfacing with the other. Third, we will look at the *life continuum as a context for therapy*. All this is based on a biblical anthropology as the core paradigm for developing a "Christian psychology." By a Christian psychology I mean a psychological understanding of personhood that is informed by the biblical story of humans as created by God, bearing the divine image, and having a destiny that defines quality of life here on earth and determines the ultimate meaning and goal of personal identity.[1]

The Integrative Self: A Developmental Model

People may be viewed as a set of subsystems, systemically related. That is, each subsystem with its relative autonomy, which makes up the person, is part of a whole—which is more than the sum of the parts. For example, the physical body is a system with its own functional relationship of parts, each contributing to the life of the body. At the same time, the physical body is often affected by the mental process, as evidenced by the many varieties of psychosomatic symptoms. The mind and the body are thus "systemically" related, though each has its own distinctive function.

One way of understanding the biblical teaching that persons are created in the "image and likeness of God" is to think of humans as related simultaneously to God and to each other. To the degree that one system or one aspect of the person operates "temperamentally," or idiosyncratically, there is disorder and alienation from the total well-being of the system. The effect of sin is to produce this "temperament" of individuality, self-aggrandizement, suspicion and fear of the other, and alienation from the shared life with the other and with God. Thus we hold that the biblical expression "image of God" applies to the entire human self, body and soul, including the social and environmental existence of the person. This is why the Bible views sin as pervading every aspect of human life, not merely the moral or spiritual dimension.

One could achieve a degree of "health" in terms of functional competence within each subsystem of the person. For example, specific therapeutic gains might be achieved by helping a client overcome severe depression with the result that life can again become useful and meaningful. Yet other problem areas, such as sexual dysfunction or troubled interpersonal relationships, might still exist. The one subsystem that caused depression has been healed, but other systems still are not adequately functioning. But unless all the subsystems are oriented to the overall system in a functional and fulfilling way, there will be only partial health from a wholistic perspective. Considered from the theological standpoint of human beings as systematically related to God and the other, spiritual wholeness and psychical health are systemically related. The apostle Paul used systemic language in a nontechnical sense when referring to the relation of the members of the Christian community to the "whole body": "If one member suffers, all suffer together; if one member is honored, all rejoice together" (1 Cor. 12:26). In scolding the Corinthian Christians for celebrating the Lord's Supper to the exclusion of some, Paul suggests that some have become sick and some have died because of these actions (1 Cor. 11:30). Our purpose here is to show in a schematic way why this is so.

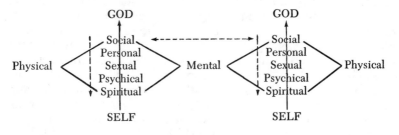

Figure 1

A schematic diagram of a systems approach to the integration of the self in this threefold way would look like figure 1.

Consider the diagram from a developmental standpoint. Reading from top to bottom, we see that the progression is from social to personal to sexual to psychical and finally to spiritual. As spiritual beings we then have an orientation to God as Spirit that runs right back through each of the other subsets or subsystems of the self.

We enter into life as infants held in a social relation to our parents. We are not yet differentiated as "persons" with a self identity that exists over and against other selves. This self identity is formed as "I" begin to distinguish myself from "you" or even "it." Further development entails sexual differentiation, with gender identity assimilated into the core self identity, again with respect to the sexual and personal identity of other persons. The development of psychical experience and capacity comes later, with a deeper capacity to feel and express emotions. Infants surely do have a psychical capacity, but their full range of experience and expression are quite limited. Small children cry easily when hurt or frustrated, but have not sufficient psychical depth to cry at weddings!

Each person represents a duality of the physical and the nonphysical (mental). Each person is also created in a social construct as the original and primary form of humanity. This is one way of understanding the statement in Genesis 2:18: "It is not good that the man should be alone." The fundamental ecology of persons is constituted by fellow humanity, or co-humanity.[2]

The purpose of this diagram is not to suggest that these are stages meant to conform strictly to the theories of developmental psychology. Rather, I am suggesting a general conformity to developmental theories of the self for the sake of showing that what we understand by the "image of God" theologically can be construed in a way congruent with these developmental tasks of becoming a mature person. The image of God is "given" in the sense that each person is born with an actual orientation toward personhood that provides the potential of becoming a person in the fullest sense. Thus we do not mean to suggest that one only has a human spirit when that stage of development is achieved, but that the human spirit given by God orients us toward him and integrates every other aspect of our personal being. The human spirit and the image of God need to be developed in the growth of the person the same as other aspects of personality. The function of the human spirit at an early age is restricted in its expression, though fully present. As the self grows, the human spirit also grows in its expressive capacity. This in no way suggests that one is less a "spiritual" being at infancy. In the same way, the image of God is present in the life of the person from the beginning, though the expression of that image will grow developmentally as the person matures.

It is quite apparent in this model that the spiritual dimension is not placed as an initial or even "higher" aspect of the self. Rather, it is shown both as the goal of personal development and as the source of the person's orientation to God and the other. If the spiritual dimension of selfhood were portrayed as the first or highest in the model, this could lead to the assumption that one could develop a spiritual life and orientation toward God with no real integration of the other aspects of the self, or even with a neglect of these aspects.

Some approaches to counseling from a Christian perspective seem to assume an anthropology that places the spiritual life as the higher or initial life of the self. This is combined with a tendency to bracket the spiritual with the mental, or rational, self. By appealing to a spiritual motivation that is essentially mental, or cognitive, counselors may seek to direct the client toward a "biblical" way of thinking as the source of solving personal problems. The assumption is that if one is spiritually oriented toward God's principles and lives "obediently" in accordance with these principles, all else will follow. For some this seems to work. But for those unable to accept this principle of spiritual obedience as the solution to all problems, the counseling may not be effective.

For example, in the case of Jay Adams, a Christian counselor who uses the Bible as a textbook for counseling, a person seeking counseling must agree to accept biblical authority as a spiritual guide before entering into the counseling sessions. From this same anthropological premise, Adams rejects psychotherapy out of hand as failing to recognize the essentially spiritual nature of all personal problems.[3] As a result, he offers no options for Christians to counsel non-Christians except that conversion to biblical authority and the lordship of Christ be a condition of entrance into therapy. Nevertheless, it should also be said that the effectiveness of the Jay Adams model with those who do receive help based on the principle of biblical authority and who achieve an integrated personal and social life points to the intrinsic therapeutic role of spiritual life open to the Word and Spirit of God. It is for the purpose of providing counseling from a Christian perspective for these, both Christian and non-Christian, who have not achieved this therapeutic integration that we propose this alternative.

In our model we propose an alternative for Christians who counsel to approach persons in an integrative way, as human persons first of all, based on a biblical anthropology rather than a cognitive belief system. The Bible consistently views persons as social as well as spiritual beings. The effects of sin, as pointed out above, are found in the social as well as in the moral and spiritual life of persons. Likewise, the effects of redemption as therapeutic intervention and healing are measured in terms of restoration of relationships and of reconciliation with God. This does not rule out, as we will show in later chapters, such spiritual resources as faith, prayer, the Holy Spirit, and the use of the Bible. Nor does it mean that conversion to Jesus Christ cannot be part of the therapeutic outcome for clients who are counseled by Christians.

In figure 1, the spiritual dimension of the self serves as the integrating motive and drive for all the other components of the self. If there should be disorder or dysfunction at any of the other dimensions—say the sexual—this will be a hindrance to the integration of the self as a function of the life of the spirit.

The difference between this model and Jay Adams's is that in this case the spiritual dimension is not located primarily in the cognitive or mental faculty of the self. Rather, the spiritual dimension is a movement of the whole self as an integrated person. Instead of spirituality in the form of "biblical thinking," this model suggests spirituality as more of a "biblical practice" of life. Biblical practice as a model of wholeness and holiness is typically described in terms of integrative life, both in the relation of the mental and the psychical life and in the sexual, personal, and social dimension. For example, in his letter to the Galatians Paul describes the "works of the flesh" in terms of interpersonal conflicts and disorders along with inner drives that reflect psychic disorder—jealousy, anger, selfishness, party spirit, etc. (Gal. 5:19–21). So, too, the fruit of the Spirit is depicted in terms of positive inner congruence with social relationships that are edifying and upbuilding—love, joy, peace, gentleness, kindness, etc. (Gal. 5:22–23).

Now, Jay Adams would certainly agree that biblical practice is what is desired as the outcome of counseling. He differs from the model presented in that he gives greater therapeutic agency to the cognitive-spiritual as the source of psycho-personal health. We are suggesting, instead, that dysfunction at the social, personal, sexual, or psychical subsystem of the self can hinder spiritual development and so undermine biblical practice as a way of wholistic and godly living. This model makes room for legitimate therapeutic focus on one or more of the subsystems as a way of facilitating spiritual and personal development. The health, ecological wholeness, or holiness of the person is thus represented by the orientation of the spirit through all the other subsystems toward God, who is Spirit, and to the other, as "soul mate," or "help meet," as the Scripture says (Gen. 2:18 KJV).[4]

Figure 1 also shows that the physical and nonphysical (mental) aspects of the self are connected to each of the components of the self. This serves to preserve a balance and positive tension between the physical and mental aspects of the personality for each of the components. If the spiritual dimension should be moved to the side and relate primarily through the mental side of the self, the religious self will become either rationalistic or mystical—both essentially movements away from the concreteness and embodiedness of the self.

In the same way, there are both physical and mental aspects to a healthy psychical and sexual life. Should these become primarily either physical or mental, this will represent a distortion and dysfunction for the self in its process of growth and development. What can be called therapeutic gains in a clinical sense are corrections made in the various subsystems of the self. These corrections facilitate positive relations among the systems. A variety of therapeutic strategies will be used, depending on the specific therapeutic gain to be achieved within each subset. For example, behavior modification works well where there are cause-and-effect mechanisms that contribute to the functioning of a subsystem. Biofeedback techniques recognize the systemic connection between the physical and psychical subsystems. Psychoanalytic-oriented therapy can uncover factors that are repressed in identity formation. Object relations psychology can provide new therapeutic strategies for persons who lack positive identity formation and continuity.[5]

Counseling the whole person thus means an approach that is informed by this systems-and-developmental model of personhood as an integrative whole. The image of God is viewed as a positive orientation to self as essentially good, to others as a context for self-development and fulfillment, and to God as a measure of personal and social health.

In this section we have described the human person as integrative by virtue of a core humanity that is—

- Developmental in its growth toward maturity in the image of God—first social, then personal, sexual, psychical, and finally spiritual;
- Systemic in nature, with each component contributing to the whole—both mental and physical combining in the "gestalt" of the self;
- Spiritually open and growing through the integration of the self with itself, with others, and toward God—making personal humanity the core of spirituality and health.

The Ecology of the Self: A Therapeutic Model

Our analysis of the dynamics of the self from an integrative and developmental perspective, as described in figure 1, contains an implicit ecological structure that needs to become more explicit as a therapeutic model. The concept of ecology in the most general sense simply means the relationship of an organism to its environment, or to a structure of interactive forces that mutually determine both the organism and its environment. In psychology the term was initiated by Allen Wicker in *Introduction to Ecological Psychology.*[6] The term is being used here in a nontechnical sense to describe the interaction of the three spheres of the self in its embodied existence, its existence with and for the other person(s), and its existence as spiritual being related to God.

The unity of the self is experienced as a process of integration, with both self identity and self activity (behavior) congruent with the three ecological spheres, as shown in figure 2.

The core of the self is present in each of the ecological spheres—the physical, social, and spiritual. The self can also be called the "soul" in a theological sense as distinguished from the "soul" of animals in a more general sense. In a biblical anthropology, both human and nonhuman creatures possess a creaturely "soul," by which is meant the basic life principle or

SPHERES OF THE SELF

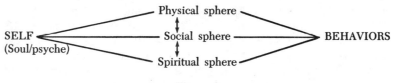

Figure 2

source. (The Hebrew term, used of both humans and animals, is *nephesh*.)[7] The human soul is the orientation of the total self as a physical, social, and spiritual being toward God as source and destiny. Charles V. Gerkin describes the self as "soul" in such a way as to include the various psychological concepts.

> To use the designation self is to emphasize the line of experienced continuity and interpretive capacity which emerges from the self's object relations. To use the term ego is to emphasize the coming together of a nexus of forces demanding mediation and compromise. . . . The term *soul* is here used as a theological term that points to the self's central core subject to the ego's conflicting forces and to the ultimate origins of the self in God. The soul is the gift of God bestowed upon the individual with the breath of life. It is thus the self, including its ego conflicts, as seen from an ultimate perspective—the perspective of the self as nurtured and sustained in the life of God.[8]

In figure 2, the self is identified as the *psyche*, the Greek word used in the New Testament for "soul," or the life of the self. It is used to describe the inner state of Jesus as he contemplates the cross: "Now is my soul [*psyche*] troubled. And what shall I say? 'Father, save me from this hour'? No, for this purpose I have come to this hour" (John 12:27). The deep ambivalence (or "ego conflicts," as Gerkin describes it) is felt by Jesus in the core of his very being, expressed by the term *psyche*, or soul. Jesus resolved this ambivalence, achieving unity of the self (soul) by integrating the perceived loss at the physical level and at the social level into a behavior that gave meaning to pain, suffering, and loss of life itself.

Earlier we used the term *psyche* in figure 1 to represent the capacity for feelings as distinguished from the personal, social, sexual, and spiritual aspects of the self. Here we are using *psyche* in a broader sense as equivalent to the self, or soul as the center and source of the life of the person. Thus there is a psychical dimension to the physical, social, and spiritual life of the self as depicted in figure 2. This is done to show the ecological relationship between the three spheres of the self as the experienced self in the world and with others.

Several things emerge from this ecological matrix of the self in the three spheres of its existence. First, the self (soul) in its totality is present in each of the spheres. If one's life (soul) is reduced to virtually a physical existence, with the loss of social relationships and even loss of spiritual perception of God ("My God, my God, why hast thou forsaken me?"), then the soul, or the selfhood of the person, is fully present up to the point of the spirit's being separated from the body (death). Likewise, the social and spiritual spheres each represents the self in its totality. Yet the nature of the ecological matrix of personhood is such that no single sphere can stand alone as the reality of the self. For example, if a person should go into a coma and be unable to respond at the social or spiritual level, we would still view the person as a total "self" rather than merely a physical being. But scientists have demonstrated that the personal development of the infant is linked with the physical bonding that occurs through being held and touched from the very beginning. This is what is meant by the ecological matrix in which the self experiences itself as physical, social, and spiritual.

Second, we must say that any pathology or disorder of the self in one or more of the spheres affects the self in all spheres. This explains why one cannot bless the "soul" of a person who is hungry without giving that person something to eat. "If a brother or sister is ill-clad and in lack of daily food, and one of you says to them, 'Go in peace, be warmed and filled,' without giving them the things needed for the body, what does it profit?" (James 2:15–16). The answer is, of course, it does not profit! If one claims a spiritual relationship with God so that "God's love abides in him," but does not provide for the physical needs of a brother or sister and instead "closes his heart against him," God's love cannot abide in him (1 John 3:17)!

In the same way, we could say that to provide for the physical needs of a person and yet deprive him or her of social and spiritual health is to violate the soul or very self of the person. The ecological spheres of the self not only mean that the self is present in each sphere, but that each sphere is essential to some degree to the health and wholeness of the self.

Third, we may say that no authentic approach to the self can bypass the ecological matrix as embodied, social, and spiritual existence. A "psychology" that seeks to describe the self and prescribe therapeutic aid for the self only in terms of the psyche as disembodied, impersonal, and nonspiritual selfhood cannot measure up to a "Christian psychology" that understands the self (soul) in this threefold way.

Fourth, we may say that there will ordinarily be pathologies that are quite specific to each of the three ecological spheres, even though the behavioral symptoms may appear in any of them. For example, a disorder that is essentially biological in origin due to, say, hormonal or chemical imbalance may cause a depression of the self so as to impair function at the social and spiritual levels. One may feel that "God has abandoned" the self, or that withdrawal from social relationships is the only escape, while the etiology of the problem may be primarily biological rather than spiritual. The ecological nature of the self results in this "pathological spillover," with the result that diagnosis becomes more complex than merely observing or noting symptoms.

The Christian who counsels will be open to the possibility that the source of the problem may be in any of the three spheres and will use therapeutic strategies accordingly. Not every disorder or problem of human behavior can be charged to spiritual failure, any more than all problems can be assumed to have a biological cause. Yet, to include spiritual openness and health as part of the therapeutic goal is not considered a violation of therapeutic and clinical practice for the Christian psychologist. So also, a wholistic counseling approach should be able to discern pathology at the spiritual level of the self and provide appropriate therapy. Here might be the place for dealing with guilt and forgiveness, for example.

A person caught in the trap of self-hatred or low self-esteem can express symptoms that might appear in any of the three spheres. Often the person projects God's judgment, internalizes and reinforces it, and uses self-condemnation as a means of atonement. In other cases, low self-esteem appears as a dysfunction in interpersonal relationships or can even produce symptoms of a physical nature. The self is failing in its attempt to achieve integration and wholeness. A therapist specializing in some form of ego psychology, or psychoanalysis, may be able to trace the patterns of the pathology and attempt therapy through a repatterning of the ego and enabling of the self to function more effectively and wholistically. There is no reason why a Christian therapist cannot offer this kind of help if adequately trained and certified.

All people get well for the same reason, regardless of the therapeutic method used! The source of healing is in the person, not the therapist or counselor. "Psychotherapy does not cure patients," suggests Thomas Paolino. "The capacity for cure lies within each patient."[9] Facilitating a movement toward health in one sphere may release the self to grow toward health in another sphere. The "ego" as a specific subject of psychological attention lies between the self and its lived experience in the world. When the self is addressed and responds at the level of its spiritual sphere, the "ego" of the self is also touched and healed. As we shall see later, effective mediation of God's grace not only is a spiritual means for healing, but touches the very core of the human self, enabling it and assisting it in the integrative task of becoming whole.[10]

In this section we have attempted to show how the core anthropological model as depicted in figure 1 can be construed as a therapeutic model as in figure 2. No attempt has been made to relate specific therapeutic theories and methods to this model, but instead we have sought to show how a variety of theories and models may be used within this model when the ecological interactions of the human self are understood in this threefold way. The ecological matrix provides a therapeutic model that depicts the integrative task of the self as—

- Open to growth in each sphere, as a physical, social, spiritual person;
- Known to self and others as the same person in each sphere;
- Developing psychological (ego) strength and health as measured by positive interrelationship among the three spheres.

The connection of the self to its life as a set of behaviors is what now must be considered as a life continuum and context for therapy.

The Life Continuum as Context for Therapy

The life of the self, of course, cannot be neatly diagrammed and displayed in a figure, as we have attempted to do. Each person's life is a pilgrimage of the self, a narrative created by the events that are experienced and the way in which these experiences are integrated into the identity of the self.[11] In Peter Shaffer's play *Equus*, the psychiatrist, Martin Dysart, has been treating a boy who blinded several horses in a psychotic episode. Through the treatment the psychiatrist discovers that the boy at an early age had become obsessed with horses when his atheist father substituted the picture of the head of a horse in his room for a picture of Christ. Now the boy experiences God as Equus, viewing him, calling him to worship, and ultimately judging him through the eyes of horses. Dysart, in reflecting on this phenomenon of self formation, says:

A Child is born into a world of phenomena all equal in their power to enslave. It sniffs—it sucks—it strokes its eyes over the whole uncomfortable range. Suddenly one strikes. Why? Moments snap together like magnets, forging a chain of shackles. Why? I can trace them. I can even, with time, pull them apart again. But why at the start they were ever magnetized at all—just those particular moments of experience and no others—I don't know. *And nor does anyone else.* Yet *if* I don't know—if I can never know that—then what am I doing here? And I don't mean clinically doing or socially doing—I mean *fundamentally!* These questions, these Whys, are fundamental—yet they have no place in a consulting room.[12]

The life of the self in the process from being to becoming is a precarious and even treacherous path, as we have said. Yet, given the right context, it is also a path of growth, healing, and discovery. The larger context of life provides therapeutic resources, sometimes minimally and sometimes adequately. In this broad context, therapy means not only healing, but the growth of the self into its fullest potential, regarding oneself positively as an integrative "gestalt" of body and soul. It is also to experience the self as affirmed and valued by others, including the reality of trust, loyalty, and shared life in community. So, too, this integrative, therapeutic context of life is meant to include spiritual values realized through worship, prayer, the peace and grace of God, and hope as assurance of ultimate value of the self as upheld by God beyond this life.

We recall here the threefold integrative task as discussed in the previous chapter. There is integration as embodied soul, as related self, and as the competence to integrate embodied and related self to God as the source of the human spirit.

The idea of life as pilgrimage is a therapeutic continuum for all persons when considered in this perspective. This therapeutic continuum stretches from the most informal caregiving that takes place through domestic, community, and friendship encounters to the more specialized forms of pastoral care and psychotherapy in a clinical setting. On this continuum, counseling is a form of support and, if needed, intervention for enabling persons to grow toward health. The resources used by the professional counselor may be more narrowly defined and focused, but the process of healing is the same. All persons get well for the same reason, regardless of the therapeutic method used. Getting well in this case means recovering the therapeutic process of life itself. The only source of healing is in the person being healed, though the process may depend on skilled intervention with appropriate therapeutic methods.

In many instances the New Testament uses the same word for salvation as for healing. The Greek word *sōtēria* can be translated "salvation" or "healing," depending on the context. But the word *therapeuō* is also used to describe an act of healing ministry by Jesus (Matt. 9:35). This shows that salvation includes therapy as one means to the gift of life at its fullest.

We will look at three aspects of this pilgrimage of the self as a context for therapy: self formation, self socialization, and self fulfillment.

Self Formation: The Hermeneutical Task

The term *hermeneutics* comes from the Greek name for the god Hermes, son of Zeus, who served as the messenger of the gods. According to Greek mythology, Hermes gave increase to herds and guarded boundaries and roads. He was also the god of science and invention, of eloquence, of cunning and trickery and theft, of luck and treasure-trove. He even conducted the dead to Hades. Indeed, Hermes seems to resemble a modern pastoral counselor!

In a more technical sense, hermeneutics is a form of literary critique in which the meaning of a text is interpreted in accordance with its intent and purpose. Here the term represents the formation of the self as it "interprets" the events and experiences of life.

At the beginning of this chapter we mentioned Andrew, a young man with AIDS, a life-threatening disease. We spoke of his response as a "therapeutic redefinition" of his life when he protested that he was not dying with AIDS, but living with AIDS. How was he able to do this? Did he suddenly acquire this therapeutic skill? Hardly. The capacity to be open to "bad luck" as well as "good fortune" is evidence of a "hermeneutical" approach to life whereby the self possesses a core of positive values that transcend sheer facts such as disease or even death. The self actually interprets facts and experiences according to its core values. Where the formation of the self has resulted in core values that are inherently positive and open to change, there will be a capacity to interpret even negative experiences in a therapeutic or healing way. This is done by accepting those experiences for what they are and building them into the larger goals of the self. For Andrew, it means to view each day as a day of living rather than as a day of dying.

The apostle Paul, when confronted with his personal "thorn in the flesh," found that it could not be removed through prayer. He concluded that he was given grace sufficient to live with it (2 Cor. 12:7–9). Not simply enduring this problem, Paul added, "I will all the more gladly boast of my weaknesses, that the power of Christ may rest upon me." Paul's self formation had taken root at the reality of God's love for him. Given the chance, he would still have preferred to live without the weakness. Yet he did not become morbidly attached to his deformity. Instead, he "made it fit" into the more wholistic pattern of his life. It sounds so simple! But how did he do it?

The hermeneutical task for Paul as a basis for his therapeutic redefinition under adversity had begun years earlier when he came to believe that he had been set apart for this ministry "before I was born" (Gal. 1:15)! Through the process of a conversion to Jesus as the Messiah there was also a conversion of Jesus of Nazareth into the inner life of Saul of Tarsus. Now the apostle Paul is able to project in a retrospective way his "story of conversion" back to his core identity. This therapeutic redefinition did not cast out the "old Saul" in favor of a "new Paul." Rather, an incredible continuity was established for him in his core identity, going back to his very conception. This enabled him to take responsibility for persecuting Christians. Many Christians apparently lost their lives through his zeal!

Having made these wrong and hurtful actions part of the whole of his life, Paul gained the capacity to include suffering and continued pain as part of the whole. We are not told how this happened. But it is worth noting that when he did arrive in Jerusalem after his startling conversion, the disciples were not prepared to receive him. It was Barnabas, whose name means "son of consolation," who interceded for him with those same disciples (Acts 9:26–30). It sounds so easy! But we can well imagine the "counseling" that Barnabas had to do to enable Paul to cope with this rejection and to enable the disciples to trust their very lives to Paul.

One of the contributions of object relations psychology as a therapeutic approach has been precisely in this area of self formation through relation to "objects" that remain present to the self despite discontinuity, separation, or deprivation for a time.[13] Charles Gerkin, who bases his counseling approach on object relations theory, says:

> To extend D. W. Winnicott's language, it is the role of interpreta-tion to sustain and solidify the line of continuing existence that provides the self with a sense of continuity at all levels of its functioning. The line of life becomes a line of interpretation—the hermeneutics of the self. Within a theological perspective I would place that process at the center of the life of the soul in all its relationships.[14]

The Scriptures tell us that Jesus, in the days of his flesh, "offered up prayers and supplications, with loud cries and tears, to him who was able to save him from death" (Heb. 5:7). This strong language describes quite clearly the psychic trauma and pain that Jesus experienced when confronted with the inevita-bility of the cross. At the very least this encourages us to know that such turmoil and pain are not due to sin, nor are they contrary to our basic human spirit. A wholistic view of the person must include such terrible depths of fear and pain if it is to be authentically in touch with persons in need.

Yet the author of Hebrews goes on to say of this same Jesus that "for the joy that was set before him [he] endured the cross, despising the shame" (Heb. 12:2). Can people who have encountered the shame of physical, sexual, or emotional violation actually learn to "despise the shame"? Only if the core of the self experiences love as a powerful therapeutic redefinition of the self as a constant and continual reality. For shame is fundamentally a matter of self-interpretation. "Although he was a Son, he learned obedience," writes the author of Hebrews (Heb. 5:8). Read another way, it means that precisely because he knew himself to be the beloved Son of the Father, he could accept with humility and dignity the obedience that kept him faithful, even to experience the shameful and dreadful death upon a cross. "Despising the shame" is not hating it, but reinterpreting it as pain. Pain can be healed when attached to a meaningful purpose—it is called redemption. Shame can never be healed as long as it is the self's interpretation of itself. Turning shame into pain, and pain into creative suffering, is a way of experiencing redemption and becoming a child of God.

The traditional theological approach has been to interpret the atoning death and resurrection of Jesus Christ as offering pardon from sin. C. Norman Kraus suggests that the removal of sin as an objective offense standing between God and humans does not yet remove shame as the deeper problem of the human self. Shame means that one has suffered loss of being, not merely loss of status. The purpose of divine forgiveness is not merely to pardon sin as a legal or objective fault, but to overcome shame, which has weakened and destroyed the inner being of the self.[15]

Counseling from a Christian perspective can bring to the therapeutic sessions, in a narrower, more clinical sense, a basis for the broader formation of the self as a life pilgrimage. This can be a therapeutic process in which continuity is restored through a vision and experience of God as the "object" of the self formation present to the self even in those earlier experiences that "split" the self off from its task of becoming a whole person. The specific therapeutic techniques to be used in this case, of course, are beyond the scope of this book. What I hope to provide here is a theological basis for clinical therapy that approaches the person on the life continuum of self formation.

Self Socialization: The Narrative Task

The process of self interpretation described above can be viewed as a task of creating the script or narrative for one's own story. Forming personal identity through narrative has been described helpfully by Stanley Hauerwas in his book *A Community of Character:*

> The necessary existence of the other for my own self is but a reminder that the self is not something we create, but is a gift. Thus we become who we are through the embodiment of the story in the communities in which we are born. What is crucial is not that we find some way to free ourselves from such stories or community, but that the story which grasps us through our community is true. And at least one indication of the truthfulness of a community's story is how it forces me to live in it in a manner that gives me the skill to take responsibility for my character.[16]

The life continuum is a process of socialization of the self. Hauerwas suggests that the concept of story can be a way of defining the concepts, values, and experiences that shape personal identity, for better or for worse. In this sense, the ecological matrix of the self, as displayed in figure 2, points toward behavior as necessarily understood in a context of socialization, or community. We express ourselves through forms of behavior that are physical, social, and spiritual (religious). Yet specific forms of behavior are not directly related to the self, but only indirectly, through the ecological matrix. While the self is present as a totality in each sphere, each sphere also contributes to the total "gestalt" of the self. Thus behavior in one sphere must be understood in terms of the ecological relationships of the three spheres.

This model also helps us to see that pathology in the form of antisocial or self-destructive behavior may have its roots in the lack of integrative self formation in the sense of having a "story" that is truthful, to use Hauerwas's term.

One way of relating the Christian story to the therapeutic process is by understanding the formation of the self as a narrative task of developing a story that gives the self a core set of values concerning oneself, others, and the future. Clinical therapeutic techniques can then be contextualized by a culture or context in which this Christian story is authenticated and experienced as one's own story. This will be developed further in chapter 4. For now we see that the context of self formation as a therapeutic process includes one's developing life story as well as the story of one's future existence.

Self Fulfillment: The Eschatological Task

In theology the term *eschatology* simply means the study of the final events that will take place at the end of the age. It derives from the Greek word *eschaton,* which means "last." We have stressed that the core values of the self include not only values that relate to self-esteem, but values rooted in relation to others and to the future. The life continuum as a context for therapy includes the future as well as the past. Too often, I am afraid, therapy has been oriented toward the factors and experiences in one's past to the neglect of the future orientation of the self. Counseling the whole person entails an approach that includes future reality as impinging on the present as much as does the past. Gerkin offers this explanation:

> The level of acceptance of eschatological identity is often signaled by a reduction in the self's preoccupation with itself and a concomitant enhancement in the self's capacity for concern for and participation with other persons. . . . Rather than being depleted by the demands and pressures upon the self that threaten the self's existence, the self is increasingly nourished and fulfilled by engagement with others in activities oriented toward the renewal of life together in the spirit of the Kingdom.[17]

For the people of Israel in the Old Testament, as well as for the early Christian community, there appeared to be a self-conscious "therapy" in one's relationship to the community. That is to say, for the Israelite, personal identity was bound up in the corporate self of the community as related to the original founders—Abraham and Sarah, for example. This relationship was part of the socialization of the individual person through ritual, story, and promise. But the very fact of promise pointed the individual forward to a destiny that gave present value to the sacrifices and struggles of everyday life.

The same can be said of the early New Testament Christian community. Not only was the community founded upon the memory of Jesus, with the rituals (baptism, Lord's Supper) oriented back to his historical presence, but the community was also looking forward toward its future signaled by the story of the resurrection and the promise of the coming of Christ to gather his own people.

The biblical anthropology presented earlier was meant to lay a foundation for this eschatological fulfillment of the person by showing that everyone's life is oriented spiritually to God as a core human value. The theological concept of eschatological fulfillment through the coming of the kingdom of God and of Jesus Christ, along with the promise of resurrection of the body, is first of all a core value of the human self before it becomes a religious, or even Christian, concept. The life continuum as a context for therapy provides for the therapeutic use of the Christian story of the kingdom of God and resurrection of the body with eternal life as a core personal value.

The newspaper story that revealed Andrew's therapeutic interpretation of his life as a person with AIDS did not tell us what "living with AIDS" meant to him in terms of the ultimate and future reality of his life beyond the almost certain death that his disease would bring. We do not know to what extent his personal integrative task incorporates the spiritual sphere—in particular, the eschatological hope of resurrection through personal relation to Jesus Christ. Certainly this dimension of his life would provide additional resources for his continued "hermeneutical" task of facing each day as a living person rather than a dying one.

Summary

In this chapter we have attempted to provide a theological basis for counseling a person like Andrew as a whole person, based on a biblical anthropology that includes the body and mind in an integrative process of spiritual life oriented to God and others. In figure 1 we presented an integrative model that was developmental in its growth toward maturity, systemic in nature by relating each component of the self to the other and the whole, and spiritually open to God and the other as the core of the self.

The ecological matrix of the self was then presented as figure 2, depicting the self relating to each sphere of life as embodied self, social self, and spiritual self. This provides a therapeutic basis for approaching the self through the behaviors related to each sphere, using appropriate methods. In this model we discovered that the ego dysfunctions described by some psychologists are related ecologically to the three spheres. One implication of this is that healthy ego development in a psychological sense is directly related to personal and spiritual growth.

Finally, we have traced out the life continuum as a context for therapy, showing the relevance of the Christian story to the life story as a pilgrimage of the self in creating one's own story. The growth of the self as an integrative project is a process of self formation and self socialization, empowered by and sustained by the eschatological reality of resurrection of the body, reconstituted social relationships, and the spiritual reality of life with God through Jesus Christ. This is what it means to be created in and live out the image of God as the form of one's own personal human story.

More simply put, the two chapters now completed have led us to conclude that—

- Personal humanity is basically therapeutic by virtue of its own integrative task;
- All people get well for the same reason, regardless of the therapeutic method used;
- Spiritual life is grounded in authentic human life, so that spiritual resources augment and complete the self's movement toward health;
- Each person is on a life continuum of growth with its own therapeutic resources and context;
- Counselors do not cure people; the capacity for health lies within each person.

We have not addressed the role of the counselor in this therapeutic context and process. Intervention for the purpose of effecting therapy and growth is almost a sacred task in light of the high value we place on the sanctity of the self in developing its own life and character. "We are born into other people's intentions," wrote Theodore Roszak.[18] And even our good intentions can violate the space that the self occupies and can manipulate its growth to fit our ideas. Can Christians counsel so as to produce change and growth without violating the personhood of another? We think so, and in the next chapter we present our case.

Notes

1. I have developed the foundations for a biblical anthropology more extensively in *On Being Human* (Grand Rapids: Eerdmans, 1982). Roger Hurding argues that there may well be a "Christian psychology" that informs pastoral care (*The Tree of Healing: Psychological and Biblical Foundations for Counseling and Pastoral Care* [Grand Rapids: Zondervan, 1988]). It is a "psychology that is deeply rooted in the way God has made us" (19). While he does not elaborate on this at length, he does provide a brief outline of what he considers a biblical perspective on our humanity: "We have *supreme value;* we are *living unities;* we have *broken relationships;* we are *restorable*" (245).

2. I have discussed the concept of co-humanity as part of the paradigm of a biblical anthropology in *On Being Human*, chapter 4.

3. Jay Adams is dean of the Institute of Pastoral Studies and visiting professor of practical theology at Westminster Theological Seminary in Philadelphia. Among his more important publications are *Competent to Counsel* (1970; reprint, Grand Rapids: Zondervan, 1986); *The Christian Counselor's Manual* (1973; reprint, Grand Rapids: Zondervan, 1986); *More Than Redemption: A Theology of Christian Counseling* (Grand Rapids: Baker, 1979); and "Nouthetic Counseling," in *Helping People Grow*, ed. Gary Collins (Ventura, Calif.: Vision House, 1980).

The controlling assumption for Adams is that divine counsel is the only option for providing therapy and the Bible is the basic textbook for counseling ("Nouthetic Counseling," 158). Nouthetic counseling is based on the Greek verb *noutheteō,*" used by Paul in several instances (e.g., 2 Tim. 3:15–17) to mean the kind of pastoral care that produces change through verbal confrontation motivated by love, for the client's health and God's glory (see *Competent to Counsel*, 51).

4. The concepts of "wholeness" and "holiness" have been the subject of some discussion in the literature on integration in counseling. "Holiness" is taken to mean the particular character of a person as the subject of sanctification, as in "sanctifying grace" applied through the Holy Spirit. "Wholeness" is a more psychological term tending toward functional well-being. The issue is whether or not one can be in a state of "sanctification" or "grace" while at the same time lacking in functional "wholeness." Those who hold that wholeness produces holiness tend to assume that growth as a function of becoming a whole person is what is meant by the theological term *sanctification*.

Professor Newton Malony at Fuller Seminary's graduate school of psychology, for example, suggests that *whole person* incorporates both psychological wholeness and spiritual holiness. "To be whole means to be conscious of and adequate in all, not just some of life's environments" (*Wholeness and Holiness: Readings in the Psychology/Theology of Mental Health*, ed. H. Newton Malony [Grand Rapids: Baker, 1983],

20–21). Seward Hiltner suggests that the concept of "health" includes "cosmic wholeness," in which one's life may be in a state of harmony with regard to the whole creation ("Salvation's Message about Health," in *Wholeness and Holiness*, 160).

My own view is that while wholeness as a psychological state is not a presupposition of holiness as a spiritual state—as though good psychological health could ensure good personal or spiritual health—holiness anticipates and seeks wholeness. I prefer not to set the terms in contrast to each other, but rather to view both holiness and wholeness as part of the tension between actuality of personal being and potential of personal being so that one can grow in both holiness and wholeness and yet be considered both "whole" and "holy" by virtue of being a person created by God and as the object of God's grace and love.

5. For a helpful discussion of some of the forms of therapy currently in use from a Christian perspective, see *The Holy Spirit and Counseling: Theology and Theory*, Marvin G. Gilbert and Raymond T. Brock, eds. (Peabody, Mass.: Hendrickson, 1985). Roger Hurding, in *The Tree of Healing*, has produced an informative and critical review of the secular psychologies and therapies, listing their basic assumptions, aims, and methodologies, along with a discussion from a Christian perspective. Hurding also includes an analysis and discussion of a variety of Christian theories for counseling, making this one of the best resource books available for pastors and Christian counselors.

6. Allen Wicker, *Introduction to Ecological Psychology* (Monterey, Calif.: Brooks-Cole, 1979). Charles Gerkin also sees the context of self development as an ecological relationship: "The quality of the self's interpretation is not simply a product of its own individual effort. The infant and mother (and/or other figures who share the mothering role) together make up a social milieu, an ecology, which shapes a certain cast to the 'I am and you are' situation. The later development of partial independence begins to shift more of the interpretive task onto the developing self. But even into adulthood, the basis for interpretation of the meaning of existence remains fundamentally social" (Gerkin, *The Living Human Document: Re-visioning Pastoral Counseling in a Hermeneutical Mode* [Nashville: Abingdon, 1984], 84–85).

7. For further discussion of the relation of soul to body and spirit, see my book *On Being Human*, appendix A, 207–14.

8. Gerkin, *The Living Human Document*, 98.

9. Thomas Paolino, Jr., *Psychoanalytic Psychotherapy* (New York: Brunner/Mazel, 1981), 13.

10. W. W. Meissner suggests that personal identity and spiritual identity flow out of the same ego source. Consequently the grace of God, to produce spiritual growth, must also become the energizing power of ego development (*Life and Faith: Psychological Perspectives*

on Religious Experience [Washington, D.C.: Georgetown University Press, 1987], 25ff).

11. Gerkin contributes vitally to this discussion when he writes, "Pastoral counseling undertaken in the hermeneutical mode [assumes] the context of human life seen as pilgrimage set within a community that shares a certain narrative vision or mythos concerning the whole life in creation. The care provided by pastoral counseling is thus only one aspect of a larger context of care provided by the community of faith and life. Rather than 'treating' an 'illness' or 'solving' a 'problem,' the pastoral counselor seeks to provide a more or less temporary intensification of a process of care and prophetic ministry to persons which the church in its ministry in other modes carries on with people throughout their lives" (*The Living Human Document*, 178).

12. Peter Shaffer, *Equus* (New York: Avon, 1974).

13. The British school of object relations theory in the neo-Freudian tradition includes such names as W. Ronald Fairburn, H. Guntrip, D. W. Winnicott, and Melanie Klein. These theories sought to locate the source of psychological problems in birth trauma and/or in the few months immediately following birth, particularly in the infant's relation to the parent (mother) as an object of attachment. The infant struggles to internalize the mother object in a way that provides continuity through the stages of separation and perceived abandonment. Successful object internalization establishes an identity that can cope with change in the object to which one relates without suffering anxiety or panic.

Frank Lake (1914–82) developed a monumental work attempting to integrate object relations theory with Christian theology. This work, titled *Clinical Theology* was first published in 1966 and has now been published in an abridged form, edited by Martin H. Yeomans with the same title, *Clinical Theology: A Theological and Psychological Basis to Clinical Pastoral Care* (New York: Crossroad, 1987). Lake's basic model is a four-stage process of human development beginning with acceptance (being) and nurture (well being) as the two input stages experienced either positively or negatively during the first few months of the infant's life. These are followed by the two output stages, status and achievement. Failure to move through the first two stages due to inadequate object internalization in the attachment/separation experience leads to "splitting" of the self, with a resulting schizoid reaction (marked by withdrawal and death wish) or by a hysteric reaction (marked by compulsive attachment or clinging). Central to his integrative approach is the figure of Christ, who becomes a new "object" by which one can pass through the stages of primal integration again and emerge with a relatively healthy self identity formation leading to more effective output in terms of status and achievement.

For those willing to struggle with some of the technical and complex concepts, the book provides a provocative text on integration.

14. Gerkin, *The Living Human Document*, 102.

15. C. Norman Kraus, *Jesus Christ Our Lord: Christology from a Disciple's Perspective* (Scottdale, Pa.: Herald Press, 1987), 205–28. Kraus says, "In no way can shame be expiated through substitutionary compensation or retaliation. . . . Only a forgiveness which covers the past and a genuine restoration of relationship can banish shame. What is needed is a restoration of communication. The rage which isolates and insulates must be overcome. Reconciliation and restoration of mutual intimate relationship through a loving open exchange is the only way to heal resentment and restore lost self-esteem" (211).

From a psychological perspective, John Bradshaw views shame as a "toxic" form of low self worth, contributing heavily to various forms of addictive and compulsive behavior. See *Bradshaw On: Healing the Shame That Binds You* (Deerfield Beach, Fla.: Health Communications, 1988).

16. Stanley Hauerwas, *A Community of Character* (South Bend, In.: University of Notre Dame Press, 1981), 148–49.

17. Gerkin, *The Living Human Document*, 189. The line between spiritual direction and psychotherapy is recognized by Gerkin, but not made an artificial or an absolute boundary. "Against that background of the psychologizing of everyday concern with problems of living and spiritualizing of religious life and devotion, the model of pastoral counseling here proposed may be seen as an alternative lying somewhere between psychotherapy and spiritual direction. Fundamentally concerned with the self's pilgrimage through the problems and crises of everyday relational life, the hermeneutical theory is simultaneously concerned with the formation of that side of the self's paradoxical identity rooted and grounded in God and the inbreaking of the Kingdom. Here, of course, the theory becomes openly and unashamedly confessional. Insofar as the horizon of understanding brought by the counselor to the counseling relationship is thus involved in confessional faith, to that extent it entails a form of spiritual direction. But insofar as that horizon represents psychological ways of attending to the inner and relational workings of the self, it is a clearly recognizable form of psychotherapy. Partaking of both, the model, both in design and intention, embraces a psycho-spiritual form of ministry" (192–93).

18. Theodore Roszak, *Person/Planet* (Garden City, N.Y.: Doubleday/Anchor, 1979), 139.

3

The Counselor as Growth Promoter

The violation of personhood begins in the cradle, if not in the womb. We learn our names and our natures at their hands, and they cannot teach us more than they know or will freely tell. Can there be families whose love is not treason against our natural vocation?[1]

Theodore Roszak has a high view of human nature and, apparently, a low view of human nurture. He is right on one count—the violation of personhood begins early and, to hear some tell it, continues through most of the growing years.

All of us lose our innocence in the cradle. Before we know how it happened, we discover a streak of perversity expressed as rebellion toward those who claim to love us and who have to live with us. Something in us has been betrayed—or is the betrayer.

Is it a need to manipulate and control, disguised as love, that constitutes the treason, as Roszak would have us believe? Or would it be treason against our human potential to leave us alone? Would it not be an act of betrayal never to penetrate the wall of defenses and call us out into the open where healing and growth can take place? Must not love and caregiving also be therapeutic and corrective in order to be genuine love? Of course! Those who love us best know this. But not all who love know how to enter the closed self of another therapeutically. And where the ordinary therapy of love in community is not enough, an extraordinary therapy is needed, a practice of extraordinary love and care. This is what professional Christian caregivers, counselors, and therapists strive to be and do.

Our purpose in this chapter is to examine more closely the role of the counselor in helping persons to grow toward wholeness. By Roszak's terms, this is the role that comes close to violating the integrity if not the sanctity of the personal life of others. In the modern concept of the professional therapist there is even more reason to question the value of such a role.

In the healing art, according to one psychiatrist, the doctor can be seen as the "prescription."[2] Indeed, in the 1950s skeptics of psychoanalysis were saying that many neurotic patients got better without professional help and that psychotherapy did not improve on this pattern! H. J. Eysenck, the British psychologist, unsettled the therapeutic world with his paper published in 1952, "The effects of psychotherapy: an evaluation." Later Eysenck stated that psychotherapy is like the "wondrous cure" of the second-century physician Galen: "All who drink this remedy recover in a short time, except for those whom it does not help, who all die and have no relief from any other medicine. Therefore, it is obvious that it fails only in incurable cases."[3]

Roger Hurding, in commenting on this, reports that when different aspects of the counseling relationship were being studied some counselors and psychotherapists appeared to facilitate improvement, others did not affect the outcome in any significant way, and a third category actually seemed to make the clients worse! The focus of inquiry then shifted to the character and role of the therapist.[4] Nonetheless, Hurding suggests, there have always been special persons who have provided the stimulus and direction for growth, though they were not always recognized as professional caregivers. Caregiving, he argues, is as essential to human growth and development as providing physical needs.

With Roszak's warning in mind and with encouragement from Hurding, a thesis can be stated for this chapter: *An effective therapeutic intervention is one in which the client's motive power to grow is facilitated by the counselor's perceived presence as a partner in the growth process.*

The anthropological framework for such a thesis has already been established in the first two chapters. Humans are integrative by nature, with the source of health and therapeutic growth found in one's own humanity. Openness to growth as personal, social, and spiritual life constitutes our basic humanity. The presence of the other is essential to this growth process; it is not an intrusion or invasion.

We will discuss this thesis in four stages: (1) growth as a sign of health; (2) the motive power for growth; (3) the counselor as the human equation in therapy; and (4) the motive power of love.

Growth as a Sign of Health

The ambiguity of such terms as *health, wholeness,* and *growth* is a well-known problem in therapeutic literature. Clinical pragmatism, says Allen Bergen, assimilates the dominant values of a social system to help define the therapeutic goals and clinical procedure. This approach seeks to diminish the pathologies or disturbances defined by the clinician, who acts as an agent of culture. Health is seen as the absence of pathology or the removal of obstacles to growth, defined as functional competence. On the other hand, Bergen suggests, humanistic idealism appeals to philosophical and ideal values as inherently good and necessary to a full human life. The clinician informed by these values determines therapeutic goals based on these values, which are based on the universal themes of humanity in the abstract.

In this case, wholeness is not defined so much by functional competence as by movement toward the "healthy" goals of ideal human life.[5] Clinical pragmatism seeks adaptation to the prevailing norms and values of the immediate cultural context. Humanistic idealism tends to ignore the social and cultural context in favor of abstract values set forth as norms by which persons should measure their own success or failure. The pragmatist sacrifices the ideal for the sake of conformity to the contemporary pattern. "Don't feel guilty for doing what everyone else is doing! If you feel better, then you are getting better." The idealist discounts the value of what is historically real for the sake of conformity to the universal ideal. "Don't think of what you are, but what you can be! If you think right, you will be all right." Of course these are stereotypes! But I suspect that each position has its representatives and a corresponding theology, even within the Christian approach to counseling.

All therapists would probably agree that therapy is meant to move a person toward a more integrated and positive approach to life. The concept of growth or health may be used pragmatically or idealistically to effect change and adjustment to life. Or we can view growth and health from a more anthropological perspective, such as we have attempted to describe in the previous chapter. We believe that this is the way forward.

We certainly can say this: therapeutic gain is essentially a forward movement that seeks to remove obstacles to that movement. Growth as a therapeutic process then becomes more of a functional term than a term with precise anthropological content. As Carl Rogers notes, "Therapy is not a matter of doing something *to* the individual, or of inducing him to do something for himself. It is instead a matter of freeing him for normal growth and development, of removing obstacles so that he can move forward."[6] I suspect that Rogers is informed more by humanistic idealism than clinical pragmatism in his concept of health. His optimism concerning the inherent value and potential of the self for growth strongly influences his therapeutic method. I would agree that growth involves a person's movement toward health, but I would assert that this is also a spiritual process of dealing with one's need for divine grace.

Howard Clinebell, professor of pastoral counseling at the School of Theology at Claremont, California, is well known for his theory of "growth counseling." According to Clinebell, a person's spiritual and personal growth includes awareness, decision, freedom, meaning, commitment, quality of spiritual life, and relation to God. This is a life-long process or "growth journey" that never reaches a fixed goal. Growth toward wholeness is sought in six interdependent aspects: enlivening of the mind, refreshment of the body, enrichment of intimate relationships, rapport with the environment, progress in relating to institutions as well as others, and enhancement of personal relationship with God.[7] Clinebell's optimism concerning the individual's orientation toward growth is only exceeded by his breadth of reach in defining growth in terms of life's fullest possibilities! At first glance it appears very much like my own concept of the life continuum as therapeutic context. What is not so clear is precisely what anthropological content is given to this "growth journey."

Professor Newton Malony at the Fuller Seminary Graduate

School of Psychology attempts to integrate personal wholeness into the larger goals of spiritual holiness by drawing on the concept of "life environments" as depicted by T. R. Sargin. These environments are physical, situational, interpersonal, idealistic, and transcendental. "The term *whole person*," says Malony, "applies to this idea. To be whole means to be conscious of and adequate in all, not just some, of life's environments."[8]

Here we may have a combination of idealistic humanism and clinical pragmatism! The concept of health or wholeness is determined by a theory of life that includes the transcendental or religious aspects of the self. Also, functional competence is defined as being "adequate" in all of the life environments. This integrative model has the advantage of including religious values and goals in the therapeutic process, but it tends to blur the distinction between clinical therapy and the life-long process of personal and spiritual development. The effectiveness of this model depends on the weight given to the term *adequate*. If by adequacy Malony means a relative degree of effectiveness in integrating each of the components into the life of the self, then I tend to agree. To function adequately may only require a minimal degree of competence. But if that competence does not develop beyond "adequate," I am not sure that we still have "health" and certainly not growth. The questions remain.

The model we have chosen in this book relies more on a biblical anthropology than either idealism or pragmatism. The core paradigm of the person as presented in chapter 2 is repeated here for our reference.

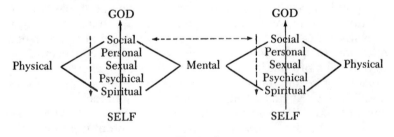

Figure 3

In this model we may define growth as integrative, relational, and open to change. The integrative dimension of growth is measured by the self's movement through the five stages of development, beginning with the social and ending with the spiritual. The integrative dimension means more than moving through these stages "adequately," to use Malony's term. Growth is not merely to arrive at any or all of the stages. Rather, integrative growth is to keep these aspects of the self in balance and integrated into the function of the self as a person. This means that there will be congruence between the self as identity and between the self as experienced in each area. For example, integrative growth would be recognized by realistic emotions and feelings at the psychical level fully congruent with the expression of the self at the sexual and social levels. This aspect of growth requires continual integrative processing of feelings, actions, and core identity as an interpretive task. Or, as we discussed in the previous chapter, it represents a therapeutic redefining of the self when confronted by experiences at any one of the five levels of personhood.

Bill, a sixteen-year-old high school student, had achieved a satisfactory level of integrative competence. In moving through adolescence he maintained healthy relationships with his peers, learned to handle his strong sexual urges, experienced strongly bonded relationships with his male friends, felt comfortable in his earliest dating experiences with girls, and was active in a campus-centered Bible study and in his church. At this point in his life his developmental and integrative growth in social, personal, sexual, psychical, and spiritual identity appeared adequate. Now, four years later, not only has his integrative growth stopped, but he is actually regressing.

After completing high school Bill left home and attended a college where he was virtually unknown and lacked the continuity of family, church, and friends. What was "adequate" in terms of integration in high school is now quite inadequate. The three (ecological) spheres of his life—physical, social, and spiritual—have begun to crumble. He suffered a football injury to his knee that will leave him with a permanent weakness, if not a disability. His comfortable relation with girls and the solidarity of male friends with whom he passed through adolescence have now opened up into unknown areas of sexual intimacy with expectations of life-long commitment. Male friendships are overlaid with competitiveness and insecurity. Philosophical questions intrude into the simplistic assumptions about a Bible that is to be taken on "faith alone." God seems to recede into the distance when he is needed the most. A mild depression and random thoughts of suicide signal Bill's disintegration.

Meanwhile, Bill's physical therapist instructs him in procedures for exercising his knee to prevent further injury and tells him to stay out of contact sports. Bill also meets once a week with a counselor to talk about his feelings of alienation and depression. On a visit home he confides in his pastor, who encourages him to "get back into fellowship with God" through regular Bible reading and prayer. As a parting thought, the pastor also suggests that Bill's knee injury might be God's way of telling him to change his major to religion and think about going into Christian ministry. Bill never did have the courage to tell him that he no longer believed in God. Bill has many losses to grieve; God is only one of them.

In each of the three ecological spheres Bill has a presenting problem. The physical therapist, psychologist, or pastor each in one's own way sees Bill primarily in terms of this problem. Each has counsel to give and a certain professional expertise with which to approach Bill. But it is Bill himself who will have to recover the integrative task and begin to move forward through growth and change. The role of a counselor now becomes much more than applying therapeutic skills in one of the three spheres of life. The very core of Bill's personal integration project has become fragmented as he has moved out of the security of this early context into his own world. Here is where our model provides insight into the kind of growth and development that a person like Bill needs to experience in order to recover his integrative task.

In addition to the integrative growth of the self as depicted in figure 3, there is a dimension of relational growth. This is growth in terms of relationship to others, again with congruence to the five developmental components—social, personal, sexual, psychical, and spiritual. For example, as he has developed sexually, integrating his sexual feelings with his personal, social, and spiritual identity, Bill has also encountered other people in each of these areas. In these new relationships he is very vulnerable. Suddenly he experiences for the first time the shock of being alone with himself. The easy familiarity with which he experienced himself as a social, personal, sexual, psychical, and spiritual being is no longer present now that the familiar context is gone. The others whom he encounters move quickly from being strangers to being roommates, classmates, or drinking mates, with little time for exploring the history and context of the self. He is drawn to others or repelled by them, like a magnetic force. He dares not allow the psychic pain of loneliness and grief over a loss to intrude into the camaraderie of social life in the dormitory. The psychic, social, and sexual become compartmentalized within Bill because his encounters with others are primarily one-dimensional. Bill is increasing the tempo and intensity of his life, but is losing the inner connectedness.

As a case in point, in his first experiences of intimacy with females outside the familiar structures of his family, friends, and male companions, Bill may find the physical immediacy of sexual encounter a powerful funnel through which he can pour his social, personal, psychical, and even spiritual needs in search of fulfillment. But what feels like integration of the self actually becomes disintegration. What is experienced as intimacy and closeness actually becomes a complicated negotiation of meeting needs while maintaining distance. Growth stops, integration fragments, and the self desperately seeks compensatory strategies to survive. Bill radically changes his personality and lifestyle. But this is change without growth, progression without development, and fusion without integration.

By telling the story of Bill, we have fleshed out the schematic model of integrative growth as a sign of movement toward health. The growth of the self is both integrative and relational. Bill experienced the first, but lost it when he failed to make relational growth. Relational growth as measured by this model of personhood is simultaneously integrative growth with respect to the self's congruence with itself in all areas. Here, too, growth will be expressed as therapeutic redefinition, or interpretation, as relationships constantly present new experiences of the self and others.

Openness to change lies at the very heart of growth. Whenever a person is open to change, there is growth potential. However, change alone is not necessarily growth, for change may merely be alteration in behavior without the two dimensions of growth discussed above. We saw clearly in Bill's case that growth must be both integrative and relational. Growth begins with openness to change; without it, integrative and relational growth simply cannot occur. The forward movement of growth toward health has anthropological content and character, as our model suggests. It is realistic, not merely idealistic; transformative, not merely adaptive and pragmatic.

Here, then, is our definition of growth as a sign of health:

- The development of the self in terms of core identity, integrating the social, personal, sexual, psychical, and spiritual;
- The relatedness of the self to others in such a way that the core integration remains intact;
- Openness to change as a condition of integrative growth and as the basis of therapeutic growth toward health.

The Motive Power for Growth

Effecting change in the personality dynamics of another person constantly challenges the therapeutic skills of a counselor or pastor. Sometimes pathology seems to be the most stable condition of all organic life. Resistance to change is rooted in the very nature of pathological structures. A neurosis is cunning and highly adaptable, able to make adjustments with computerlike speed to retain its own set of defenses. This instinctive adaptability can easily deceive the unwary counselor into thinking that growth is occurring when actually the patient has only adjusted his or her behavior to relieve therapeutic stress.

In a public lecture in the late 1960s the psychiatrist Viktor Frankl told of his transition from psychoanalytic therapy to what came to be called logotherapy. "I discovered that many patients were unwilling to terminate therapy, even after long periods," said Frankl, "because they lacked a positive will to meaning in their life. The thing that they feared the most was being well. Their sickness at least gave them a project on which they could focus their attention." Frankl's existentially oriented psychology led him to develop what he called a "psychotherapeutic anthropology" that precedes all psychotherapy.[9] What Frankl saw as untapped in the traditional psychotherapy was the role of the human spirit in positing a "will to meaning." This movement of the spirit can be understood as the core motive of the self in growth and openness to change.

The function of spirit as essential to the life and power of the person is consistently depicted in the Bible as a life force that issues out of the "heart," or the inner life of the person. One cannot cut away the life of the spirit as a "religious appendix" that serves no necessary function. "This means that the spirit must be distinguished from the soul or psyche," writes theologian Helmut Thielicke. "It must not be psychologically or psychopathologically derived from the psyche."[10]

The heart in biblical psychology appears to be the source and center of the person's imagination, intentions, will, and actions. Indeed, when the heart has become evil, then all of a person's thoughts and actions become sick and "unholy," or "unclean" (cf. Prov. 4:23; 6:18). David asks God not to remove his Holy Spirit from him and to create in him a new heart (Ps. 51:10–11). Jesus reminds his disciples that one does not become "unclean" through that which enters into the self; instead, what comes out of the self, out of the heart, makes one unclean: "For from within, out of the heart of man, come evil thoughts, fornication, theft, murder, adultery, coveting, wickedness, deceit, licentiousness, envy, slander, pride, foolishness" (Mark 7:21-22). In the same way, one is responsible to "keep one's heart," for "from it flow the springs of life" (Prov. 4:23). The source of the heart's positive and "healthy" motivations comes from a "new and right spirit" (Ps. 51:10).

What the Hebrew language meant when referring to the "heart" (leb) as the center and source of life, is what is meant by the psycho-spiritual dynamics of the self. The way a person "thinks" in this construct is not separated from who one is or how one feels. Rather, the conceptual and cognitive life is linked with the feelings, instincts, and motives of the person as embodied soul and ensouled body. The "heart" is expressed in actions that reveal motives and intentions. It is the core of the self in the most fundamental and comprehensive sense. The biblical concept of the heart is close to what I earlier called the "soul" as the core or center of the self. I think that the Greek word psyche as used in the New Testament can also be seen as representing this center of the life of the self.

When considered from this anthropological perspective, the

self is inner driven, not stimulus-response controlled. There is a stimulus-response factor that is appropriate to each of the subsystems of the self, by which certain changes in behavior can be produced. Specific therapeutic gains can often be produced through an intervention that makes use of this dynamic. But when we seek the motive power for growth as openness to change, we must probe deeper into the self than the psyche, as Frankl has reminded us. It is the self as spirit that integrates the various facets of personhood and produces openness to change.

How is the human spirit encountered therapeutically so as to release motive power for change and growth? In *Dynamics in Pastoring,* a work that has already become a standard reference in the field of pastoral theology, the Dutch scholar Jacob Firet offers us a model.[11] Firet's concern is for what he calls role fulfillment for the pastor. Because pastoral care is part of this task, what Firet says can also be applied to the entire continuum of counseling as we have understood it in this book. For it is in the dynamics of the growing and changing person that a ministry of the Word of God is made effective.

Firet distinguishes between the "hermeneutic moment" as a moment of understanding and the "agogic moment" as the moment of change and growth. What does this mean? We have already discussed the formation of the self as a hermeneutical task. That is, it is the task of reinterpreting the self therapeutically through encounter with new events and experiences. When we hear an idea or come to understand a concept in such a way that the new is assimilated into our already existing core of knowledge, we have the "aha!" experience. "Now I see what you are getting at!" is often the response when we are trying to make a point.

Many times one can listen to a sermon, to good advice, or to a therapist's comments and have the feeling, "I understand that. It makes sense. I see what you mean and I agree." Yet one can go away without changing the pattern of behavior that contradicts the wisdom and truth of what has been understood. No real change and growth have occurred. But Firet emphasizes that God's Word intends to effect change and growth, not merely to produce new information or new concepts in the mind. This is why the pastoral caregiver must go beyond the "hermeneutic moment" to the "agogic moment."

While the concept of pedagogy is familiar to us, the word

agogy is more recent and less familiar. *Agogy,* which basically means "guidance," describes a situation in which a person is not merely "addressed" or "talked at," but actually encountered in such a way that there is "guidance from one kind of action to another." Through the intermediary role of the counselor, an "agogic moment" can occur. "It is a motive force which activates the person on whom it is focused, so that that person begins to change."[12] What I earlier called the integrative process of growth is close to what Firet means by the term "agogic." It is *growth produced in the self by the guidance (agogy) of another.*

Firet warns against construing this kind of guidance as "nurture," because nurture presupposes an "ideal type" toward which the nurturer guides the person. As soon as a nurturing guidance becomes intentional, the person may stop growing and may wrongly depend on the nurturer as the actual power that produces change. In contrast to nurture, the agogic situation believes that the motive power for change lies within the client, not in the counselor. The counselor merely mediates that power and facilitates the growth process.

Let us define this process more fully. The "agogic situation," or growth process, is a human and personal encounter, whether ordinary or extraordinary, that releases a motive power that generates change. This change opens up the constricted world of the one who lives only marginally. The constricted person develops into a self-directed and fully functional participant in community, and his or her narrow self is expanded to a larger and more authentic existence. For example, in the case of Bill, a counselor who is herself an integrated and growing person can intervene into his "closed" self and become the agent of change and growth for him. A counselor who understands the power of grief to heal can guide Bill in the process of grieving his lost physical prowess (the injured knee). She can release in him a new motive power to intregrate this loss into his life and so transform it from something alien to part of his "story." The point at which this transformation occurs is what Firet means by the "agogic moment."

Firet describes three components in the agogic situation. First, a *motive power* comes into the situation in the form of a word, address, or symbolic action; second, *another person* acts as an intermediary for this motive power; and third an *effect* is marked by change and growth.[13] The Holy Spirit comes directly to persons as movement on the human spirit, suggests Firet. The motive power that enters the agogic situation comes from God as the source of human life itself. Yet persons recognize the effect of growth and change in a new motivation that is truly their own.

We see an example in David's expressing in a psalm, "Put a new and right spirit within me" (Ps. 51:10). Here David is referring to his relationship with Bathsheba and the killing of her husband. When the prophet Nathan confronts David about these sins, he creates the "agogic situation" by telling a story of a rich man who took the only sheep of a poor man to feed a stranger. David says, "The man . . . deserves to die." Nathan responds, "You are the man!" David acknowledges the truth: "I have sinned." Nathan then gives the final word of grace, indicating that change and growth have occurred: "You shall not die" (2 Sam. 12:13). All three components of the agogic situation are present. A *motive power* released in David allows him to integrate his own terrible deed and accept God's grace and forgiveness; Nathan acts as an *intermediary,* having earned the right to confront David in this way; and Psalm 51 testifies to the *effect* produced in David's life.

How do we recognize that an agogic moment or situation has occurred? Because the agogic moment affects the life, attitude, and behavior of the person, we can only recognize the moment after it has occurred. A client may come to a therapy session and say, "I could hardly wait to get here to tell you this. I woke up this morning and something was different. The feeling of that awful burden that I had been carrying was simply gone. I can't explain it, but I feel different." The counselor herself may not be aware of any precise moment in the previous sessions when a breakthrough occurred. There were, to be sure, times when the client seemed to gain new insight and when the therapeutic interpretation seemed accurate. But these were only "hermeneutic moments" with no immediate relief or change. Still, therapeutic insight and interpretation are valuable contributions to the therapeutic process. The agogic moment ordinarily does not happen without such insight.

In contrast to therapeutic insight, the agogic moment actually releases motive power to begin change and growth. The agogic moment requires above all an encounter between the "growth promoter" and the client that is fully human on both sides. There must be real *parity* between the one who hears and the one who speaks, between the one who counsels and the one who is counseled. This encounter is what Firet calls the "pre-agogic" situation; it means that *all action toward a human being with a view to his or her humanization has its starting point in dealing with a particular person as a human being.*[14]

Although the counseling relationship clearly differentiates between the therapist and client, the therapist (or growth promoter) must overcome this disparity and create an environment for the agogic situation. Says Firet, *"The growth promoter who does not enter the relationship as equal, does not enter the relationship: he not only does not come close to the other; he cannot even maintain distance; he is simply not there."*[15] The concepts of "being there" and "distance" suggest a therapeutic relation in which both the speaker and hearer, both the counselor and the counselee, are mutually defined through the encounter at the core level of human selfhood. This is more than a therapeutic strategy to gain confidence. It is an essential component of the process that produces growth and change as a therapeutic outcome.

Let us review what we have said about the motive power for growth:

- Resistance to change must be overcome by releasing a motive power from within the self;
- The motive power to change lies within the self in the form of "spirit" or "soul"; in this "center" the self thinks, wills, and feels;
- The self is inner-driven, not stimulus-response controlled;
- The motive power of the self is released through the encounter and guidance of another as agent of change;
- This encounter, called the "agogic moment," produces change by
  —releasing motive power within the self,
  —relying on the guidance of another person,
  —producing an actual effect of growth in the person.

The Counselor as the Human Equation in Therapy

Our focus in this chapter is on the counselor as growth promoter. Our thesis is that an effective therapeutic intervention is one in which the client's motive power to grow is facilitated by the counselor's perceived presence as a partner in the growth process. We have looked at the process of growth and change using Firet's terminology of the agogic moment. Instead of using this technical term, I will simply call it the "growth process." I will continue to assume that the threefold process of growth includes a release of motive power, the role of the counselor as intermediary, and a perceived effect of change and growth in the counselee.

The people who face each other in the counseling room have names. They have personal histories. They are somehow always vulnerable. They can be offended and hurt. Or they can be respected and granted the benefit of the doubt as mysterious beings, not capable of being resolved into a problem or a profession. They all have feelings as well as faces. They all have hopes and dreams as well as failings and fears. All of this, though it be unspoken, constantly attends the encounter of the counselor and the client and cries out that this relationship, too, despite the urgency of divine address or the misery of human need and weakness, demands that this humanity be recognized, affirmed, and cared for.

This could be mere rhetoric and sentimentality if it were not also fundamentally true and if the issues at stake were not so crucial.

The Swiss psychiatrist Paul Tournier is well known for his therapeutic distinction between "person" and "personage," as well as his emphasis on the humanity of the therapist. He urges us to bring the "personage into harmony with the person," not by looking inward "where the true nature of the person always eludes us," but by turning outward "towards the world, towards our neighbor, towards God." The "personage" is what others experience through our actions and presence; the "person" is who we actually are. This inner "person," Tournier says, is the real person who must be disclosed in order to overcome the personage.

Tournier found through his own therapeutic experience that "confession" on the part of the therapist often lessens a client's resistance to growth. He tells of a case in which he counseled a woman for weeks without progress. She had been referred to him by a colleague. In a time of prayer, Tournier discovered that he had been overconcerned with "being too much successful" in the eyes of his colleague. He shared this insight with his patient and discovered that the atmosphere between them improved considerably.[16] This is an example of what Firet means by "parity" between the counselor and counselee. Humanization must occur for there to be actual growth, and it occurs most effectively when the counselor engages the other as the person she or he is.

When we considered the anthropological basis for growth earlier in this chapter, we reproduced the core paradigm of personhood as developed in figure 3. From this perspective we defined growth as integrative, relational, and being open to change. This provides a more substantive basis for understanding what growth toward health means. Growth is not merely change, but the enhancement and enlargement of the self through integration. Change in behavior does not always mean change and growth at the integrative level.

Referring again to figure 3, we note that the construct of the self as related to the other constitutes core humanity itself. Therapeutic intervention into the core humanity of another therefore requires that an approach be made "humanly" and not merely "technically" or "professionally." The technical and professional training and skills that the counselor must bring to the therapy session can also be introduced through his or her own presence in the encounter as a person.

This does not violate the integrity or freedom of the counselee's "self," because the freedom and growth of the self are oriented toward the other person. That is to say, growth is not only integrative with respect to the self's congruence with itself in each of the levels of personhood, but it is also growth through relatedness to other selves. In fact, as Firet correctly states, change and growth only occur when this encounter takes place as part of the "agogic moment." For such a relationship to be effective, says Firet, a person must turn to another in trust to let her participate in the process of her own change and growth. A relationship can only produce this growth when mutual trust is engendered. In this encounter there must be a presence of "authority," not in the sense of a hierarchy of psychical, physical, technical, or even spiritual expertise, but in the sense of actually being an *auctor*, a "promoter of the prosperity" of a life in the process of becoming.[17]

By restating our basic thesis for this chapter, we can emphasize this point more clearly: *an effective therapeutic interven-*

tion is one in which the client's motive power to grow is facilitated by the counselor's perceived presence as a partner in the growth process. The effectiveness lies in the client's *perceiving* the counselor as a growth partner.

Even as the knife of a surgeon can cut but cannot heal, the psychic scalpel of the therapist can expose an atrophied and deformed human spirit, but cannot implant the power to trust, love, and act in faith. Most of us learn to trust and love and come to faith without extraordinary means of intervention. We suppose that we have a certain autonomy of selfhood because we have not had to surrender to the care of a professional therapist. But this is self-deception. From the beginning, we have had the personal space of our lives invaded by "growth promoters"! Yet we did not mind. We responded openly and freely to those who became partners in our own growth and development. But what we experienced ordinarily and somewhat routinely is the same thing that some of us need in a special and extraordinary sense when the process of growth and change stops. It is when we become stuck that we need the intervention of a skilled "growth promoter."

In these therapeutic situations, the "growth process" (agogic moment) begins with encounter in which the counselor mediates the "power that motivates growth" directly and discerningly. The counselor's therapeutic skill provides the discernment and precision to mediate the power accurately. Hence we can appreciate the value of intensive training as a psychologist, therapist, or pastoral counselor. These people need all their skills and knowledge in their ministry of mediating the motive power that produces change and growth. This motive power is love.

The role of the counselor as growth promoter can be summarized as follows:

- Counselors are open to the real humanity of their counselees, and this is perceived by the counselees;
- Counselors are present in the counseling situation so as to reveal their own humanity;
- The core humanity of each person is structurally open to the other; thus the counselor does not "invade" the counselee but is present as a growth partner.

The Motive Power of Love

The power that motivates persons can be indiscriminate and even destructive. In its most positive sense this power may be viewed as a "self-actualizing" potential in which the drive to move through basic human needs to higher needs is considered the motivating force in therapy (e.g., Abraham Maslow). In more Freudian terms, this power may be viewed as blind libidinous instinct or craving that needs to be connected to positive and healthy ego needs through analysis and transference (e.g., Melanie Klein). Or, it may be viewed in a more mystical sense as a kind of "daimonic" impulse or drive, which can be either destructive or creative (e.g., Rollo May). In behavioristic psychology, power is not an attribute of the self, but a phenomenon of stimulus-response mechanism. The power to produce change lies almost totally with the stimulus (e.g., B. F. Skinner).

All these concepts of power as a therapeutic resource tend to be individualistic and phenomenological. That is, they seek sources for altering a person's behavior within the personality itself or, in the case of behaviorism, totally outside the personality.

In the anthropological model we are using, power is not simply a person's need, craving, or search for creativity. Nor is power totally outside the person. The power of selfhood is "response power." The image of God as a divine endowment posits a power of "response-in-kind" as the essential motivation of persons. In the biblical story of creation, Adam, the solitary male, is "powerless" to change and grow even though he has "control" over his environment, can name the animals, and hear God's commands and obey them. What is lacking is what I call "response-in-kind" power. The biblical text says that Adam lacked a "partner" or "helper," or "one corresponding to him," as the Hebrew word literally says (Gen. 2:18). With the creating and positioning of the other person as one whom he could encounter directly, Adam became "empowered" to respond out of the depth of himself to one who had the power to encounter him as such. This response-in-kind empowerment links the motivating power of the self as the source of change and growth to human encounter and relationship.

Whereas God's address and command to Adam did not empower him in this way, the encounter with the other human did. This, of course, is precisely what the creation story means to tell us. God and human personhood are as unalike as they are alike. The divine image does not lie solely between God and an individual human, but also in the relationship of persons. The quality of this relationship is indeed grounded in the motive power of God's own love—this is what the image of God means to convey as a material gift of human empowerment. In the human encounter of one with the other, the core motivation of the self to love is released as response-in-kind.

We now have the answer to Roszak's charge that the personhood of one is violated by the intervention of another. The problem is not an ethical one, as Roszak seems to assume, but an anthropological one. If people are structurally open to the other as necessary to the growth and integration of the self, then love that seeks the other's growth and health is not an invasion, but a prompter. Christians who counsel from this perspective make interventions humanly, not merely professionally. This is all the more important to remember for those who have spiritual and pastoral motivations in counseling.

Love is a motivating power only for God and for those who bear his image. "We love," says the apostle, "because he first loved us" (1 John 4:19). We are urged to love one another because "love is of God, and he who loves is born of God and knows God" (4:7). Also, "if we love one another, God abides in us and his love is perfected in us" (4:12).

Clearly, such love as a motivating power for growth is more than an affection or an "attitude." All human expressions of love should seek growth, in oneself and in the other. This requires the "real presence" of the other, in both word and deed. The person who releases love as the motive power is open to change, which means open to the Spirit of God as the source of renewal, growth, and change. A counselor who is cautious and closed to this spiritual openness as a dynamic of the therapeutic encounter has already sacrificed the greater possibility of empowerment for growth to the lesser goal of therapeutic efficiency.[18]

When Jesus commissioned his disciples to minister the reality of the kingdom of God, he sent them out without title or professional status. He sent them out in the same form in which he himself was present in the world—becoming human for the sake of the salvation of humans. "Whenever you enter a town and they receive you, eat what is set before you; heal the sick in

it and say to them, 'The kingdom of God has come near to you'"
(Luke 10:9; cf. also Luke 17:21; Matt. 10:7).[19]

Summary

In this chapter we have argued the thesis that an effective
therapeutic intervention is one in which the client's motive
power to grow is facilitated by the counselor's perceived
presence as a partner in the growth process.

- We defined growth as integrative, relational, and openness
  to change;
- We examined the concept of the agogic moment as the
  release of the motive power to change;
- We sought to understand the role of the counselor as a
  partner in the growth process;
- We discovered that God's love seeks its fulfillment in the
  human task of growth and that this saving and sanctifying
  love is released through the reciprocal love experienced
  between the counselor and the client in the therapeutic
  encounter.

This love is not treason or treachery committed against the
human self. It liberates, empowers, and enriches personal life.
Christians who counsel are sent with this gracious permission
and commission. It is indeed a high calling.

Notes

1. Theodore Roszak, *Person/Planet* (Garden City, N.Y.: Double-
day/Anchor, 1979), 139.
2. Michael Balint, *The Doctor, His Patient and the Illness*
(Marshfield, Md.: Pitman, 1957), 5: cited by Roger Hurding, *The Tree of
Healing* (Grand Rapids: Zondervan, 1988), 188.
3. Cited by Hurding, *The Tree of Healing*, 28–29.
4. Ibid.
5. Allen E. Bergen, "Psychotherapy and Religious Values," in
*Wholeness and Holiness: Readings in the Psychology/Theology of
Mental Health*, ed. H. Newton Malony (Grand Rapids: Baker, 1983),
306f.
6. Carl Rogers, *Counseling and Psychotherapy* (Boston: Houghton
Mifflin, 1942), 29.
7. Howard Clinebell, *Basic Types of Pastoral Care and Counseling*
(London: SCM Press, 1984), 31–34. See also, "Growth Counseling," in

Helping People Grow, ed. Gary Collins (Ventura, Calif.: Vision House, 1980).

8. H. Newton Malony, ed., *Wholeness and Holiness: Readings in the Psychology/Theology of Mental Health* (Grand Rapids: Baker, 1983), 20–21.

9. Donald F. Tweedie, Jr., *Logotherapy: An Evaluation of Frankl's Existential Approach to Psychotherapy* (Grand Rapids: Baker, 1961), 35. For further reading in the concept of logotherapy, see Viktor Frankl, *The Unconscious God: Psychotherapy and Theology* (London: Hodder and Stoughton, 1977); *Man's Search for Meaning: An Introduction to Logotherapy* (Boston: Beacon Press, 1959); *The Doctor and the Soul: From Psychotherapy to Logotherapy* (New York: Alfred A. Knopf, 1955).

10. Helmut Thielicke, *Being Human . . . Becoming Human* (New York: Doubleday, 1984), 446.

11. Jacob Firet, *Dynamics in Pastoring (Het agogisch Moment in het pastoraal Optreden),* trans. John Vriend (Grand Rapids: Eerdmans, 1986), esp. 99ff.

12. Ibid., 101.

13. Ibid.

14. Ibid., 161 (emphasis in original).

15. Ibid., 165 (emphasis in original).

16. Paul Tournier, *The Meaning of Persons* (London: SCM Press, 1957), 35–36: cited by Hurding, *The Tree of Healing,* 330.

17. Firet, *Dynamics in Pastoring,* 112.

18. Charles Gerkin comments perceptively on the "gap" between the self and the other that must be interpreted positively from the perspective of object relations theory when he says: "Thus a gap is formed between the self and the mother as well as the self and God, and this gap must be interpreted. This interpretation comprises the task of the life of the soul as seen theologically as it comprises the task of the self as we have seen it from the psychological perspective of object relations theory. But, as in the analogous relationship with the earthly mother, this task of sustaining the life of the self or soul is not simply an autonomous activity. Rather the life of the soul is facilitated by God, who both asserts otherness and mirrors the deepest longings of the human spirit" (*The Living Human Document* [Nashville: Abingdon, 1984], 95).

19. The Roman Catholic theologian Hans Urs von Balthasar expresses the case for salvation as present healing in the midst of continuing imperfection when he says, "Thus man, healed and made whole in the salvation of God, and thus in this simple basic sense holy, rests in a mysterious suspension he does not himself understand and which on that very account is strangely exhilarating. He is clearly aware

of earthly imperfectibility, which does not become for him the oppressive prison. The thought of having to perfect himself at any cost does not become an obsession. Knowing of the house built up in grace for him with God, he can cheerfully inhabit his tumbledown hut and free himself through time" (A *Theological Anthropology* [New York: Sheed and Ward, 1967], 101).

This may be one way of expressing the relation of wholeness to holiness, but one should also be careful not to let it become permission to leave persons in untherapeutic environments with only spiritual assurances as a form of comfort. This would be to give a stone when a child asks for bread!

PART TWO

———

SPIRITUAL DYNAMICS
IN COUNSELING

4

The Kingdom of God as Therapeutic Context

As we turn our focus to spiritual dynamics in counseling, we need to clarify the context and culture that bear on the therapeutic interventions made by Christian psychologists and therapists. What we have called the "growth process" (agogic moment) involves a process of change and development of the client in a therapeutic relationship. There is an "ecological" dimension to the self that involves relationship to others as well as to God. This necessarily entails a social and cultural context in which the change takes place.

S. L. Halleck writes in *The Politics of Therapy,* "There is no way in which the psychiatrist can deal with behavior that is partly generated by a social system without either strengthening or altering that system. Every encounter with a psychiatrist, therefore, has political implications."[1]

This was certainly true for Jesus! The religious authorities condemned his healing of the man blind from birth (John 9) because it occurred on the Sabbath. Jesus' healing challenged a social and religious system that tolerated the sick and deformed to preserve its institutional life. On one occasion, when confronted with a man having a paralyzed arm, Jesus challenged the authorities with a question: "Is it lawful on the Sabbath to do good or to do harm?" (Mark 3:4). When they did not reply, he immediately healed the man. This healing directly challenged the prevailing ethical and religious culture of Jesus' society. Often he explicitly commanded those healed from mental illness to return to their homes and communities and there testify of their healing as a sign that the kingdom of God had manifested its power (Mark 5:19).

Therapeutic gains do not occur in a cultural or social vacuum. Christians who counsel are keenly aware of this—too keenly aware, in many cases, for their own comfort. They realize that they cannot intervene therapeutically without a conscious or unconscious intention to help the client adapt to his or her own cultural context. The very fact that a person seeks therapy or is urged by others to seek help indicates some degree of cultural and social maladaptation. "Implicit in every therapy is a theory of culture," suggests Alvin Dueck.[2]

From a Christian perspective, the issue of a cultural theory with regard to therapeutic goals becomes critical. The counselor's attempts to extend therapeutic gain to include growth toward specific personal and religious values and goals could be viewed as inappropriate or even "unethical" from the perspective of secular culture.

The social and cultural context that the client brings to the growth process will affect the process in at least two ways. First, any growth or change in the client will require integration back into the culture and context from which the client is coming. This often involves therapeutically redefining one's identity and relationship to that culture. But failure to make this integrative movement will leave the client alienated from the only culture he or she knows.

Second, the culture that the therapist brings to the situation will affect the growth process in some way. The long-range "growth goals" as negotiated between the therapist and client may require modifying the culture of either the client or the therapist. When the culture of the Christian counselor includes values and goals assumed to be essential to human health and wholeness as theologically defined, there may be a confrontation of cultures in working out the therapeutic goals. The counselor will have to determine how far these growth goals can be made part of the therapeutic goals without making this confrontation disruptive and nontherapeutic. Even Jesus could not do more for some people than to provide mental and physical healing. Beyond that he urged the transformation of the culture itself to provide a context for growth (as seen in the Sermon on the Mount, Matt. 5–7).

When a Christian counselor has a client who is suffering

mental and emotional abuse in a marriage relationship and the other partner in the marriage will not respond to therapeutic intervention, a separation or even divorce may result. Counseling an alcoholic to sobriety will greatly affect the client's marital or family relationship. If a codependent is involved, that person, unable to sustain a relationship with a recovering alcoholic, may leave. The counselor's own values and cultural framework will be influenced as well. Therapeutic gains are social and cultural realities that affect both counselor and counselee. For Christians who counsel, the biblical theme of the kingdom of God provides a therapeutic context in which to consider these factors.

In this section we are shifting the focus from therapy as a process of integrative growth to the environment of therapeutic gain. This environment is, in fact, the culture in which both the therapist and the client exist. The culture is the particular ethos, worldview, values, and common language—among other things—that make up the context of individuals.

Christians describe this culture as the kingdom of God, a theme that runs throughout Scripture. We will look first at the culture of the kingdom of God with respect to counseling goals, and then at three specific themes of the kingdom: righteousness, wisdom, and community.

The Kingdom of God and Counseling Goals

The concept of the kingdom of God is central to the Judeo-Christian tradition. The kingdom is a social reality over which and through which God exercises his power and presence, rather than merely a realm over which he reigns. God promised a land, but he established a people before he gave them a land.

The kingdom of God is a culture that takes form in world culture. That is to say, there is a culture unique to a society and people whose personal, social, and religious life is oriented to this particular God who makes covenant with them. But this kingdom culture only exists as a particular form of "world culture." The cultural matrix of the Semitic people, descended from Shem, a son of Noah, became the world culture in which the kingdom culture took form.

However, no essential language, race, sexual role, ethnic origin, or worldview belongs to the culture of the kingdom of God. This was not made clear in the Old Testament, although it was implicit in the original covenant promise to Abraham—"By you all the families of the earth shall bless themselves" (Gen. 12:3)—and was quite explicit in the prophecy of Joel—"I will pour out my spirit on all flesh; your sons and your daughters shall prophesy . . ." (Joel 2:28).

The relativity of all world cultures became clear through the incarnation, death, and resurrection of Jesus of Nazareth. Though Jesus was born a male Jew and was socialized into the Palestinian culture of the first century, his resurrection and the sending of his Spirit fulfilled the prophecy of Joel and broke down the wall of cultural particularity as a criterion of the kingdom of God (cf. Eph. 2:14–22; Gal. 3:26–29).

Let me repeat the point: The kingdom of God is a culture with its own social and religious life that takes form in existing world cultures. This culture of the kingdom uses existing cultural forms and *corrects* and *adapts* these forms to the content and reality of the kingdom of God. The kingdom of God understood in this way has a therapeutic aim that seeks the health and wholeness of individuals in the context of the community that provides their core identity. God enters into the personal, social, and historical life of people in order to release a motive power for wholeness (*shalom*), righteousness, faith, and love of God and neighbor. This is what we have called the growth process.

This is a critical insight for Christians who counsel. It means especially that the context of each person's life is not alien to the culture of the kingdom of God. People can be accepted as persons in the social context in which they live. This means that Christian counselors can authentically relate to non-Christians at this level. The kingdom of God does not discriminate between those who believe in God and those who do not, but treats each person as someone created in the divine image and as an object of God's love and care. This also means, however, that the kingdom of God works from within the existing social and cultural matrix of each person to bring liberation and healing, especially in the forms inflicted by that person's own social setting. The kingdom of God is not primarily a religious culture, but a power that liberates and frees persons within their existing culture to experience the "human" culture that belongs by right of God's creation to each person.

No longer are individuals oppressed by impersonal and tyrannical world powers; they are liberated (as in the Exodus) to become a new people whose social relationships become the source of personal identity and power becomes transformed into covenant love.

No longer are people subject to the blind and capricious powers of nature; they are aligned with the power of a creator God who intervencs into these natural forces and sustains the fragile life of his own people.

No longer are people possessed by powers and spirits that defile and destroy; they are filled and directed by the good and holy Spirit of God.

No longer do moral failure, outbreak of cruelty, and breakdown of family leave hopeless victims and unmediated guilt; the same God who demands holiness in life and action provides atonement, healing, and restoration through rituals of forgiveness and renewal.

With God incarnated through Jesus of Nazareth, this culture of the kingdom became a living power and presence through his person and ministry. Through the calling of the twelve disciples, Jesus reconstitutes the kingdom community and culture. He delivers the ethical mandate of the kingdom as the Sermon on the Mount and invites everyone, without discrimination, to enter the kingdom. The conflict occurs between the culture of the kingdom and the prevailing culture of religious Judaism, where the concerns for justice, forgiveness, righteousness, and healing have been forgotten.

Jesus did not specialize in individual therapy as a clinical procedure—though he did not turn away from offering such help. His concern was for the growth goals that belong to persons as created in the divine image. He called for the integration of the entire self and pointed to the healing and purifying power of the inner life directed outward toward others and toward God. He demanded the integration of religious truth with social concern. He sought the integration of prayer with feeding the hungry and healing the sick. He enacted the integration of social unity over the barriers of racial, sexual, and religious discrimination.

Jesus left no person standing in the spot where they were healed, but either sent them back to be integrated with their own people again, as a sign of the kingdom of God, or called them as followers into the new community of the kingdom.

This understanding of the kingdom provides a context for

developing an approach to therapy from a Christian perspective. The kingdom of God is a therapeutic context that offers, as Jesus claimed, "the way, the truth, and the life" (John 14:6).

- This way is the way of *wisdom,* which leads to the good and fulfilled life;
- This truth is the truth of *righteousness,* which gives moral worth and value to life;
- This life relates the individual to the *community* of faith and hope, a community extending beyond, yet including, this present existence with its suffering and sorrow.

These three "ways," constituting the heart of the Christian life and grounded in Jesus himself, give us a threefold paradigm to explore further the culture of the kingdom of God with respect to counseling goals.

The Way of Wisdom: A Discerning Praxis

If people who seek help from counselors could express in one word what they would like, beyond relief from pain or depression, it probably would be wisdom. They would be quick to point out that wisdom does not mean knowledge, though knowledge helps. You may need knowledge to know how to take the first step, but you need wisdom to know how to take the second step before you take the first!

In the Old Testament, wisdom meant discovering and living the kind of life that brought health, happiness, and fulfillment. The book of Proverbs extols wisdom as fruitfulness, meaningful work, moral sensibility, and security for body and soul.

The kingdom of God provides a context for discerning and practicing wisdom. The wisdom of the kingdom is not abstract and theoretical; it is practical and within reach of each person through the right actions. "Wisdom," says Samuel Southard,

is reflection upon human possibilities and limitations in the light of God's revelation. It is guided both by realistic observations of ourselves and explanations of our attitudes and behaviors that are drawn from revealed knowledge of God's original intentions for his creation. The context for the wisdom of God is the power of his love shown in understanding of the self and others—both friends and strangers.[3]

Here again, those who seek counseling will often lament their inability to act and behave in ways that result in happiness and well-being. They know better than most philosophers that wisdom is discovered in the living of life, not in reflecting on it. This discovery of the way of living is called *praxis*. Wisdom is a discerning praxis, and as such it is one important aspect of the culture of the kingdom of God.

The concept of praxis originates with Aristotle, who distinguished between two kinds of action. The first he called *poiesis,* the act of making something that results in a product. The *telos,* or final value or character of this activity, is not included in the product. The second kind he called *praxis.* This kind of action includes the telos intentionally in the action as an outcome and also as a criterion for the quality of the action. In praxis, one not only is guided in one's actions by the intention of realizing the telos, but also discovers the telos through the action itself.[4]

We could illustrate this distinction in the construction of a house. We measure the competence of the builder by the technical specifications and quality of the house as a product of professional craftsmanship. The end use of the house in terms of the character of the people who use it (its telos), is not a factor contained in its making. The builder would presumably devote the same skill and diligence to constructing a brothel or a church. The one who merely builds the house is not liable for its final use or purpose (telos). The way of wisdom is discovered through an authentic praxis in which God's purpose is more and more realized in the living of life.

Praxis is not merely a "practice" in which one makes a product or applies a theoretical knowledge; it means discerning the truth as a final outcome of one's action. The action itself contains its own good end, and if the end is not "good," the action cannot be the right one. For example, when Jesus healed on the Sabbath, he was acting in accordance with the telos of the Sabbath, that is, God's purpose for the Sabbath in terms of reconciliation and restoration of life to its God-intended value. This was a form of praxis. The religious authorities who challenged Jesus "practiced" the keeping of the law like a blueprint, ignoring the telos of the law of the sabbath. This was a form of *poiesis,* as Aristotle would say. This blind keeping of the law concealed from the self-righteous Pharisees the true purpose of the law. Even more serious, the action failed to yield the wisdom to see Jesus as the one in whom the work of God was actually present.

The Old Testament emphasizes that God in his actions intends good for his people. Likewise, the good life in word and deed will lead the people to the goal of *shalom*, a concept of peace and prosperity as a divine gift.

Jesus reiterated this concept of wisdom embodied in praxis when he said, "You will know them by their fruits" (Matt. 7:16) and "Why do you call me 'Lord, Lord,' and not do what I tell you?" (Luke 6:46). He used the analogy of the good and the bad tree to make his point: "For no good tree bears bad fruit, nor again does a bad tree bear good fruit; for each tree is known by its own fruit" (Luke 6:43–44).

The kingdom of God is revealed through a praxis that embodies the telos, or maturity of a life through its actions. The New Testament Greek word *teleios* (mature, perfect) was used by those who translated the Old Testament into Greek (the Septuagint) to render the Hebrew word *salem* (shalom), which means "sound, complete, whole." The stress is on the concept of being whole, perfect, or intact. It is used of the heart that is wholly turned toward God (1 Kings 8:61; 11:4) and of the person who is wholly bound to God (Gen. 6:9; Deut. 18:13).

Teleios is often used in the New Testament to mean "mature, adult, fully developed" (1 Cor. 2:6; 14:20; Phil. 3:15). Paul uses the word to say that he has not yet become fully "perfect" (Phil. 3:12). But then he adds, "Let those of us who are mature [*teleios*] be thus minded" (v. 15).

There is both an anthropological and an eschatological concept of maturity or perfection. From the anthropological perspective, maturity is not a process of ethical perfection realized by degrees. Rather, maturity signifies the undivided wholeness of a person in his or her behavior (cf. Matt. 19:21; James 1:4). When applied to individuals, *teleios*, or maturity, does not denote the qualitative end point of human endeavor, but anticipates eschatological wholeness in actual living.

For example, a baby is "perfect" if it is healthy and growing, even though it has not yet reached its "perfect" or "complete" maturity. Through the praxis of living, the child not only will grow, but through growth will actually discern and discover a way of living. No person's wisdom can be given to another; each must discover it through the praxis of living life itself.

Jesus encouraged his disciples to "be perfect" even as the heavenly Father is perfect (Matt. 5:48). In his high priestly prayer Jesus asked that his followers be "perfected in unity" so that the world might recognize the presence of Christ in their lives (John 17:21). The concept of maturity, therefore, not only must relate to an eschatological goal, but also must be a Christological reality given in the present time through the gift of the Holy Spirit. The gift of the Holy Spirit is then itself confirmed through a praxis of living whereby the fruit of the Spirit—love, joy, peace, gentleness, goodness, etc.—are experienced as part of what we have called growth goals.[5]

The "wisdom" discerned through praxis is not a maturity that comes with age or experience alone, but is what I have earlier called a growth process. It is a gift of discernment by which one's life is secured and upheld from an ultimate source—God's love and grace. This is a praxis of faith, by which one's attitudes, emotions, and actions become ordered and integrated through appropriation of this reality. This is to "know the truth" (John 8:32). It is to "walk in newness of life" (Rom. 6:4); to "walk by the Spirit" (Gal. 5:16); to "walk in love" (Eph. 5:2); and to "walk in the day" rather than in darkness (John 11:9).

The metaphor of walking carries exactly the meaning of praxis as the discernment of wisdom. To "take up one's bed and walk" (John 4:8) is not merely for the exercise, but to be integrated back into life, to gain the "maturity" that belongs to those who are fully functioning at the personal and social level. The physical healing that enabled the paralyzed man to walk also reintroduced him to his society and culture; he could no longer "carry about" with him the old culture of being a cripple. In carrying his own bed he now has a praxis of life where he will discern the wisdom of life as his personal goal and purpose as measured in terms of his social and communal life. The apostle Paul suffered an apparently incurable physical problem that he called his "thorn in the flesh." By his own testimony he says that after praying three times for it to be removed, he came to the understanding that this was to be a means of grace: "My grace is sufficient for you." Therefore, concluded Paul, "my strength is made perfect in weakness" (2 Cor. 12:9). This is the way of wisdom by which one can gain the inner strength and coherence of life to cope with what cannot be removed or changed.

Now, then, how does the kingdom of God act as a context for

therapy? Surely we must see that therapy offers more than psychological restoration. The goals of therapy go beyond removing physical or emotional dysfunction. Integrating self with self, with others, and with God is a praxis that discerns meaning and purpose. The way of wisdom is the telos that reaches back into the actions (praxis) of therapy to enable the client to establish a coherent meaning to life. This itself can be transforming, even when not every situation in life can be transformed. There are losses that can only be grieved, including a failed marriage, the loss of a child to raise because of abortion, or damage done to others through one's carelessness.

The moral law supports the moral judgments in such cases. But the moral law does not itself contain the moral freedom or wisdom to provide healing and restoration. The kingdom of God brings moral wisdom, not merely a relentless application of the moral law. The church will often be tempted to think its primary responsibility is to uphold the moral law of God and thus leave those without moral virtue or standing exposed as victims or failures. But if the church as the sign of the kingdom of God in the world is to embody the moral wisdom of the kingdom, it will need to offer restoration and renewal to those who have no moral standing.

To say that "God hates divorce" (cf. Mal. 2:16) does not give the Christian community the right to deny the grace of God to those who have experienced this tragedy and failure of marriage vows. The moral wisdom of God receives greater emphasis in the Old Testament than his moral outrage! The story of Hosea contains a powerful message of mercy and grace extended to a people who have "committed adultery" with God as their marriage partner, yet are the objects of God's love and renewal in grace. The restoration of a person who has shattered a marriage, aborted a fetus, or damaged another person's life has high priority with God, for it is the restoration of his image in humanity. The tension between upholding the divine order in its perfection and upholding the divine intention in restoring humanity is a praxis of moral wisdom. Christians who counsel are agents of redemption when they function in this way.

Therapists who wish to bring a Christian perspective to bear in the therapeutic process need to have this "maturity" or wisdom that comes through praxis before they set themselves up in "practice." So, too, the criteria to assess and measure effective therapy will consider the client's growth goals in terms of the wisdom that belongs to those who experience the kingdom of God.

The Gospels tell of a demon-possessed man who lived naked among the tombs and bore the broken chains with which his former neighbors had tried to control him. When Jesus healed the man, he was found "sitting at the feet of Jesus, clothed and in his right mind" (Luke 8:35). We marvel at the healing of this man's emotional and mental condition. But who provided the clothes? This man's clothing symbolized his reentry into the community, his acceptance with trust and loving care, and his newly discovered praxis of community. In the end, this "healing," marked by his clothing and acceptance into the community, is as great a marvel as the healing of his tortured mind. In a sense, this case is a parable of the culture of the kingdom of God as a therapeutic context. Jesus could not have done it alone. And the man was not "made perfect" until he was clothed and restored to community.

This is the wisdom and the healing praxis by which one's life is "made whole," which is a mark of the culture of the kingdom of God. This is the *way* that Jesus offers as the discernment of wisdom for life. We now look at the *truth* as a person's moral horizon in the kingdom of God.

The Way of Righteousness: A Coherent Moral Vision

The biblical concept of truth is lodged in the larger concept of righteousness. The righteousness of God is his acting "rightly" so as to bring forth the truth as a result. We cannot be "in the truth" unless we are rightly related to God and to our neighbor. The opposite of truth is unrighteousness, which is a life devoted to deception and deviousness. This is a basic theme in Paul's letter to the Romans (especially chapters 3–6).

A life congruent with the truth of God's purpose as lived out in praxis has a moral vision that is shared with the community and culture with which one is identified. In the Christian community and culture, moral vision and moral discourse permeate all structures and relationships. Stanley Hauerwas makes this point when he says:

The church as a community of moral discourse gives meaning to its ethical terms. To use such terms as freedom and equality as values that are Christian and hence appropriate in a theory of government or therapy neglects the fact that these terms have material content in Jesus' definition of the Kingdom and as they are incarnated in His life and death. Ethical terms are not self interpreting but require a tradition to give them content.[6]

In the environment of the kingdom of God, personal goals are thus subject to kingdom goals while, at the same time, kingdom righteousness is exemplified in the integrity of social relationships. While the kingdom is concerned with the inner righteousness life of the individual person, it is even more concerned with justice for the oppressed, fairness in trade and commerce, regard for the poor and the "stranger within the gate," and genuineness in approach to God through the worship and rituals of community life.

The kingdom of God imposes a "coherent moral vision" on the existing cultural and social structures, stressing righteousness as an ethical link between persons and a religious connection between the people and God. In the culture of the kingdom of God, the moral and spiritual apostasy of one person affects the righteousness of the community. This is seen in the dramatic incident when Achan stole and hid some of the things taken from the enemies in the victory over Jericho. His single action caused the defeat of Joshua in the next military campaign, and the writer says that in this situation, "the people of Israel broke faith . . ." (Josh. 7:1–26). In many other incidents, the actions of a few resulted in the loss of righteousness for the entire people.

The concept of a coherent moral vision, then, is not an abstract set of moral principles. It is a moral vision of the social structure of community in which individual lives are bound up in a coherent and interconnected whole.

The righteousness of a single person is derived from the righteousness of a people as a whole. However, this righteousness is not the result of the perfecting of individual moral lives. The righteousness of the people solely depends upon the grace of God, who constitutes them as a people. The covenant, as the binding metaphor of this relation between the Lord and the people, is the basis for the moral vision of a people who "belong to Yahweh" and who are therefore a holy people because he who called and constituted them as a people is holy.

This can be seen from another perspective as well. The individual partakes of the righteousness of the community as a privilege and gift. Circumcision sanctified a person symbolically both by "cutting away the flesh" of natural origin and by creating a new identity as a covenant person. The community, not the individual act of penance, provided the source for renewal of faith and the renewal of moral and spiritual integrity.

The community functioned both as administrator of justice and mediator of mercy between God and the individual. No private contrition or familial bond could sufficiently dissolve the ethical relation of the individual to the community. Achan repented of his wrongdoing, but the community nonetheless stoned him to death for his sin. Parents might excuse their children's rebellious acts, but they must nonetheless hand their children over to the elders of the community for discipline (Deut. 21:18–21).

Yet the community was also commanded to provide cities of refuge for the "manslayer" to find protection against the avenger (Num. 35). Righteousness is not only retribution for wrongdoing to satisfy a sense of moral justice; it is an act of restoring lost personhood. The community, as the source of a person's moral dignity, provides that moral worth through concrete actions of social inclusiveness.

In dealing with "outsiders" and those without any claim to righteousness, Jesus himself provided a "circle of refuge" for the sinner. To self-righteous critics who accused him of indiscretion, he said, "The tax collectors and the harlots go into the kingdom of God before you" (Matt. 21:31; cf. also Luke 7:29–30).

The one who mediates between the individual and the community performs a "priestly" service, both as an advocate of the individual who approaches the community for healing and restoration, and as representative of the community as an "agent of righteousness." This priestly service is closely linked to the growth process, in which a motive power to experience change and growth is released. As an intermediary, the one who performs the priestly service shares a common humanity and mediates the righteousness of grace and healing.

For every high priest chosen from among men is appointed to act on behalf of men in relation to God, to offer gifts and sacrifices for sin. He can deal gently with the ignorant and wayward, since he himself is beset with weakness. Because of this he is bound to offer sacrifice for his own sins as well as for those of the people. And one does not take the honor upon himself, but he is called by God, just as Aaron was (Heb. 5:1–4).

This person embodies the "moral horizon" that constitutes the community of the kingdom of God. But the person does not function primarily as an ethical agent, bound to ethical codes of professional practice alone. This person is an agent of righteousness. As a therapeutic gain, one may remove psychological guilt, but to establish the person "in righteousness" places the person in truth. That is, the gift of forgiveness and peace is affirmed by one's belonging to and participating in the kingdom of God. Such forgiveness goes beyond even contrition and confession, which themselves are not sufficient to establish righteousness. The righteousness of the kingdom of God is a social and communal reality mediated through and by the one who performs this priestly service.

Christians who counsel can also represent this culture of the kingdom of God. They need to think of righteousness in terms of a life that is given a "moral horizon" as a growth goal in addition to the growth goals belonging to the process of therapy. The wisdom that people seek when they come for counseling will often be hidden to them, and perhaps to the counselor as well. A skill even more important for the counselor than clinical intuition is the discerning praxis of this wisdom that will orient the client to a trajectory of health and growth extending beyond specific therapeutic gains.

Didn't Jesus suggest that, with his authority and presence, every Christian could act as an "agent of righteousness" (cf. John 20:21–23; Acts 1:8)? The early church seemed to think so. "But you are a chosen race, a royal priesthood, a holy nation, God's own people, that you may declare the wonderful deeds of him who called you out of darkness into his marvelous light. Once you were no people but now you are God's people; once you had not received mercy but now you have received mercy" (1 Peter 2:9–10). We will have more to say about this in the final chapter of this book as we develop more fully the role of the counselor as a form of pastoral care.

Christian counselors should represent the coherent moral vision embodied in a community that offers righteousness beyond therapeutic gain. Such counselors provide the growth goal of righteousness through authentic forgiveness and affirmation by a community representing the kingdom of God.

Does this mean that a Christian therapist must in every case provide therapy through the institutional form of the Christian community—say a local church setting? Not necessarily. In the parable of the good Samaritan, the Samaritan became the agent of righteousness, not the priest or the Levite, both of whom represented the institutionalized religious community.

It does mean, however, that the concept of "private practice" will be radically qualified for the Christian therapist, because the mediation of righteousness requires a living community as a context in which the therapist lives and to which the therapist is accountable. It also means that, to lead the client past therapeutic gain, the counselor must establish on the trajectory of growth the goal of righteousness as embodied affirmation of belonging.

There can be no definitive model for the way a Christian therapist serves in a professional capacity. Many work on the staff of mental health or psychological clinics where the services are offered to the public without a context of community or church support. In these cases, individual therapists will have to think out for themselves what it means to provide this service as a Christian, taking into account growth goals beyond mere therapeutic gain. The role of the Christian as a professional counselor will be discussed at greater length in chapter 10.

Kirk Farnsworth, who offers a concept of "embodied integration" based on an incarnational model, suggests that one of the best strategies for bringing our counseling practice under the lordship of Christ is to establish a group of believers to whom we are professionally accountable. This would provide a Christian forum for discussion, prayer, and shared concerns and also place the counselor in a context and culture that extends the Christian community.[7] But what about the growth goals of the client? The counselor may try to provide this linkage for the client if it does not already exist. Who will "clothe" the client when therapy comes to an end? Just as important is the question, what community will provide the "moral horizon" of health (righteousness) for the client during therapy?

These questions have no easy answers. The Christian who

counsels, however, cannot define therapy so narrowly as to ignore the culture of the kingdom of God as a context for therapy. The concept of "private practice" will also need to be reexamined when viewed from this perspective. If we use the adjective "Christian," we must recognize it as a *verb* of action that includes a praxis of community life.

The implications of what we are saying here also apply to the church. A Christian community that is not providing this "priestly" service of therapy "on the streets," so to speak, is failing to be neighbor to those who are in need. In the culture of the kingdom of God, the community cannot itself sustain righteousness without being also the "good Samaritan."

We are tracing out the implications of the kingdom of God as a culture that provides a context for therapy from a Christian perspective. Using the formula statement of Jesus—"I am the way, the truth, and the life"—we are developing a context for therapy that includes wisdom, righteousness, and now community. This community of the kingdom fulfills the individual's quest for identity, meaning, and hope.

The Way of the Community: An Embodied Identity

The emergence of "identity" psychologies in the early and middle part of this century was as much a response to the growing emphasis on the individual self and the thirst for experience as it was a weariness with the earlier naturalistic and biological attempts to explain human behavior. Behavior no longer preoccupied the therapists, but rather the phenomenon of the person as an experiencing self.[8] The humanist and existential psychologists found a ready market for a variety of new therapies in contemporary Western society where the older, more traditional ties of community identity were broken or rejected outright. The quest for "reality" even provoked a "reality therapy" (William Glasser).

Alvin Dueck suggests that naming reality is the central task of any healer. When the search for reality at the experiential level moves the self inward rather than outward, the person loses reality. In our ecological model of personhood (chap. 2) it was argued that people operate in a three-sphere matrix: the physical, the social, and the spiritual. The self (*psyche*/soul) is totally present in each of the three spheres, but the "reality" of the self is experienced as a praxis of intentionality, belonging, and identity that includes all three. This is what "embodied identity" means. The embodiment is not only in one's own physical body, but in the "body" of the community as a corporate identity from which self identity is derived and on which it is always somewhat dependent.

For example, the identity of Abraham, Isaac, and Jacob—the founders of the new "family" and community of the kingdom of God—was given embodiment through the covenant promise of God. The ritual of circumcision was one form of creating a new identity. The new identity, of course, was actually the naming of reality by which the individual was integrated into the tradition of the community as being in continuity with Abraham, Isaac, and Jacob. It is interesting to see that this ritual affected the identity of the self (*psyche*/soul) at three levels. Identity was literally "cut into the flesh" through circumcision, which was both a ritual of incorporation into the family and community and a sign and seal of the spiritual reality of covenant promise by which one became a member of the kingdom of God. Circumcision, like the Christian ritual of baptism, is not performed on oneself; it is performed by significant others who represent the community or "body" that gives the person primary identity.

The community that represents the culture of the kingdom of God names this reality through the story, in which the tradition is carried forward through its living members. Personal identity is thus derived from the community identity of a people who have as their essential being a history of community with God. This identity is firmly grounded in this particular history of a people of God. This is one reason why the concept of history is so important for the Hebrew people.

Losing this community identity and participation in a living history will result in a sense of anomie or disassociation for the individual. The person may move from finding his or her reality in community to finding it in the reality of the inner life. Brooks Holifield suggests that this tendency can be found in the development of a distinct emphasis in pastoral counseling over the past several centuries in North America.

> The story proceeds from an ideal of self-denial to one of self-love to self-culture, from self-culture to self-mastery, from self-mastery to self-realization within a trustworthy culture, and finally to a later

form of self-realization counterpoised against cultural mores and social institutions.[9]

Holifield also suggests that the contemporary preoccupation with psychology might be traced to the influence of experiential piety in religion.

The German theologian Wolfhart Pannenberg has analyzed the effect of "penitential piety" as related to the loss of a sense of community identity in Western society. He points out that the Protestant tradition has emphasized attaining an individualistic spirituality based on a sense of deep personal guilt over sin and suggests that a better model for spirituality would be celebration of one's life in community. This he calls "eucharistic piety."[10]

There is indeed some suspicion that modern culture's tendency toward self-realization owes something to a religious inwardness that has become separated from the righteousness of the kingdom of God. The culture of the kingdom demands a righteous concern for the "fatherless," that is, those whose identity as members of the community is threatened. This righteousness integrates marginal persons into the "mature" life of the community; it does not segregate them through discriminatory practices or institutional dormitories.

"Our believing is conditioned at its source by our belonging," writes Michael Polanyi.[11] Therapeutic gains that do not establish or reinforce a trajectory of growth in terms of participating in community life as a culture of the kingdom of God fall short of the growth goals that have been defined as essential to the maturity of the self. It is not enough to give a name or to create an identity for an individual. The naming of reality by which personal identity is formed and sustained is a function of community, not the client or the therapist. The character of this community will determine the significance of the identity and reality by which the members are named.

For the early church, the ritual of Christian baptism was sometimes enacted as a "household" or "family" ritual (cf. Acts 16:33). But even if performed with an individual, it was always with the intent of baptizing the person *into* the community, and it was always an act on behalf of the community. For many people, the culture of the kingdom of God represented a break with the previous family and kinship ties. This necessitated a praxis by which a new sense of family and kinship became a concrete reality.

The church has never fully developed its function as a "therapeutic bridge" for individuals who are without a strong sense of identity and belonging in modern society. In fact, many of the church's evangelistic methods may actually contribute to the breakdown of the social identity of persons. The remarkable proliferation of clients from within the Christian church who are seeking therapeutic relief from personal and emotional stress may be one indication of this.

While this phenomenon provides a "ready market" for Christian therapists, one has to question the root cause for such a failure of psychological health among church members. It is the concern of this book to present the case for a Christian approach to therapy that will address the actual structures of Christian community itself, both as a contributing cause to the lack of emotional health among its members and as a resource for providing a context where growth goals can be realized beyond mere therapeutic gain.

For all its concentration on the concrete present and the history in which one's present is grounded, the kingdom of God is a culture that embodies a strong sense of the future. This future does not merely extend the present into some ideal state of existence beyond today, although that expectation exists. But the concept of the future in the culture of the kingdom is that of a reality that is coming into the present.

The kingdom of God presents the future as advent, as a reality that is coming into the present out of the future. It is given as promise and carries signs in the present of its coming to us. For Christians, this advent has occurred in the coming of Jesus Christ as the incarnation of God himself and, therefore, as the embodiment of the future that belongs to all who are in the kingdom. The physical and psychical healings performed by Jesus can be understood as dramatic signs of ultimate wholeness and healing.

Promise, then, does not mean escaping the present, but using the future as a basis for belief and as a growth goal by which the self can experience integration and wholeness. Promise enables and empowers us to grasp with hope the present and all its imperfections and uncertainties. The maturity of faith integrates hope into a realistic and creative approach to life.

How can people experience *now* this hope that provides wholeness and faith? Through forgiveness of sin, for one thing. Absolution is not merely a formal pronouncement, because it liberates us from the consequences of our actions and from psychological and spiritual anguish. It assures us that our hope for forgiveness and freedom from sin will not in the end be betrayed.

Beyond the therapeutic gain that comes from dealing with the inner psychological dynamics of guilt through confession, there is the growth goal of absolution as an act of the community. Here, too, the therapist must mediate between the client and the community, which uses the therapist to embody its culture as a people of God.

Hope can also be experienced now in the promise that life itself is a value and good that cannot be lost through one's own feeling of insignificance or the threat of suffering and even death. The kingdom of God does not make suffering a good, but it affirms the one who overcomes suffering through patience and steadfast hope.

Does my small life count? Does what I do, despite my failures and even deliberate digressions from the good, really mean something in the end? I should hope it does! The gift of God's Spirit, the community upholding my baptism, and the reality of belonging that grips me even when I suffer confusion, disorder, or sickness—all these compel me to hope and empower me to live.

Summary

These, then, are the themes of the kingdom of God as a therapeutic context for Christians who counsel:

- A discerning wisdom that gives meaning and coherence to those seeking help; this is the *way* that Jesus came to be and share;
- A righteousness embodied in the moral structures of God's people; this is the *truth* that Jesus came to be and create;
- A sense of identity communicated through a story in which each person has a part; and a hope that compels faith to value life and to love community; this is the *life* that Jesus came to be and to give.

In subsequent chapters we will explore some of the spiritual dynamics that provide resources and a context for therapy from a Christian perspective.

Notes

1. S. L. Halleck, *The Politics of Therapy* (New York: Harper & Row, 1971), 36.

2. Alvin C. Dueck, "Ethical Contexts of Healing: Peoplehood and Righteousness," *Pastoral Psychology* 35, no. 4 (Summer 1987): 249. I am greatly indebted to Dr. Dueck for his contribution to my thinking about the kingdom of God as a context and resource for therapy as well as for the overall emphasis and some of the specific themes of this chapter.

3. Samuel Southard, *Theology and Therapy: The Wisdom of God in a Context of Friendship* (Dallas: Word Books, 1989), ix. Southard also says, "And this is why some theologies are defective in wisdom. They do not prepare counselors for realistic testing of mind and heart. They do not deal with the question, how do we receive and respond to God's revelation? This misses a consistent theme of wisdom, that human claims of righteousness may conceal as well as reveal the self" (2).

C. Stephen Evans makes a distinction between wisdom and shrewdness. A shrewd person knows how to manipulate situations so as to gain the most and lose the least. True wisdom, says Evans, means understanding "one's own life, an understanding which may be painful. But the fact that wisdom cannot be guaranteed by a technique does not imply that nothing can be done to encourage the development of wisdom" (*Wisdom and Humanness in Psychology: Prospects for a Christian Approach* [Grand Rapids: Baker, 1989], 71).

4. Aristotle, *The Nichomachean Ethics*, IX, vi. 5. For a more extended discussion of the concept of praxis as applied to the development of competence for ministry, see my article, "Christopraxis: Competence as a Criterion for Theological Education," *Theological Student's Fellowship Bulletin* (January–February 1984): 10–13.

5. For additional information on the concept of maturity or perfection, see *Telos* in *The New International Dictionary of New Testament Theology*, vol. 2, ed. Colin Brown (Grand Rapids: Zondervan, 1976), 59–66.

6. Stanley Hauerwas, *A Community of Character: Toward a Constructive Christian Social Ethic* (Notre Dame, Ind.: University of Notre Dame Press, 1981), 134.

7. Kirk E. Farnsworth, *Wholehearted Integration: Harmonizing Psychology and Christianity Through Word and Deed* (Grand Rapids: Baker, 1985), 90.

8. In Germany in the late nineteenth century, Wilhelm Dilthey (1833–1911) was outspoken in urging the need for a psychology that sought to appreciate individuals as living entities capable of personal integration. In the early part of this century, other German psychotherapists continued an emphasis on the whole person, including Wilhelm Stern, Kurt Goldstein, and Edward Spranger. Other psychiatrists and psychologists developed humanistic psychologies following this tendency, including Alfred Adler, Karen Horney, Erich Fromm, Kurt Lewin, Gordon Allport, and Carl Rogers. For an excellent survey of some of these psychologies see Roger Hurding, *The Tree of Healing* (Grand Rapids: Zondervan, 1988), chaps. 6–7.

9. E. Brooks Holifield, *A History of Pastoral Care in America: From Salvation to Self-Realization* (Nashville: Abingdon, 1983), 12.

10. Wolfhart Pannenberg, *Christian Spirituality and Sacramental Community* (London: Dartman, Longman and Todd, 1983).

11. Michael Polanyi, *Personal Knowledge* (London: Routledge and Kegan Paul, 1958), 322.

5

The Grace of God as
Therapeutic Intervention

"My grace is sufficient for you." The thorn in the flesh would remain, but the apostle Paul would learn to live with it and even confess that he was content (2 Cor. 12:9). Learning to live with a physical disability and learning contentment are two quite different things. For Paul, the grace of God was not merely a sedative for discomfort; it transformed his soul.

For my friend Susie, the same is true. Afflicted with cerebral palsy since birth, she speaks with extreme difficulty and walks with lurching, spastic movements. When she completed her master's degree in theology, I suggested that she might minister to handicapped persons.

"I don't have that much in common with handicapped people," she responded. "Most of them haven't forgiven God for who they are, and I have."

Susie is writing a book that will share her perspective on life and Christianity. The opening chapter is titled "Being Normal in an Abnormal World." Having a "thorn in the flesh" doesn't make us abnormal or less than a total person. Somewhere, somehow, Susie and the apostle Paul realized that wholeness is not the same as perfection.

The purpose of this chapter is to show more clearly how this grace of God that effects an inner wholeness can be related to therapeutic intervention. We will discuss first how dysfunction relates to the concept of "whole person." Then we will look at God's grace as a dynamic of the growth process and of

reconciliation. Finally we will examine the intervention of grace
and conversion in the therapeutic process.

Being a Total Person When All the Parts Are Not Working

Therapeutic gains are relative and pragmatic. Growth goals
are essential and realistic. This is as clear a distinction as can be
made between healing and wholeness, or between function and
self-perception. The concepts of "growth process" and "growth
goals" are similar to what in chapter 3 we called the "agogic
situation," following the lead of Jacob Firet. This growth
process includes the release of a motive power for change,
involves the humanity of the counselor as intermediary, and
produces change and growth in the client. Thus growth goals are
related to the integrative and relational aspects of the self as
open to change and as defined by the nature of personhood as
presented in chapter 2.

Specific therapeutic objectives are relative to this essential
trajectory of growth and have their value in promoting integration and growth. It is in this sense that therapeutic gains are also
pragmatic. They are means to an end rather than being an end in
themselves.

The reality of the self is essential to the well-being of the self
as a relational being. When this reality is experienced as the
core of one's identity, it is "whole," though not always perfect in
function. Many levels of dysfunction limit a person's freedom to
move within his or her own environment. These limitations can
be physical, psychical, or spiritual, or some combination of each.
The essential reality of the self as the core of identity can be
expressed and experienced by others in its totality despite
certain levels of dysfunction.

This is obviously the case with regard to physical disabilities.
Physical impairment, even dismemberment, does not destroy
the "totality" of the self in its core identity. There are limitations
of function, to be sure, and these limitations constitute in many
cases severe losses at the experiential level for which the self
must compensate. This is also true for those with emotional and
mental disability or impairment. No parent with a Down's
syndrome child will tolerate the suggestion that the child is any
less a total person, despite the retardation of mental processes.

My friend Susie perceives herself as normal because she

experiences a positive and tangible form of self-love through the people who help her with the simplest functions of dressing and eating. Most of us, being physically and mentally able to live without the direct touch or presence of another person, live with a high degree of autonomy. We are free to choose whether or not we want to be touched or helped, or even whether we want to be with other people. We think this is normal. Susie thinks it is abnormal for people to live in an isolated and private world, moving out to touch others only when there is need or desire. She experiences grace as a whole and normal person despite physical and mental frustrations and failures.

Psycho-spiritual forms of distress, including sinful attitudes and dispositions, do not destroy the totality of personal identity. God continues to address as fully personal those human beings who are spiritually estranged and hostile. If we were not essentially total persons, even as sinners and spiritually decrepit people, we could not continue to create meaningful human relationships and enter into social-personal community.

But there is a limit. The dysfunctions at every level can become so severe that the totality of the person is virtually concealed from view. The core of the self identity can become so out of focus and tormented that this "wholeness" cannot be sustained, except through the intentions of others who insist that the self remain as it "really" is. Those who live with people in an acute stage of Alzheimer's disease, for example, sustain the totality of that afflicted person in a kind of vicarious way.

The point is this: therapeutic gains, whether through physical therapy, psychotherapy, or pneuma-therapy (spiritual disciplines), are only relative gains. The gains in these areas can never be total or permanent. There is a value to the gains, to a point. At the point where the cost of further gain is so great and the gain so little, continued therapy may not be a pragmatic value to the totality and reality of the self. This point, of course, must be negotiated by each person to the extent that there remains a core of identity on which to make the assessment.

The Growth Process as a Dynamic of God's Grace

The essential reality of the self and the core of identity gives content to the growth goals, which are not related directly to the therapeutic gains in any kind of deterministic or causal way. For example, a self-perception as a whole person, essentially good and with a positive and hopeful attitude toward life, cannot be produced though reducing anxiety alone. Psychotherapy can reduce psychic trauma and enable persons to regain a fairly high degree of function in daily living and work. But therapeutic technique will not cause a person to perceive herself or himself as whole and filled with self-love.

This is exactly the reason why Viktor Frankl concluded that many people do not permit themselves to "escape" from therapy. The "decision" that one is whole and that life is good and has meaning is so difficult and threatening that the client prolongs the treatment. When Frankl stopped treating the psyche alone and instead challenged the person to meaning, he discovered that in many cases people could live with their anxieties and even neuroses if there were meaning and purpose in their lives. And so logotherapy was born.

The merits or limitations of logotherapy are not the issue here. Frankl's experience, however, points to the well-known phenomenon of people "suddenly" deciding they are well enough to function without further therapy. In my judgment, this points to what I call a contingent relation between psychic health and personal wholeness. By "contingent" is meant a relation in which there is some kind of correlation, but not a causal or deterministic one. Being a whole person as a psychic-somatic unity is contingent on some orientation toward or relation with a source or power beyond the psychic-somatic entity itself.

The apostle Paul's "contentedness" with his life situation, tormenting and inconveniencing as it was, resulted from his perception that God had given him "grace." Susie put it somewhat differently when she said that she had "forgiven God" for who she is. But she had come to this inner place of wholeness and self-acceptance because she had experienced the love of others even as a small child. Realizing her physical limitations and the acute loss that this meant to her in many ways, she experienced God as free from the responsibility to heal or change her. Thereby she could experience God and his grace through the care and love of other persons. Their love represents the love and grace of God on which her life depends. They serve as intermediaries in the growth process.

I repeat, therapeutic gains are relative and pragmatic while growth goals are essential and realistic. The long-range integration and growth of the self may at times need specific therapeutic intervention. Because the grace of God is experienced as a dynamic process of change and growth, grace can also aid the therapeutic process in its relative and pragmatic task of assisting this growth. God's grace can be experienced as a form of intervention through the growth process. This provides a context for therapeutic procedures to function so as to contribute to the growth goals.

The growth goals presuppose the totality of the self as a whole person, even though the self is not perfect in all its functions. This point is so vital to what follows that it must not be missed. Being a whole person, or a total person in this dynamic sense, is the very construct of personhood. In addressing the other person as a self, one presupposes that the other is "really" a person and that the potential of response inheres in the self. The growth process can only exist where there is "equi-human" address, as Jacob Firet has put it. The totality of human selfhood must be equal and fully present on both sides of this process to provide a context for therapeutic gain and to provide the motivation and right moment for "escaping" from therapy, to use Frankl's term.

The biblical concept that the image of God constitutes personhood thus establishes each person's core identity as an essential, not merely functional, aspect of the self. To create and enter into the growth process with other persons is, from a Christian perspective, to recognize and affirm the essential *grace* of God by which persons exist. This grace is not a movement by God toward persons prompted by sin or by need alone. It is by and through the grace of God that the self exists at all in the freedom and mystery of personhood. Sin works against this grace, denying the freedom and responsibility to love.

Grace is the freedom of God expressed creatively as the "encounter" that preserves humanity in personal relation with God and with other persons. Theologians have called this "common grace," though it should not be confused with some impersonal attribute that belongs to nature. Common grace is the positive, personal, and continual intervention of God that prevents the cosmos and its creatures from slipping into chaos and "falling out of" the reality of being created and related.

This is one way of understanding the biblical meaning of sin and the "sinner." Because God continues to intervene when persons act self-destructively and negatively, he preserves a "real history" of the person instead of mere fate. Actions that deny and destroy love as the bond of relationship with God and the neighbor rebound to God himself. This is at once terrifying and hopeful. It is terrifying, because now the self must confront the essential and real instead of pragmatically accommodating its fate. Yet it is hopeful, because now the grace of God, which is the original basis for one's essential and real existence, intervenes in this self-deception and self-destruction.

In his perceptive book *Life and Faith*, W. W. Meissner suggests that a theology of divine grace must be accompanied by a psychology of grace. "Grace not only alters our theological condition, changing us in reference to the supernatural," he writes, "but it delves into our very nature and makes contact with the depths of our psychic reality."[1] A psychology of grace means more than transposing theological insights and terms into psychological language. Grace is divine action motivating the receptive psyche. Meissner adds that

> the action of grace must make a difference to the living of the Christian life. It must alter our experience and the course of our life cycle. This does not mean that the action of grace is itself immediately experienced, but it does mean that we are somehow changed and presumably spiritually assisted and advanced by its influence.[2]

What Firet called the "motive power" released in the "agogic moment," Meissner calls the effect of grace as a psychological dynamic of change in behavior.

Corresponding to the work of Erik Erikson in a psychology of personal identity development, Meissner argues that we must have a psychology of spiritual identity development that views the grace of God as the ego's source of energy and direction. Spiritual identity, he suggests, flows out of the same ego center in the self as personal identity. Where lack of a healthy ego impairs the development of personal identity, spiritual identity will also suffer. This is the core of Meissner's integrative model. While therapeutic intervention using strictly psychological means can assist the ego in developing a personal identity, it cannot assist in developing spiritual identity, for this can only take place through the intervention of divine grace. Such therapeutic intervention only partially recovers the essential function of the ego, for spiritual identity is also necessary to the complete identity of the self as created in the divine image. Psychoanalytic therapy cannot produce spiritual identity, says Meissner, but the intervention of grace can promote this spiritual development and also assist in the ego's task of personal identity development. This is true because spiritual identity is a function of the ego and thus is directly related to both divine grace and the psyche. Therefore, using "means of grace" in the therapeutic process will promote both personal and spiritual growth.

> Grace is the energizing and relational principle on the spiritual level for the proper functions of the ego. Development of spiritual identity, then, is achieved through the same ego-functions that are involved in the natural psychological identity. The relation between these two levels is based on the operation of the common functions: in terms of psychological identity, these functions operate on their own, but in terms of spiritual identity, there is an added component supplied through grace.[3]

While I do not totally agree with Meissner's assumption that grace merely "perfects nature," so that the ego's natural state is "without grace," I do think his emphasis on the psychological effects of grace on both personal and spiritual growth contributes greatly to our understanding of the integration of grace into the therapeutic process.

The grace of God creates anew the growth process out of the autonomy and self-preserving motivations of those who flee from God and conceal themselves from their neighbor. For this reason O. Hobart Mowrer has said that "sin is the lesser of two evils" as compared with sickness. When sin is understood as a personal construct rather than an impersonal "condition," the possibilities of "radical redemption" are opened up.[4]

Because the self is real from the very beginning, the potential for growing into a mature person is based on the totality of the self as person. This "potential" is the freedom of the self to move on the psycho-spiritual continuum in a process of change, growth, and development. When people are confronted by the reality of grace, they are confronted by the reality of God. One cannot have grace without God. But grace presupposes the freedom of the person to respond, and therefore grace creates and gives freedom as the motive power of love. Freedom to love does not come from autonomy and self-will, but from the growth process in which we experience the reality of our personal being in the relation as necessary to the relation.

The theologian Otto Weber puts it this way:

> The epitome of that kind of existence in which we are free but not autonomous, in which we are neither the functionaries nor the autonomously cooperating partners of God, is *love*. It accords with the state of man's existence which is defined by the Spirit. Thus it is the form in which the good command of God arrives at its right in us—just as the "law" reaches its goal and its end in Christ (Rom. 10:14), love is the "law's" fulfillment (Rom. 13:10; cf. Matt. 22:40 and John 13:34).[5]

While love is the motive power for change and growth, it is not a product of therapeutic gain, nor is it a result of psychic healing. Love is the effect produced by grace, which gives freedom to respond, where the response itself is expected and even demanded by the relation. This is why Jesus commanded us to love one another. This command to love is not an ethical demand, but one that comes through the intervention of grace. Grace intervenes into our self-isolation and penetrates our self-deception to give us freedom to love in response. This is because, as Meissner has shown, grace energizes the ego to make new and healthy responses in terms of both personal identity and spiritual identity. Love is therefore a goal that is transformative in nature and a process of development along the psycho-spiritual continuum.

The goal of this development is included in the process. That is what constitutes this growth as *praxis* rather than merely the "making" of a product. Praxis is the process of creating the truth through being and doing. The growth process therefore is a form of praxis. The praxis of growth takes place when a motive power for change and growth is released by which the self grasps the reality and totality of personal life as essential to the core of identity. It is as normal as the first step of a baby, as difficult as the first "word" learned by Helen Keller in the silent darkness of total impairment of sight and hearing. It is as ordinary as gaining a new friendship, as extraordinary as experiencing God.

The Intervention of Grace as Reconciliation

Why is the grace of God that leads to wholeness and love so difficult to experience? It may be because the human self is so proficient in self-deception! Psychotherapists who work with people seeking emotional healing often find that self-deception is a common problem in their clients.

"Wounded individuals who seek relief through psychotherapy," says Walter Becker, "usually present distortions, smokescreens, misperceptions, and evasions in their experience and description of reality."[6] Healing growth must, therefore, come through correcting this self-deception, which manifests itself in many ways, including reaction formation, repression, and rationalization. Becker concludes that the task of psychotherapy is to lead people to a more realistic, authentic perception of themselves. I believe this is true, but I would argue that this problem cannot be resolved through therapy alone.

Fundamentally, self-deception, which is one way of understanding the psychology of sin as a prevailing disposition, is not merely a denial of reality but is also a denial of grace. Self-deception is a form of spiritual autonomy. The self retreats into a private place and perceives reality through the prism of the self alone. The primary deception is not what the self perceives, but the self's being autonomous and private. Grace is the creative freedom that relates the self and will not permit this autonomy of self-perception.

One of the basic self-deceptions is the religious self. I suggest that a significant number of neurotic and even psychotic people manifest their distortions in some kind of religious experience or perception. For this reason the therapist cannot assume that the religious self is a reliable source of wholeness on which to build. In my judgment, those who seek to integrate theology and psychology by integrating religious values and perceptions into therapy can mistake religious life for integrative life. Religious behavior and religious values can be incorporated into the psychological construct of the human personality, both in theory and in practice. The question is whether or not this merging of psychology and religion is really the integration of God's grace into the human integrative task itself.

The Episcopal clergyman Carroll E. Simcox puts it this way:

"Christianity begins where religion ends—with the Resurrection." The reference here is specifically to the resurrection of Christ rather than to that transition to experiencing God as a companion which is the final stage of religion. There is a connection between the two, but they are not identical. The believer knows that God's companionship is not a delusion because he or she knows Christ as real and present, in the power of his resurrection.[7]

The religious self as well must be corrected, or "sanctified" by grace. While the theological concept of "atonement" is considered a religious ritual and experience, religion itself needs "atonement," otherwise it becomes another form of self-deception. For this reason the theological construct of reconciliation through grace is more far-reaching and productive than the concept of "atonement for sin."

The doctrine of the atonement, while a valid and necessary component of a theology of redemption from sin, is too narrow a construct on which to develop a strategy and practice of intervention by which saving grace can enter into the psychotherapeutic process.

Why is the doctrine of the atonement too narrow for this? Precisely because the doctrine itself tends to reflect an inherent dichotomy between an objective atonement in terms of God's saving action in Christ on the one hand, and a subjective appropriation of this work in the person on the other. This is true whether one views the atonement as a vicarious act of God's love that took place "on behalf" of sinners or as an example for motivating sinners to love. Here we see the swing between the objective and subjective sides of the issue, with no real union of the two. Again, Otto Weber helpfully comments:

> Jesus' work is not to be compared with a legacy which was set up "objectively" for our benefit and which we must then lay claim to on the basis of our own knowledge and our own decision. Nor can it be compared with a payment which someone else has made in our favor, and which now appears, as it were, on our account record, and which we then may dispose of as we please. The personal character of reconciliation opposes all such views.[8]

God's saving activity includes the behavior of those who participate in it, says Weber. This "subjective" aspect of the salvation of God is also part of the saving activity of God, not merely a human appropriation of an objective truth.[9] A doctrine of so-called substitutionary atonement, continues Weber, does not mean that Jesus' life and death are a "substitution" for my life, but an "intervention" into it through the incarnation and resurrection of the "crucified God," to use Jürgen Moltmann's term.[10] In this way knowledge and love are not subject to the same polarity or dichotomy, but unite in the personal character of God's saving activity, which is always contemporary. How can this be?

The atonement is not based on the historical event of Christ's death alone. The basis for the atonement is the *person* of Jesus Christ, the one who died on behalf of all human beings and then was resurrected. The atonement is not an "objective" thing that we as "subjective" persons need to appropriate by our own cognitive act of belief. It is Jesus Christ, the living God, who graciously encounters us in the growth process.[11]

We sometimes think of atonement abstractly as a concept or doctrine rather than as the saving activity of God in the incarnate, crucified, and resurrected Christ—an activity that is personal and contemporary. If this happens, attempts to persuade clients to "believe" in the atonement as a basis for feeling forgiven will come to grief over the subject-object polarity that Weber warns against. For the kind of intervention that occurs with God's saving activity does not take place through a cognitive grasp of an abstract truth. Rather, the intervention is through the power and presence of the Holy Spirit. And the Holy Spirit is not communicated through ideas or concepts, but through persons.

Here we see what is implied in the statement "when religion comes to an end, Christianity begins." For if grace is rooted in religion, there will be no real intervention. And when God does not intervene into the human situation, religion can be only a subjective experience, with no objective (ontological) reality originating in God. The counselor who views atonement as merely an objective (metaphysical) value or concept and introduces it into the therapeutic process as a form of "God talk" will fail on two counts: by thrusting a religious concept into the therapeutic process and so confusing the therapeutic dynamic; and by seeking to ground Christian faith in mere dogma.[12]

My purpose to this point has been to show that a *doctrine* of atonement is too narrow a focus on which to build a relationship between God's saving action and psychotherapy. Rather, atonement is a *continuous activity* of God's saving grace, which took place "once and for all" in the incarnation, crucifixion, and resurrection of Jesus Christ, but which also includes the sanctifying work of the Holy Spirit in the Christian's life.

Where religion comes to an end and where Christianity begins is at this point of intervention, or sanctification. Religion cannot of itself sanctify; it can only point toward the need for sanctification as a gracious intervention and source of healing. The Christian experience of sanctifying grace, of course, is not a substitute for religion. The religious life of a Christian in whom the Holy Spirit dwells is itself sanctified. This means that God has related the person to himself in such a way that the deepest religious needs and aspirations of that person are authentically affirmed and fulfilled.

This is why I prefer the theological concept of reconciliation to the narrow theme of atonement as a way of understanding grace as intervention and transformation of the self. Reconciliation suggests encounter, it requires dynamic movement from both parties, and it encompasses the whole self as a psychosomatic unity. Reconciliation thus comprises the growth process described in the preceding chapter. And reconciliation allows for a mediator, a role that the Christian therapist is well qualified to fulfill.

The relation of the grace of God to the therapeutic process can be summarized as follows:

- The integration of the self as a whole person includes adjusting to facts, experiences, and limitations in life that cannot easily be changed;
- Therapeutic gains can be made that will enable the self to reinterpret and cope with these factors and experiences;
- These therapeutic gains are relative to the process of the integration and growth of the self along the life continuum; these gains are useful to the degree that they achieve this goal;
- The grace of God brings a new, creative resource to the ego's task of growth and integration, at the level of personal and spiritual identity;
- The theological concept of sin has its psychological effects

in isolating and weakening the ego's power to recover authentic personal and spiritual identity and growth;
- The doctrine of the atonement from sin through Christ's life, death, and resurrection has its psychological effect through the grace of forgiveness and healing, which gives motive power to the self to experience new life and hope;
- This is reconciliation at the personal and spiritual level.

The Intervention of Grace and Conversion

The specific intervention of grace that heals the individual's relation to God, others, and self can be understood as a kind of "conversion." Setting aside the narrower concepts of conversion that tend to stereotype a form of religious experience, we can view conversion as a transformation of the self through a process of change and development.[13]

The origins of conversion as a phenomenon of orientation toward God that encompasses the whole of one's life will always be somewhat ambiguous, especially from a cultural, sociological, psychological, and anthropological perspective. The theological perspective views the origins of conversion with relative indifference, for it is not a critical issue for theology. What is essential is that the source of the power motivating change and growth be grounded in love, particularly in the love of God as expressed through Jesus Christ. Conversion is the self's orientation toward the true source of wholeness, which, for Christian theology, is God as revealed through Christ and experienced through the power of the Holy Spirit. Conversion, therefore, is more than a psychological or religious phenomenon. It is that intervention of divine grace that effects change and growth. It is the experienced salvation or healing that is God's gift to all through Christ.

It is well known that the Greek word *soteria* as used in the New Testament means not only "deliverance," but "healing." The frequent association of the word with deliverance from physical illness in the Synoptic gospels strongly points to this relationship (cf. Mark 10:52; Luke 8:48; Matt. 9:22). When Peter is asked by which authority he had healed the lame man at the gate of the temple (Acts 3:1–10), he answered that it came by the name of Jesus Christ, whom God raised from the dead. Peter then said that "there is salvation in no one else, for there is no other name under heaven given among men by which we must be saved" (Acts 4:12). God's saving work in Jesus Christ was "at work" through the Holy Spirit's intervention in the lives of the apostles. Thus healing occurred not merely through conveying information about Jesus, but also through the Holy Spirit's "filling" the apostles with power (Acts 2:4; 3:33, 38; 4:8).[14]

Through the Holy Spirit, Christians represent in their encounters with others the presence and transforming power of Christ. The Christian counselor experiences the sanctifying grace of Christ through the therapeutic relation. This sanctifying grace breaks the self's bondage to sin and bonds it to God, allowing the self freely to seek the meaning of the religious experience.

Conversion, which lies at the heart of sanctification, is not a one-time event. Nor is it a crisis to be induced for the sake of alleviating anxiety or distress. Rather, as Karl Barth has said, conversion

> is the affair of the totality of the whole life-moment of [persons]. To live a holy life is to be raised and driven with increasing definiteness from the centre of this revealed truth, and therefore to live in conversion with growing sincerity, depth and precision.[15]

Conversion must begin outside the self, because it is not a natural movement of the religious self. Instead, it results from God's intervening grace, which enables the religious self to turn away from its own striving to receive the gift of God's saving work. But this beginning has no end; it does not merely become an "event" of one's historical life. Conversion is the work of the sanctifying Spirit of Jesus Christ, which opens up the narrowness of individual existence to existence in grace and community of life. Thus the call to sanctification in the New Testament is no mere private matter, but is addressed to the collective, or communal, person.

From this we can see that conversion as the saving work of the sanctifying Spirit of Jesus Christ is a work of grace that promotes mental health in healing the estranged and narcissistic individual. The evidences of this ongoing conversion in a person's life are, first, a confession of faith in Jesus as the truth in which one believes as an objective fact, and second, a profession of faith that is marked by love of God, neighbor, and self.

When the therapist discerns no evidence of such conversion in the life of the client, the Holy Spirit may yet enable the client to experience the saving work of Christ. A client may profess faith in Christ at any point on the continuum of growth. Such a conversion is not a "shortcut" to mental health, but a resource of divine grace to enable the therapeutic process to become a sanctifying work of grace.

Here is where the significance of the growth process can again be seen. When the therapist is a Christian and when presence and encounter take place between the therapist and the client at the growth level, the therapist mediates the grace of God. This kind of intervention is appropriate for a Christian therapist because it does not use therapeutic technique to produce conversion to Christ, nor does it make conversion an object of therapeutic gain. It is also true, however, that the context for the therapy experience will need to be defined explicitly for the client at the outset so that the growth goal of experiencing the grace of God is established as a horizon in which the therapeutic work can be done. Conversion is not a therapeutic gain. But the grace of God can work through the intervention of a therapist who is a believer in Christ, and conversion can be a result.

If the client is already a Christian, Christ's sanctifying grace can search out the sin that may lurk behind the symptoms of mental illness. The therapist may practice the intervention of forgiveness and enable the client to move positively through therapeutic techniques of healing toward mental health as therapeutic gain and personal wholeness as a reality of self-perception. "Absolution" may also take place, the therapist mediating the grace of God that affirms wholeness.

The theological and liturgical form of absolution is expressed through the pronouncement of forgiveness of sins based on personal confession of sin and the seeking of God's grace. The psychological effect of absolution as "realized forgiveness" includes release from the self-defeating and self-denying cycle of guilt, shame, and contrition. This manifests itself in renewal of self-esteem, in openness to change and growth at the personal and spiritual levels, and in behavior that reflects this inner experience of grace and forgiveness.

To say that a Christian counselor may serve as an intermediary for this "absolution" is not to suggest that the therapist replaces the priest or that psychological release from feelings of guilt replaces authentic forgiveness of sin. Rather, it is to suggest that the effects of grace as psychological health and wholeness manifest in personal and social relations constitute precisely what the Bible means by conversion, repentance, and forgiveness of sin. Absolution that is merely "pronounced" and not "experienced" falls short of being the transforming and renewing grace of God it is intended to be. In my view, Christians who counsel can become an important agent in that process of "realized forgiveness."

When the Christian therapist practices the intervention of grace as a sanctifying process of conversion, the Christian client need not experience a dichotomy between religious experience and psychotherapy. Rather, the therapist will share with the client an experience of the real presence of Christ through the Holy Spirit's intervention.

In the growth process there is no confusion between the sanctifying work of the Holy Spirit and therapeutic technique, and no confusion between therapeutic gain and the growth goals of personal and spiritual wholeness. This Christian approach to therapy does not use psychological techniques to achieve religious results. Rather, the growth process is the dynamic context of encounter in which the therapist creates the environment for the grace of God to intervene in a gracious and transforming way.

Summary

In this chapter we have seen that the counselor can mediate the grace of God in such a way that intervention is made into the restricted and often dysfunctional life of another person. This reality of God's grace is not only a motive power for change and growth, but also a therapeutic resource that makes therapeutic methods even more effective in establishing a trajectory of lifelong growth and wholeness.

"My grace is sufficient," said the risen Christ to the apostle. This was heard as the Word of God and produced in the hearer the reality of grace. The Word of God, too, provides a strategy of intervention for the Christian therapist. The role of Scripture in the therapeutic process will be the subject for the next chapter.

Notes

1. W. W. Meissner, S.J., M.D., *Life and Faith: Psychological Perspectives on Religious Experience* (Washington, D.C.: Georgetown University Press, 1987), 5.

2. Ibid., 7.

3. Ibid., 58.

4. O. Hobart Mowrer, *The Crisis of Psychiatry and Religion* (Princeton, N.J.: Van Nostrand, 1961). Mowrer writes, "So long as we subscribe to the view that neurosis is a bona fide 'illness,' without moral implications or dimensions, our position will of necessity continue to be an awkward one. And it is here I suggest that, as between the concept of sin (however unsatisfactory it may in some ways be) and that of sickness, sin is indeed the lesser of two evils. We have tried the sickness horn of this dilemma and impaled ourselves upon it. Perhaps, despite our erstwhile protestations, we shall yet find sin more congenial" (50–51).

5. Otto Weber, *Foundations of Dogmatics*, vol. 2 (Grand Rapids: Eerdmans, 1983), 327.

6. Walker Becker, "Healing and Spiritual Disciplines," *Journal of Christian Healing* 6, no. 2 (Fall 1984): 35.

7. Carroll E. Simcox, "On Being Both Christian and Religious," *Christian Century*, (18 April 1984): 398–400.

8. Weber, *Foundations of Dogmatics*, 2:229.

9. Ibid., 233.

10. Jürgen Moltmann, *The Crucified God* (New York: Harper & Row, 1974).

11. Otto Weber warns against making the atonement purely "objective" as an abstract concept. "If it were the case that God, in the person and the work (the personal work) of Jesus Christ, simply set up a 'fact' and then made this fact available to us through the Holy Spirit in the Church, it would be our task to recognize, agree to, trust in, and 'appropriate' that 'fact.' God would not have acted for us in a valid way, but would have merely given us a 'chance,' or sent forth a power which we would have to permit to have its effect on us. The subject-object polarity this implies would make God's grace in its relationship to us an object, to which we would have to address ourselves, or which inhered in us. But, as we saw, God has by no means caused merely a 'chance' to be made available to us nor initiated the momentum which then leads to salvation. No, he has made Christ Jesus 'our wisdom, our righteousness and sanctification and redemption' (1 Cor. 1:30). In the Holy Spirit, our own freedom is God's work, the gift of his free grace" (*Foundations of Dogmatics*, 2:412).

12. H. Newton Malony, for example, suggests that "God talk," as the introduction of a set of religious values based on the assumption of divine reality and love, can appropriately be used as part of the psychotherapeutic task. I view this as an attempt to build on an inherent religious aspect of the self, which may already be part of the deception of the self and thus needs to experience the intervention and

correction of grace. See "God Talk in Psychotherapy," in *Wholeness and Holiness: Readings in the Psychology/Theology of Mental Health*, ed. H. Newton Malony (Grand Rapids: Baker, 1983), 269–80.

13. I have discussed the theological concept of conversion in the essay "Conversion: Essence of the Christian Story," in *Theology, News and Notes* (Pasadena, Calif.: Fuller Theological Seminary, June 1986), 8ff. See in this same issue the essay "Conversion: The Sociodynamic of Change," by H. Newton Malony, 16ff.

14. For a discussion of the use and meaning of *soteria* in the New Testament, see "Redemption" in *The New International Dictionary of New Testament Theology*, ed. Colin Brown, vol. 3 (Grand Rapids: Zondervan, 1975), 205–21.

15. Karl Barth, *Church Dogmatics*, vol. 4, pt. 2 (Edinburgh: T. & T. Clark, 1961), 566.

6

The Word of God as Empowerment for Change

She was a young woman in her early twenties. She walked into my office for her first appointment carrying one of the largest Bibles I have ever seen. She sat down, holding this enormous Bible against her chest with both hands wrapped around it, as though it were either a shield to ward off enemy spears or a life jacket to save her from drowning. As it turned out, she probably intended the Bible to be the latter, though I suspect it acted more as an anchor dragging her under than a life preserver.

She had been referred to me by a psychologist who was on the staff of a counseling center not far from the church of which I was pastor. The psychologist, a Christian, explained to me that the woman had received several hours of therapy with no apparent results and had no financial resources to pay even a nominal fee. The center could no longer keep her as a client on that basis. Would I be willing to provide her with some pastoral counseling? Of course. This was not the first time as a pastoral counselor that I had been asked to provide free therapy!

Week after week the woman appeared, clutching this Bible, her grasp on it growing more convulsive each time she came close to naming the thing that possessed her. She would sit for several minutes, hunched over the Bible, unable to speak or respond.

Finally, in a session in which I discerned and named for her the thing that she found so terrible and self-destructive, she looked up and said, "Yes, that is it—is God going to kill me?"

"What do you think?" I responded, not breaking eye contact for even a second.

For a long while she looked at me. Then she said, "No, I guess not. So, what do we do now?" Then I noticed that the Bible was lying in her lap and that her hands were folded, resting on top of it.

When she came the following week, she did not bring the Bible with her. From that time I began to think that she would be healed, and I believe that in due time she was.

I relate this story to focus our discussion on the role of the Bible in counseling and psychotherapy. In this case the woman brought the Bible right into the counseling session. I found out later that she had been doing this also with the psychotherapist. While it certainly had symbolic significance for her, it appeared to have no positive effect on the process of therapy.

As we worked together on her emotional and mental health, she disclosed a severely conflicted self-concept in which her view of God as judge predominated. She began to ask what "God would think" or "what God would say" about certain things we discussed. I would then select incidents in the life of Jesus and read them to her from my Bible, asking her what she thought God was saying to her. I sought to awaken in her a response, or "hearing" of the Word of God, not merely to "tell" her what the Bible said.

The use of printed material (bibliotherapy) in counseling is widespread, both as "homework" and as a basis for intervention during the therapy process. Does the Bible fall into this general category of "literature," and can it be used by Christian counselors in similar fashion? Does the Bible, because it represents a religious set of teachings based on the Judeo-Christian tradition, provide a therapeutic device that enables the therapist to deal with the religious life and values of the client?

I find that there is a great deal of confusion and uncertainty regarding the Bible and counseling. Some Christian counselors view the Bible as a handbook of moral and spiritual injunctions by which one can bring a disordered and disobedient life into conformity with the Word of God. The primary emphasis in this case, quite obviously, is on obedience. The emotional and mental life is considered to be a reflection of one's spiritual and moral life. If one is morally and spiritually in conformity with

God's Word and God's rule for life, then the other problems will be resolved. This is a caricature, to be sure, but many counselors do use the Bible as a tool by which the individual's life is examined and to which submission is sought as a spiritual discipline.

Where this method is used, success is indicated by those who respond and become faithful members of a Christian community in which the teaching reinforces the basic principle of obedience to the Bible. Those for whom this method does not work tend to be viewed as resisting God or as spiritually and morally delinquent.

By and large, the students of mine who are preparing for a ministry of psychotherapy find this approach scandalous. They have come to regard emotional disturbance as the result of a complex system of factors that are not directly related to the self's moral or spiritual inclinations. Or they feel it is an oversimplification to cast emotional problems into the mold of a spiritual problem. In their view, neither the compulsions and obsessions of the mind nor the dysfunction of the psyche are treatable as symptoms of disobedience to God. Depression is not merely a sign of sin. There are chemical imbalances, neurological disorders, and psychical traumas that must be taken into account. Many who hold this view conclude that the Bible has no place in the therapy hour. But this, too, is a caricature. Yet many Christian therapists have found no way to integrate the Bible with therapeutic practice.

In the middle range between these approaches there is considerable uncertainty and not a little anxiety among Christian psychologists and counselors concerning the use of the Bible in counseling. Many do find ways of integrating Bible readings as homework for their clients, or find it helpful to suggest meditation on biblical passages as conducive to therapeutic gain. Some have found it meaningful to incorporate specific biblical passages or teachings into their counseling as a standard practice. Thus they integrate their Christian faith into their therapeutic practice without substituting the Bible for psychological analysis and therapeutic insight into human problems.

The purpose of this chapter is to work with this middle ground, avoiding the two extremes. At one extreme the Bible is viewed as a tool by which most, if not all, emotional problems can be resolved. On the other extreme, the Bible is excluded from the therapeutic practice as irrelevant to the purely psychological or psycho-somatic problems of persons in distress.

In approaching the issue from this perspective, I intend to discuss first the nature of the Bible as Word of God, then the Word of God as the counsel of God, and finally some approaches to the use of the Bible in the therapeutic context.

The Bible as Word of God

It is common to make the equation that the Bible is the Word of God. But it is equally common to assume that the Word of God is merely the Bible. The two statements are not the same. The Bible is a collection of writings that represent a broad cross section of literature, centering on the history of the people of God in the Old Testament and the history of Jesus of Nazareth and the early church in the New Testament. To say that the Word of God is merely the Bible is to focus on the Bible primarily as a literary work, used for religious edification, teaching, moral instruction, and the formulation of doctrines. Those who view the Bible in this way use it as a "collateral" source of information and support for the client alongside other literature that may be used for somewhat the same purpose.

Others might use the Bible as an "authoritative text." That is, the Bible has a special kind of authority that no other literature has, because it is the revelation of God in written form. The concept of "inspiration" supports this view, in which not only the ideas of the Bible are inspired by God, but the very words— the text itself—is God's authoritative word. Proponents of this view see the Bible in much the same light as Muslims see the Koran. The Bible would have somewhat the same authority as a prescription written by a medical doctor, though the element of "inspiration" is not involved in the latter case. The text becomes God's "prescription" for our instruction and edification. The purpose of inspiration as a technical theological concept is to guarantee the authenticity of the text and, consequently, the "prescription."

The question of authority is a critical issue for the use of any text, whether the Jewish-Christian Scriptures or the "holy book" of any religion. Authority is not a self-evident or intrinsic quality of a Scripture text. Rather, it is a complex set of factors such as tradition, religious institution, and personal belief system, to name just a few. The text that a Muslim might cite from the Koran, for example, would not be recognized as authoritative by a Christian for whom only the Old and New Testaments are authoritative. The reverse might be true for a Muslim.

When the Bible is used in counseling as an authoritative text rather than merely as literature that informs and inspires, one must look carefully at the nature of the authority claims that attend its use. Both the counselor and the client would have to recognize the Bible as authoritative, but their belief systems may interpret the authority in different ways.

From the perspective of pastoral counseling or of psychotherapy offered as a service of the church, it is easier to use the Bible as an authority. But the Christian psychologist in a private practice has to carefully think through using the Bible as authoritative text. If care is not exercised in this use in counseling, the authority attached to the text of Scripture might be confused with a bias of interpretation or teaching that the counselor imposes on the text. Or the confusion may come from the other side. The client may have a quite different perspective of the role and authority of the Bible than the counselor. My concept of the authority of the Bible is probably quite different from that of the young woman who entered my office clutching it desperately in her arms.

This is not to suggest that the Bible should never be used as authoritative text for giving specific guidance or prescribing spiritual direction for a client. My point is that we should clearly understand the source and context of authority when we use the Bible as a text for these purposes.

Besides viewing the Bible as literature or as authoritative text, we may see it a third way, as the Word of God. Here we make a distinction between the Bible as literature and authoritative text, and the Word of God that encounters us through the literature and text of the Bible. The Scripture has not replaced God himself as the one who seeks us and speaks to us through his Word. Geoffrey Bromiley has helpfully reminded us of this fact in saying,

> The Bible does not replace God. He has not just given us the Bible and left us to it. He himself is still the one with whom we have to deal. . . . Even as we consult holy scripture, we are really

consulting God himself in his self-revelation as he came and comes to us through holy scripture. God indeed says what scripture says, but this does not imply a direct equation of God and scripture.[1]

The Word that became incarnate in Jesus Christ (John 1:14) was a radical reaching out of God's Word into the human predicament, says Seward Hiltner, and as a consequence, all persons, "actually seeing and touching, might grasp the intent of the word of God that had been given all along but never before in such complete and comprehensive fashion. This was and is the conviction of the Christian."[2] Hiltner adds that Western Christianity tends to confuse the words of the Bible with the Word of God. This confuses the authority of the Word of God as inspired Scripture with the text of Scripture, as though to have the text or to use the text one is in control of the Word of God.

Karl Barth comments on this same point.

> Because the Word of God meets us in the form of the scriptural word, assimilation means the contemporaneity, homogeneity, and indirect identification of the reader and hearer of Scripture with the witness of the revelation. Assimilation means assuming this witness into our own responsibility.[3]

This, of course, means that the purpose of the Word of God is to be *heard*. The text of Scripture is not authoritative in the abstract sense of possessing some intrinsic power that can be manipulated by the one who uses the Bible. Rather, the authority of the Word of God manifests itself in its power to affect the "hearing," which is the assimilation of the Word into one's own responsibility, as Barth has said.

The difference between hearing the Word of God as a command to be obeyed, or as instructions to follow, and the assimilation of the Word, of which Barth speaks, is an essential difference. The assimilation of the Word is not merely appropriating it as a conceptual truth or moral rule into one's belief system; it involves a transformation of life. It also involves assimilating one's life into the event of the Word of God as an encounter with the reality of God.

Jacob Firet puts it this way:

> The issue in hearing and understanding the word, without which the word is powerless, is an intensely yielded and dedicated listening such that a person achieves rapport with the word from within the core of her existence.[4]

This kind of hearing is the "actualizing of salvation," Firet says. It is the kind of hearing and response represented by the good soil in the parable (Mark 4). This clearly points again to a growth process in which an encounter provides a motive power to change and grow. "My word . . . that goes forth from my mouth," says Yahweh through the prophet, "shall not return to me empty, but it shall accomplish that which I purpose" (Isa. 55:11).

We can read the Bible, memorize it, and follow its teaching as guidelines for behavior and yet not actually have "heard" the word in the sense of being transformed and changed by it. We can follow its teachings without knowing the Lord who speaks through the text. Jesus warns his "hearers" of this very danger when he says, "On that day many will say to me, 'Lord, Lord, did we not prophesy in your name, and cast out demons in your name, and do many mighty works in your name?' And then will I declare to them, 'I never knew you; depart from me, you evildoers'" (Matt. 7:22–23).

For this reason I did not use the Bible as an authoritative text to counsel the disturbed young woman clutching the Bible. Rather, I sought to "release" the Bible from her grasp, so to speak, that she might sense the need and the occasion to "hear" the Word of God. Even then, when she pursued the matter, she did not ask, "What does the Bible say?" about this matter, but "What does God say?"

In our counseling we need to look for the moment when the client seeks the Word of God, has a "faith in the Word of God" that will lead to the occasion for the Bible to be used. Hiltner writes,

> I wonder if this faith is not, in however secular a sense, an implicit belief that the word of God will speak although not necessarily in the time span we would ideally hope for. Such a view is not dissimilar to a belief in revelation in the theological sense. The counselor must have patience, even at times near the limits of his endurance. But if he has this faith and is doing everything he can based on knowledge, then he does well to endure and wait for God's word, or its secular equivalent, to break through.[5]

I am not sure what Hiltner means by a "secular equivalent" to the Word of God. Perhaps he means that the Word will break through in a nonreligious form or situation. If so, I fully concur, for God's Word itself breaks into the world culture, coming in a human language, a "nonholy" form, in order to encounter the person within one's own human and, yes, secular context. We surely do not need to create a religious "point of contact" for the Word of God to speak and be heard!

We are told by Luke that a great multitude came to Jesus to "hear him" and "to be healed" (6:17). "He who has ears to hear, let him hear," said Jesus (Mark 4:9). In hearing there is health, we could say, with respect to the power of the Word of God in the counseling process. But this means we do not begin with teaching general or universal concepts supported by Bible texts and then move to more specific guidelines or prescriptions for health. Rather, the act of hearing is always a specific act and thus the Word of God always comes with a specific "address" to it.

The Word of God as the Counsel of God

The fact that God has spoken and that the written Scriptures are the Word of God does not mean that God does not continue to speak through the Scripture. God has spoken and still speaks, the Reformers believed, especially Calvin. According to Calvin, the highest proof of Scripture as the Word of God is the fact that God in person speaks in it (*dei loquentis persona*).[6] The authority of Scripture is thus the "counsel" of God in it, we might say.

The action of the Word is God's "interacting" through it with the person who hears. The counsel of God is not merely advice or instruction, which remains in a kind of neutral zone waiting to be appropriated by the hearer. Nor is the counsel of God identical to the voice of the prophet, or "counselor." The role of the therapist in the growth process, like that of the preacher, is as an intermediary in this interaction of the Word with the hearer. "When God comes in his word," says Firet,

> then by that token he has turned in love toward people; then he has acted on behalf of people; then he has communicated with people. When God comes in his word, then by that token salvation is there; then people are being healed and situated in the peace, the righteousness, and the life of the Kingdom.[7]

The word of God is not merely a movement of sound waves, a vibration in the air. The counsel of God is not merely a word of wisdom or even a heavily weighted admonition. It is the dynamic presence of God that penetrates self-deception and unmasks the pretenses of the heart. "Is not my word like fire, says the Lord, and like a hammer which breaks the rock in pieces?" (Jer. 23:29). The word of God is "living and active" (Heb. 4:12), it is the "power of God" (1 Cor. 1:18), and it is able to "save your souls" (James 1:21).

The Word of God cannot be isolated into a text and then used out of context as an authoritative command. The context of the Word is not merely its literary context, but the context of "hearing"—the context of encounter, presence, and faith. To view the Word of God as the counsel of God is thus to understand that the Word is itself the motive power that engenders change. It produces understanding *and* change because it is a word of truth. It is not a deceptive word, nor does it permit deception in the one who hears it.[8]

The Word of God is not merely a biblically based form of counseling, as though it could be added to therapeutic technique as a Christian form of psychology. The concept of counseling as a pastoral therapeutic has already been "psychologized" through the introduction of psycho-therapeutic dynamics into pastoral care. The reverse of this, attempting to "Christianize" psychotherapy by adding Scripture as a religious context and therapeutic tool, does not approach what I have in mind here. The Word of God is a personal encounter and the transforming presence of God himself.

The growth process (agogic situation) is created not only by quoting or reading the Bible, but through the encounter of one human being with others in which one intermediates the reality of God for the other. Where this situation exists, it is because of the presence of faith inspired by the Holy Spirit. This encounter demands the Christian's active belief, so that God's Word may manifest itself as being heard, believed, and enacted through the life of the Christian.

This encounter breaks the "silence of the gods," as Kornelis Miskotte once put it. "When the gods are silent they are silent everywhere; when YHWH speaks, he speaks somewhere, at some definite place; and in this 'somewhere' is to be found the Word which was always the life and light of men."[9]

The purpose or power of the Word of God, says Miskotte, is to give knowledge and life. All religions include some knowledge, but not all can lead to life. The unique nature of the Word of God is that it is a knowledge of God, which leads to essential life.

> The courage to live grows out of the strength of knowing, which is essentially identical with the ability to know oneself as one who is known, to accept oneself as one who is forever accepted, to affirm oneself as one who is affirmed by God. This is the way in which and this is the reason why all the abundance of the tree of life lies in the knowledge of YHWH.[10]

The gospel of John tells us that the Word that became flesh is the source of life (1:4). Jesus himself said, "I came that they may have life, and have it abundantly" (John 10:10). When dealing with the religious scribes, who had become specialists in using the Scripture as an authoritative text, Jesus said, "You search the scriptures, because you think that in them you have eternal life; and it is they that bear witness to me; yet you refuse to come to me that you may have life" (John 5:39–40).

When Christians who practice counseling and psychotherapy enter into the growth process expecting the Word of God to be present, to be heard, and to heal, they use Scripture to facilitate this effect.

When I believe that the client coming with an implicit need to "hear" the Word of God, even if this need is expressed in nonreligious concept or words, I am better prepared to let the Word of God be heard. I am encouraged to believe that the Scripture will awaken that hearing to an authentic experience of God, who is the source of essential life, not just the pragmatic form of life.

How is this done? With clinical intuition and spiritual discernment, coupled with a knowledge of the Word of God as "story" or "paradigm."

Using the Bible in a Therapeutic Context

We recall that Jacob Firet distinguishes between the agogic moment and the hermeneutic moment. The word *hermeneutic* basically means the practice or art of interpreting something and expounding the meaning of it. The hermeneutic moment is the situation, or moment, that releases the motive power for *understanding*. The agogic moment releases the motive power for *change and growth*. This is what I am calling the growth process.[11]

There is, however, another way of seeing the hermeneutic moment as part of the dynamic of the Word "coming to us" and thereby producing a response in us. Gerhard Ebeling, for example, suggests that the Word is not really the object of understanding, as though we could grasp it abstractly with the mind and thus bring it under our control. Rather, the Word brings something to understanding; it has a hermeneutic function. The Word as the reality of God passes *through* language and relates the hearer to the source of the Word—that is, to the being of God in his Word.[12]

In the Old Testament the Word of God had the power of blessing or cursing, but it was not some magical or secret word. The Word was intelligible and came in a situation where the hearers could be affected by the hearing. They had a "choice," in effect, either to hear with faith and so take the way which leads to life and health or, in "not hearing," to take the way that leads to self-destructiveness and futility (cf. Deut. 30:1ff; Isa. 45:19; 48:16).

The surprising thing about the Word of God is that it does not come in strange sounds or unintelligible syllables, but instead sounds ordinary and familiar. "God speaks our mother tongue" (note the experience at Pentecost, Acts 2:8, 11).[13] The Word of God is heard in a relationship that already has a basis of understanding, a relationship that was there before. In this relationship a genuine encounter takes place; in this growth process the hermeneutical moment takes place.

The point is this: The Word of God seeks hearing and response. It demands that those who hear the Word will assimilate it into their lives. For this to take place, there must be a context for addressing the totality of the person's life, treating the individual as a unity.

In the approach to counseling I have attempted to develop in this book, an encounter is created through a counseling or therapeutic relationship in which persons are addressed as a psycho-spiritual unity. The therapeutic techniques used can aim at specific therapeutic gains in a context that also addresses the larger goals and values of personal life.

The growth process produces the context for the hermeneutical moment. Or to put it another way, the encounter through the counseling relationship releases a motive power for change that is also the motive power for understanding. Faith, or a person's openness to God as the source of life, is thus the motive power for understanding. To say that one has heard and understood the Word of God without believing and growing toward the life of faith is to deny the truth.

This rather technical discussion explains to me the dynamics of what took place when I counseled the young woman who was desperately clutching her Bible. I think she saw me as a person who has a relationship with God, probably because of my pastoral role. She appeared to verify this through our first sessions together, in which she found it possible to trust me at the human level also. A growth process resulted where the reality of God entered in despite the unreality of her own structure of confusion and distress.

The Bible was displaced from the role of standing between her and God, and she found it possible to question directly, through me, her relation to God. Then, when she began to ask what God meant in her life, she entered into the hermeneutic moment, when understanding could take place as an intervention into her confused perceptions of self and God.

When she questioned whether God would now "kill her," I forced her to answer the question herself out of the reality of the growth process. She was thus confronted with the choice of understanding the Word of God as a blessing or a curse. When she was able to say, "I guess not," she had come to a new understanding of God and herself, and a motive power for understanding was released. As she continued to work on her self-perception on a clinical basis, she also came to evidence a motive power for change and growth.

I introduced the use of the Bible through a series of selected stories that I read to her without comment. Then I asked her to interpret these stories from the context of her growth process. If I had asked her to read the Bible for herself, either silently or out loud, it would not have had the same effect. The Scripture needed to be displaced from the center of her distortion and placed in the context of the growth process. I accomplished this by reading the Bible to her so that the Word of God came to her in the "familiar" voice of our relationship. By this means a new "hermeneutical moment" had been created for her. She did not have to agree or disagree with my "interpretation"; she had to provide the interpretation herself.

This seems quite consistent with Jesus' method of using parables and stories to bring his hearers to a new understanding. In telling the story of the Good Samaritan, for example (Luke 10:25–37), Jesus ended with a question, "Which of these three, do you think, proved neighbor to the man who fell among the robbers?" When the man answered, "The one who showed mercy," Jesus simply said, "Go and do likewise."

Over and over again, Jesus forced his listeners into the hermeneutic moment—they had to announce the interpretation and so assimilate themselves into the event of a story. The stories were created out of a landscape familiar to the listeners, and they were told by Jesus, a person familiar to them through his teaching and ministry.

True, the Bible also contains "prescriptions," admonitions, doctrines, and guidelines for living. But these "prescriptions" are addressed to believers who are presumed to be in a position of understanding. Where understanding has become distorted— and this is one way of understanding both emotional and mental problems—using Scripture as authoritative text does not seem to be effective.

Counselors who wish to bring a Christian perspective to their practice can use the Bible effectively as a "hermeneutical moment." To be most effective, the counselor should be so familiar with Scripture that she can "tell" its basic stories or paradigms in the context of the therapy process without using the Bible itself. Doing so liberates the Word of God from its encasement in the "literature" of Scripture and embodies it in the language and relationship already "in place." This is particularly effective when we are counseling non-Christians or those who view the Bible in a distorted or stereotyped way.

The Bible is used most effectively when the hermeneutical moment has already occurred and both the therapist and the client can approach the text in their "co-humanity."

It is up to each counselor to decide whether to use the Bible in therapy. There is, however, no reason not to use it, provided that this Word has not become "dis-incarnate" and is not brought in as something alien to the therapeutic relation itself. The Word of God should be a friend. If it sounds strange to the ear, the ear has become estranged from the heart. The Word, even in its strangeness, can provide healing and growth.

If heaven and earth were created by the "Word of God" (2 Peter 3:5), then the Word of the Lord that "tells" the glory of God through this world can also be a "law of the Lord" that brings blessing and wholeness to his human creatures.

> The law of the LORD is perfect,
>   reviving the soul;
> the testimony of the LORD is sure,
>   making wise the simple;
> the precepts of the LORD are right,
>   rejoicing the heart;
> the commandment of the LORD is pure,
>   enlightening the eyes;
> the fear of the LORD is clean,
>   enduring forever;
> the ordinances of the LORD are true,
>   and righteous altogether.
> More to be desired are they than gold,
>   even much fine gold;
> sweeter also than honey
>   and drippings of the honeycomb (Ps. 19:7–10).

Notes

1. Geoffrey Bromiley, *God and Marriage* (Grand Rapids: Eerdmans, 1980), 2.

2. Seward Hiltner, *Theological Dynamics* (Nashville: Abingdon, 1972), 172.

3. Karl Barth, *Church Dogmatics,* vol. 2, pt. 1 (Edinburgh: T. & T. Clark), 736.

4. Jacob Firet, *Dynamics in Counseling* (Grand Rapids: Eerdmans, 1986), 37.

5. Hiltner, *Theological Dynamics,* 176.

6. John Calvin, *Institutes of the Christian Religion,* I.vii.4.

7. Firet, *Dynamics in Counseling,* 29.

8. Firet says, "God does not speak deceptive words; he never says anything offhandedly to pass the time. His word is truly word and word of truth. His word names his name: he helps us understand who he is, what he is for us; he thus makes us other people who may live in the knowledge of his name and who may call on the name. His word reveals the truth: he leads us out of our delusions into understanding and discernment of reality; he changes us so that we do not need to run our lives by what is deceptive and changing. The word of God

actualizes salvation; he makes us understand that all things are new, and causes us to walk in newness of life. His word is the form of his presence: it is our prerogative to know him in his word and to live with him, drawing our life from his word" (Ibid., 95).

9. Kornelis Miskotte, *When the Gods are Silent* (London: Collins, 1967), 478.

10. Ibid., 364.

11. Firet, *Dynamics in Counseling*, 95ff.

12. See, for example, Gerhard Ebeling, *Word and Faith* (Philadelphia: Westminster Press, 1963), 305ff.

13. Firet, *Dynamics in Counseling*, 96f.

7

The Healing Praxis
of Prayer

In the modern view, says theologian Donald Bloesch, "if you speak to God, that's prayer; if God speaks to you, that's schizophrenia."[1] As a phenomenon of the religious instincts of humanity, prayer as a form of addressing the deity, by whatever form and by whatever name, is probably found in every culture and in every age.

Christians also pray. Jesus prayed, as did the people of Israel. Jesus taught his disciples to pray, and the early church practiced prayer as a central part of their community life as well as a form of ministry to the sick.

"Is any among you sick?" wrote James. "Let him call for the elders of the church, and let them pray over him, anointing him with oil in the name of the Lord; and the prayer of faith will save the sick man, and the Lord will raise him up" (James 5:14). Jesus and the early Christians considered prayer to be effective both in the lives of people who pray and in the lives of people who are the object of prayer.

In chapter 1 I mentioned Martha, who told her Christian counselor, "You never prayed with me." Yet she testified that therapy caused changes in her life that her own prayers failed to bring about. Sue Johnson, as a Christian who counsels, wants to know whether prayer is appropriate during a counseling session. She prays for her clients as part of her own life of prayer, but she has not yet discovered the place of prayer in therapy itself. This chapter is written to answer questions about prayer as related to the therapy process.

Should a Christian therapist think of prayer as a means to healing persons through the therapeutic process? Does prayer heal memories and renew the emotional life as well as alter the mental process so as to produce mental health?

In addressing these questions I will discuss first the nature of prayer as Christian praxis and then the use of prayer as a healing praxis.

Prayer as a Form of Christian Praxis

Praxis, we will recall from chapter 4, is not merely applying a theory in practice, nor making a product according to a design. Praxis is discovering truth through actions so that truth, as the *telos* (goal) of the action, is revealed. For praxis, the goal is included in the act itself, bringing together the means and the end in a unity of action. The praxis of Christian truth is therefore transformational in nature. Christian praxis is encountering the reality of God through the actions in which that reality becomes manifest. Praxis does not bring the reality of God into the situation through applying a procedure, but discovers and makes manifest the reality of God through action.

In this view, prayer does not become a way of manipulating God to create a certain effect. Prayer is a growth process in the sense that the motive power for change or growth is not lodged in the one who prays, but comes to the one who prays (and the one prayed for) as the power and reality of God.

Prayer is a dialogical activity, says Donald Bloesch. It necessarily involves words and is a "two-way conversation" between the Creator and the creature.[2] This implies that God does indeed talk back to the one who prays! But we should not be misled by the emphasis on "talk" in this understanding of prayer.

1. Prayer as Shared Life. Jacques Ellul, a lay theologian in the Reformed Church of France, argues, with Bloesch, that prayer is a form of communication with God, though he suggests that prayer is not a formal discourse using a common language. Rather, he says, prayer is shared life with God and therefore is not confined to verbal statement. The verbal form of prayer is not useless, Ellul says, but if God did not turn the language of prayer into an encounter with him, the words of a prayer may only be a monologue and not a dialogue at all.[3] We are reminded of the way in which Jesus described the Pharisee who "stood and prayed thus with himself" (Luke 18:11).

The predicament of "modern man," says Ellul, is that we are in a crisis of language in which words can no longer attain the level of speech.[4] T. F. Torrance agrees, saying we have suffered a culture split wherein language has become detached from being with the result that words have only a syntactical relation and no real semantical relation with personal reality.[5] This means that words only connect with other words in the grammatical form (syntactical) and do not really refer to a reality beyond this grammatical form. (A semantical relation is between a word and a reality that it signifies.) If the words of our prayers only have meaning in a grammatical or existential form, then God as the (semantic) reality of prayer is not involved at all.

For Ellul, this means that often we are only using the "language of prayer" but not real prayer itself. Only words are spoken, not prayer through words. When we "talk with God" in prayer, we may only be using words that have not yet become "speech." To become speech, continues Ellul, prayer must be an authentic address of the "I" to the "Thou" that constitutes the reality of God. For prayer to be authentic "speech" whereby we "hear" what God says in answer to prayer, we must let go of the manipulation and power of words. We must be open toward God, realizing that we cannot pray for an "objective good" but only for the will of God. Ellul puts it this way:

> In the act of praying, I am signifying that the good is not an objective reality known in advance, with evil as an equivalent opposite, as though I had a choice to make between two things. I am signifying that, to the contrary, evil is a condition, a situation which affects me, and that it is not visible to the eye like a tumor in healthy flesh. I am signifying that the good is not a source for objectifiable commandments, but that the good is the will of God. Even if I am not a theologian, that is what I mean when I pray.[6]

The will of God, for Ellul, is precisely the only justification for prayer, for it creates in us the need to pray and answers our prayers by orienting us toward a life of wholeness and holiness. This shared life with God is also the source of our own good and the good of our neighbor. While this sounds quite mystical, it really is concrete and practical. I can bring specific needs to God in prayer—the need for physical healing, for courage in bearing a burden, or for a solution to a problem. But these "needs" are not identical with the "shared life" with God that constitutes prayer. Even Jesus concluded through prayer that the will of God was more to be desired than to have "this cup removed from me" (cf. Luke 22:42). Paul, to whom we referred in chapter 5, prayed three times to have his "thorn in the flesh" removed, only to discover through prayer that the grace of God is sufficient. As Ellul reminds us, the "good" is not identical with the need that prompts prayer, but the good is experienced through prayer in the form of shared life with God—in some instances, in the form of the need met and the "thorn" removed!

Ellul speaks of prayer in much the same way as I have spoken of Christian praxis—as an encounter with the reality of God through action. Prayer is not a way of manipulating the power of God so as to "produce" a result, but a means of encountering God through language and words.

There is a kind of "primitive prayer," says Ellul, that was marked by an "economy of scarcity." The individual person generally suffered from an impoverishment of goods and of "good luck." Thus, as the beggar expected a handout from the passing stranger, the one who prayed expected a handout from God. So, too, primitive prayer was bound up with an infantile and paternalistic relationship with God. In such prayer the person acts like a little child afraid to accept responsibilities, putting the decision making on God.[7]

As a result, in a materialistic age when goods and good luck can be secured through a variety of means more reliable than prayer, the modern person may view prayer as superstitious and magical. It may be comforting to "talk with God," but it is more helpful to talk to one's therapist. In this context, if the therapist turns to prayer and begins to "talk with God," some may think this reinforces the "infantile" need to project on God the responsibility for solving one's problems. But if we view prayer as a "shared life" with God and others and as a "growth process" in which God is really involved, "God talk" will not intrude into the therapeutic moment, but will have integrity based on the integrative nature of the process itself.

2. *Prayer as Victory Over Nothingness.* Does prayer contribute to the therapeutic process itself? I believe it does. Prayer is

more than "talking with God." Prayer is crossing a boundary; to use the suggestive phrase of Ellul, it is the means of "making a lawful entrance . . . into the closed world. The sacred is, in reality, the delineation of the boundary of something forbidden, of a mystery, the establishing of a certain number of fixed points of reference, the designation of a meaning."[8]

On the other side of this boundary, which seems to close in upon us, leaving us powerless and oppressed, lies the mystery of life with its resources of hope, faith, and love. Christian prayer is not the instinctive, primitive prayer of the poverty-stricken. Nor is Christian prayer an infantile movement away from personal responsibility and decision making toward an invisible "parent" who will take over. Christian prayer is communication with Jesus Christ, who "crossed the boundary" through his incarnation.

Christian prayer stands over and against primitive prayer, which seeks to cross the boundary through superstition, magic, or even human sacrifice. Christ's incarnation creates a basis for prayer in the continual coming to our situation by that same living God. Jesus' prayer to his Father in John 17 reveals that the boundary separating the divine mystery from our human situation is now overcome. All prayer to God now takes place within that "dialogue" and relationship between Father and Son that continues to empower Christian prayer. Jesus not only upholds the human situation through his own flesh-and-blood relationship with the Father, but also gives an insight into the mystery of the will of God, that we should be kept from the evil one (John 17:15) and "sanctified" in the truth of his word (v. 16). Finally, he shares his intimacy with the Father with those for whom he prays—his disciples and also those who will believe in him through their words (v. 20).

Christian prayer, therefore, is based on the incarnation of God in Christ, yields insight into the will of God for our wholeness and holiness, and creates an intimacy by which the life of God himself is communicated to those who pray.

A woman (let's call her Diane) who felt trapped in her marriage came for counseling. Her husband constantly abused her emotionally, but she followed what she thought was a biblical mandate to "be submissive to him" in hopes of changing his attitudes and actions. She had very little self-esteem, which she interpreted as a spiritual form of humility before God—not to "think of [herself] more highly than [she] ought to think" (Rom. 12:3). Her strong sense of spiritual obedience to God in this situation led her to a deep sense of despair and even doom, for despite her "prayers" for God to change her husband, he continued to humiliate and abuse her. Diane was caught in the "nothingness" that Ellul describes, where God was on the other side of the boundary and her prayers appeared futile.

Diane asked me to pray for the transformation of her husband so that she would be able to fulfill her calling of God to live in this marriage. Instead I led her to pray that God would come to her on "this side" of that boundary of despair and reveal his will for her. At first she protested that God's will was perfectly clear—she was to be submissive to her husband as a way of changing his behavior. But, in fact, he already professed to be a Christian and was a seminary student preparing for the ministry! I read some Scripture passages, in the manner suggested in the previous chapter, and asked Diane to interpret for herself what God desired in terms of her worth as a person and the quality of her life as a woman and a wife. She discovered that Jesus was "on her side," so to speak, willing her to move toward a position of health and wholeness. Her own prayers offered during the counseling sessions began to explore this "shared life" with God through Christ.

As her sense of worth grew along with an assurance of God's will for her and her children, Diane was able to confront her husband with his responsibility to share this life of wholeness with God and with her. Reacting with anger and even threats of violence, he left seminary and abandoned the marriage, with the result that she finally initiated and received a divorce. While she grieved a lost relationship, she discovered through the praxis of prayer a new shared life with Christ that continues to be a source of growth and life for her.

3. *Prayer as "Making History."* Ellul suggests that we see Christian prayer as a form of "making history" through the power of the Word of God incarnate and present through proclamation and sacrament. The Word proclaimed and embodied in sacrament must also be enacted in prayer, Ellul says, for the incarnation of God in Christ to be a continuing and present reality.[9] Because prayer constitutes the meeting place

between God's Word and the human word in the form of dialogue, it has the power of "making history." By "history" Ellul means purposeful and meaningful human existence that embodies God's design for the present and his will for the future.

> Prayer gives consistency to life, to action, to human relations, to the facts of human existence, both small and great. Prayer holds together the shattered fragments of the creation. It makes history possible. Therefore it is victory over nothingness.[10]

This "victory over nothingness," as Ellul puts it, is the source of all true healing of persons. The struggle for personal existence is a form of combat against this "mystery" of nothingness that seeks to undermine all efforts at self-validation and self-affirmation. The therapist who is a Christian can enter into this "combat" because the incarnation of God in Jesus Christ has crossed over the boundary and entered into this arena of personal existence, where the threat of "nothingness" is always present.

The apostle Paul says that Christ is the "image of the invisible God" and that he is before all things. "In him all things hold together," or cohere (Col. 1:15, 17). As the incarnation of God, Christ has "disarmed the principalities and powers," triumphing over them (Col. 2:15).

4. *Prayer as "Deliverance From Evil."* The Christian therapist has the Spirit of Christ present as a discerning Spirit, yielding insight into the struggle for existence against the powers of nothingness. Christians pray to exercise this insight through intimate communion with the Spirit of God in Christ. Christian prayer is therefore much more than meditation; it is much more than focusing and centering one's being on a God or the concept of a God who is hidden beyond the boundary of our temporal and tangible word of experience. Christian prayer, along with the proclaimed Word and sacrament, is the continuing power and presence of incarnation as a healing and integrating force, overcoming the fragmenting and destructive "powers of evil."

In Christian prayer, the petition "deliver us from evil" both acknowledges our vulnerability to the destructive powers around us and attacks those powers through the presence of Christ in us.

When the disciples implored Jesus, "Teach us to pray," they did not want to learn a method. Rather, they wanted to experience the same effect in their lives that they saw in his life. They saw that he overcame the powers that tempted and tormented them. They observed in him an intimacy with God as Father that enabled him to be whole and holy in the face of fragmenting forces around him and conflicting voices within him: "Now is my soul [*psyche*] troubled. And what shall I say, 'Father save me?'" (John 12:27). They saw the liberation and healing that prayer brought to others when all other "methods" failed (for example, see Matt. 17:14–20, where Jesus heals the epileptic boy after the disciples had failed).

Should a Christian pray in the context of psychotherapy? The answer is yes. A Christian who is undergoing therapy should pray, and should be taught to pray, in the same sense as Jesus taught his disciples to pray. A Christian therapist should pray with and for the client so that the process of therapy might become a structure of "history" through which the client triumphs over the power of "nothingness" and experiences the reality and power of the kingdom of God.

This is exactly what occurred for Diane. As long as her spiritual life remained attached to the destruction of her self-worth under the assumption that this was the "will of God," she had no real personal history. As she began to experience God's power in her life, she began, through prayer, to construct a sense of history. She now discovered that God was working with her, not against her. Despite the loss of her marriage, she discovered through prayer a "shared life" with God, giving her life a historical structure, rather than leaving her trapped in a cycle of doom and despair.

5. *Prayer as "Preparation of the Way."* When Christian prayer is seen as a "preparation of the way" rather than as a "method" or technique, the matter of when or how to pray in the context of the therapy hour will not be a problem. It is in the "preparation of the way of the Lord," said Dietrich Bonhoeffer, rather than in "method" that the kingdom of God comes to us with power, healing, and hope.[11] The "when" and "how to" of prayer are matters of having appropriate clinical intuition, a sense of spiritual discernment, and confidence in one's own form and

style of prayer. Whatever method of prayer is used, it should be congruent with the context and process of the therapy itself.

The deeper issue related to the process of psychotherapy is how one views prayer as it relates to God's work of healing. When prayer is understood as a form of "preparation of the way," through which our "closed-off" world is invaded by the liberating and healing power of God, then we will understand what Christian prayer is. When we understand that Christian prayer is not our "talk with God," but real "speech"—in which he is present in such a way that the language of prayer as a boundary is broken through by a real dialogue and communion with him—then we will know why we pray.

What do I expect when I pray with and for a client in a counseling session? I expect that concepts and images of God as an invisible but powerful source of healing and hope become real to me through the human and personal reality of speech. That is, I expect that concepts of God become communion with God—his presence taking hold of our presence. Thus the way is prepared for our response to his Word, as a new insight into our need, our worth, and our relatedness to him. The client will experience the reality of God as a partner in the process of mental and emotional healing.

I expect, when I pray with and for a client, that the feeling that God is an accuser or judge will be replaced by the feeling that God is an advocate of the client over and against the accusing and incriminating conscience. I expect that the client will be astounded to discover that a prayer for the forgiveness of sins carries with it the assured response—your sins are forgiven, on earth and in heaven. Thus the way is prepared for a transfer of power from the powerful to the powerless, from the eternal and unreachable ideal, to the historical and assessible self. The client will experience a feeling of relief and rest, with new psychical energy to continue the therapeutic process with a renewed spirit of anticipation and hope.

I also expect, when I pray with and for a client, that the unexpected will often happen. I expect that there will be surprises. In some cases and in some situations there is the surprise that nothing seems to have happened. At other times there is the surprise that healing appears to be almost instantaneous. The sense of surprise enables us to practice prayer even when there appears to be no visible effect, and to resist the temptation to make out of prayer a method for manipulating the Word of God. In both cases we are only preparing the way.

Prayer as a Healing Praxis

Some Christian therapists practice a form of prayer related to the therapeutic gain of "healing of memories." This prayer as a healing praxis works to remove the traumatic emotional experiences in the past that continue to plague a person in the present. Many Christian therapists feel that prayer releases Christ's power and that they can use guided imagery as a form of prayer in order to provide a kind of "inner healing."

It appears axiomatic to behavioral scientists that negative and self-destructive images can actually destroy mental health. Likewise, it appears to many that constructing positive images tends to produce good mental health. The recent literature on "inner healing," which focuses on the healing of negative memories (images) through the creation of positive self-images, testifies to the therapeutic implications of the imaging process. More recently, Christian counselors have been attracted to the therapeutic possibilities of inner healing. At the popular level this trend is represented by the book written by John and Paula Sandford, *The Transformation of the Inner Man,* identified on the cover as "The Most Comprehensive Book on Inner Healing Today."[12]

It should be noted, however, that the Sandfords do not agree that the self-image of a person can be healed or renewed. On the contrary, they insist that inner healing does not erase old memories, but transforms them by relating them to a totally new self-image—that of being completely victorious through the grace of Jesus Christ.[13] "The inner being is not good that it should be restored," argue the Sandfords, "but it is put to death in order that a new being may arise within us."[14] In support of this astounding statement they cite Romans 7:18–19: "For I know that nothing good dwells within me, that is, in my flesh. I can will what is right, but I cannot do it."

My response is that this does *not* say that the "inner being" is not good, but rather that nothing good dwells within. The Sandfords do not cite the text that follows: "For I delight in the law of God, in my inmost self" (7:22). The same Paul who confesses his psychological and spiritual ambivalence can nonetheless claim that his inner being *is* good, because it "remembers," or delights in, the law of God.

We are reminded here of the way the Old Testament describes the mental process. For the Hebrews, the mental process involves "receiving" an image or perception into the soul, so that what "rises up" in the heart becomes an intention or will to act. For us to say that it did not "come upon my heart" or "come into my heart" is to say that it was not our intention or will. God says, through the prophet Jeremiah, that the people of Judah did evil, because they did that which "I did not command, nor did it come into my mind" (Jer. 7:31).

When the people responded to Jehoash's plea to contribute to the repair of the temple each was to contribute (in addition to the money assessed) "the money which a man's heart prompts him to bring into the house of the Lord" (2 Kings 12:4). The Hebrews did not first of all "think" as a neutral or abstract mental process and then "decide" or will an action. Instead, for them, the soul, or inner being, received impressions that then "rise within the heart" as an intention.

This is exactly what is meant by praxis. The goal of the action is included in the intention so that no dichotomy exists between the concept or idea and the action in which the idea is completed. Memory is thus grounded in concrete actions and outcomes, rather than merely in abstractions of the mind.

When the soul "remembers" something, it does not have an objective memory image of some thing or event. Instead, an image is called forth in the soul and assists in determining its direction or action. To remember the works of Yahweh and to let one's acts be determined by his will is the same process. That which is not remembered passes out of the soul and has no bearing on determining the will or action of a person. The Israelite cannot "image memory" as an abstract image without affecting the direction of life. An Old Testament scholar, John Pedersen, says of this mental process of the Israelites:

> New and large experiences make one forget the lesser; they are displaced from the soul and exercise no influence. When the new heavens and the new earth are created, then the Isarelites shall no more remember the former, and it shall not rise in their heart (Isa. 65:17; Jer. 3:16). It means that the new order of things shall fill their soul, so that the old no more stirs any emotion in it.[15]

Although the phrase "healing of memories" is used as a therapeutic goal, I believe that a more biblical concept would be the "healing of memory." Memory itself, not memories, is the key to health. Scripture seems to emphasize the forgiveness of God, which can be the basis of self-forgiveness.

We are told that God has forgiven us, and I believe it. Does that mean that his memories have been healed? "Remember not the sins of my youth," cries the Psalmist (Ps. 25:7). "Thou hast cast all my sins behind thy back," testifies the prophet (Isa. 38:17). "As far as the east is from the west, so far does he remove our transgressions from us," writes David, who had as much reason as anyone to hope that God had healed his memories (Ps. 103:12)!

Old Testament sinners were confident in the presence of God, not because God had a selective memory or because he had purposefully forgotten the sins of his people, but because in "remembering" his own people he could not at the same time remember their sins. With God, forgetting is not an action of his will; only remembering is. "O Lord GOD, remember me, I pray," Samson cried out, even though he had been blinded through the folly of his pride and disobedience. "He [God] has remembered his steadfast love and faithfulness to the house of Israel" (Ps. 98:3).

God does not say "I will forget," but "I will remember." In his remembering lie salvation and healing. In being remembered by God we are at the center of his vision and occupy the totality of his affection. Those whom God remembers fill his vision as objects of his desire and love. They are seen by God as whole. God has no imagination of evil, because he has no intention of doing evil. God has no distorted image in his mind, because he has no will to distort in his heart.

Thus prayer helps us to focus on God as the totality of our lives, measured by his promises for our good. "Memories" in the form of disconnected mental images are "flooded" out of the self through the flow of this total goodness of God directed toward us. Prayer is itself the work of memory directed toward promise.

We do not find it natural to pray in this way, however. Our "imagination" is hooked to the disconnected thoughts and experiences of the past and roams freely over the undirected and fragmentary desires and sensations of the inner self. "The imagination of man's heart is evil from his youth," declared God following the judgment of the flood (Gen. 8:21). The power of "imaging" in the human heart went awry, and as a result, people have "exchanged the glory of the immortal God for images resembling mortal man or birds or animals or reptiles" (Rom. 1:23).

From this perspective, the healing of *memory* is more appropriate as a therapeutic goal than the healing of *memories.* The difference may be largely semantical to many, but from a Christian perspective memory relates to the positive core of self-identity and thus to the essential reality of the self as having not only a past, but a future. Because the determination of God is the basis for self-identity, his promise of the future becomes the orientation of memory. This, however, does not discount the value of therapeutic procedures dealing with a person's "frozen" emotional experiences, which continue to support neurotic patterns of behavior.

Therapeutic gain achieved through some kind of cathartic experience under the supervision of a therapist can be quite necessary, and yet quite insufficient to achieve the growth goal of the "healing of memory." The healing praxis of prayer supports therapeutic gain achieved through therapeutic procedures, but it continues to release emotive power to grow and develop as memory itself is liberated from a "thought pattern" that deflects it back upon the self. When the "memory"—to the Hebrews the core of the mind itself—is "filled" with God's love and promises, then a healing praxis takes place beyond therapeutic gain.

Two implications of what we have been saying for the therapeutic process can now be underscored. First, there is the implied theory that emotions result from perceptions, with behavior issuing from the emotion as a "purpose of the heart." Emotions, therefore, are not "free-floating" or "autonomous" components of the self that drive behavior; rather, they are systemically related to the mental processes of perception, intending, and acting. The Scottish philosopher John Macmurray says that emotions are basically rational in that they can be directed toward the objective reality of other persons. Emotions become irrational when they are broken off from our actions with other persons. Even the emotions and feelings that are most closely related to my self are given objective and rational status when integrated into my shared life with others.[16]

Ordinarily, we are concerned with the emotional health of a person because of the kind of behavior that constitutes the presenting problem. But in dealing with emotional disturbances we must also take into account the relation of emotions to perception and will. At this point we might want to take another look at the Rational-Emotive Theory as advocated by Albert Ellis. Despite his contention that religion is a source of mental confusion rather than mental health, it may well be that some aspects of RET are quite congenial with a biblical anthropology and a Christian approach to therapy.[17]

A second implication for the therapeutic process is the theory that memory is not a function of the mind, but *is* the mind. For the Israelites, to remember, to imagine, and to think are all part of the same mental process by which the self is directed toward action. The result is "wisdom," the property of the soul, or a skill in shaping the very thought that leads to the right result. John Pedersen insightfully comments, "Wisdom is essential in the making of a soul. If a man lacks wisdom, then he has no heart. . . . Wisdom is the faculty of the whole of the soul, just as the will is the direction of the whole of the soul." Pedersen relates this to the psychological process:

> All mental activity points in the direction of action. But what is the place that *action* occupies in the psychological process? According to European psychology action first originates in the region of ideas; then it is penetrated by feeling, which in its turn makes it to be determined by volition; this again leads to resolution, which is followed by action. Thus the activity of the soul is completed; the result of the action lies entirely outside its sphere, being added as a new element.[18]

For the Israelites it was quite different, says Pedersen. The soul perceives the result of the action as a good, so that the intention rises in the heart to produce the action. We do not contemplate action in itself as a mental state, but we "imagine," "call to mind," or "remember" the result of an action.

The healing praxis of prayer works in just this way. When prayer focuses on the concrete results of God's actions in our lives, we actually become whole by contemplating this wholeness. Expressing in words the results of God's love and grace, prayer names the reality that belongs to the healed self, rather than merely describing the pain and lamenting the loss.

When Jeremiah laments his affliction and complains, "My soul continually thinks of it and is bowed down within me," he immediately "remembers" the faithfulness of Yahweh.

> But this I call to mind,
>   and therefore I have hope:
>
> The steadfast love of the LORD never ceases,
>   his mercies never come to an end;
> they are new every morning;
>   great is thy faithfulness.
> "The LORD is my portion," says my soul,
> "therefore I will hope in him" (Lam. 3:21–24).

The healing for Jeremiah did not come about through an attempt to replace the negative images (memories) with new and positive images, but through his "remembering" the good that Yahweh had done and that he had promised to do for him. Jeremiah recovers the "memory of wholeness," which is itself a mental process through which his emotions and actions can be reoriented to a good and productive life. Thus he achieves the "wisdom" characteristic of the righteous and blessed man.

I have suggested that there are two implications of our understanding of the mental process from the perspective of an Old Testament anthropology. First, perceptions cause emotions to arise within the self that lead directly to appropriate action in order that what is perceived (imagined) may be accomplished. Second, "memory images" are not one function of the mind, but "memory is the mind."

How do these two implications inform a Christian therapist who seeks to heal persons through the praxis of prayer? Let me suggest several specific ways that come to mind.

1. We should focus on results of actions rather than actions themselves. The Israelites did not really think about the actions of God, but rather about the results of those actions. Joseph did not think about the actions of his brothers, who sold him into slavery, but contemplated the result of the actions as good despite their intentions. "You sold me. . . . you meant evil against me; but God meant it for good" (Gen. 45:5; 50:20).

Jesus told his disciples that to hate is already to have committed murder, and to lust is already to have committed adultery (Matt. 5:28; 1 John 3:15). When we perceive desires and emotions in terms of the results of actions, we perceive things quite differently. I once asked a person who hated his mother how he planned to dispose of her body. Shocked, he protested that he did not want her dead, but neither did he think she actually suffered from his feeling of hatred. I think that he ended up not liking her very much, but was content to leave her alive while he got on with his life.

To pray in a case like this demands forming positive, concrete intentions toward the one who has caused pain. Praying does not take our pain away, but it frees us from the captivity of painful memories and emotions. To this end Jesus told us to "pray for our enemies." To be sure, praying won't necessarily make us feel affectionate toward our enemies, nor will we necessarily come to regard them as friends. But in praying for our enemies we release ourselves from the captivity of our own emotions and free our emotions to be directed toward God. For we do not pray to our enemies, but to God on their behalf.

2. We should focus on the benefits of God's actions through Jesus Christ, not on concepts of God. When the apostle Paul was caught in the undertow of his ambivalence, nourished by his own self-condemnation, he experienced a healing of his memory by contemplating the "law of God" and then acknowledging his love for it, out of the depths of his own being (Rom. 7:22). In the Old Testament, Israelites would praise Yahweh, but they would love and meditate on his law (cf. Pss. 19:7–14; 119). Consider the vivid images of Psalm 23, where David remembers the Lord as a shepherd, with green pastures, still water, an overflowing cup, and a banquet table, all consummated by a life lived in the house of the Lord forever!

When we focus on the benefits of God's actions, historical memory joins with eschatological memory to heal present memory. The Israelites comprehended past benefits of God and future benefits in the same act of thinking, or remembering. Healing memory means much more than relearning or forgetting bad memories. Memory is healed when it "remembers the goodness of God" in upholding one's present and future life. When memory heals, emotions arise within the self that become intended actions, which include the blessings and good anticipated. Thus modification of behavior results when we image the results of behavior as a benefit or blessing on our lives.

Worshiping and praising God for his benefits give the mind "rest" from attempting to integrate fragments of good into a whole. The good is one thing and is willed by God. Prayer is "willing the good" as directed toward us by God.

We should not doubt the therapeutic and practical wisdom of "meditating" on God's Word and God's benefits. "Blessed is the man who walks not in the counsel [precepts] of the wicked," says the psalmist, "but his delight is in the law of the LORD, and on his law he meditates day and night" (Ps. 1:1–2; cf. 119:15, 78, 97; 143:5). When the psalmist says, "I have laid up thy word in my heart, that I might not sin against thee," he is not speaking of rote memorization, but of receiving the Word into his heart as the story of God's actions and the promise of his benefits (Ps. 119:11). There is every reason to think that such an exercise as part of the therapeutic process would have similar healing power today.

Here prayer and the use of Scripture can be helpfully combined. When we fill our minds with Scriptures that speak of God's goodness and blessings, prayer becomes the praxis of healing. Thus a helpful "homework" assignment for a patient would be to write out prayers after meditating on Scripture.

3. A Christian therapist can act in the role of a prophet as well as a priest. The therapist as a priest can not only become the advocate of the client through listening, affirming, and interpreting, but also serve as the advocate of the benefits of God. In this prophetic role the therapist may challenge the memory of the client when that memory has become selective and partial. He or she may even debate the client's perspective on life by looking at both the past and anticipated results of God's actions.

After listening sympathetically for an hour to a man's litany of self-condemnation and self-accusation, I suggested that if all that he said was true, then God had failed miserably in what he set out to accomplish. Could God's intention to forgive and grant complete healing as the consequence of the prayer of confession be such a failure? Which was true, his own self-condemnation based on what he felt, or the promise of God that stood contrary to his own feelings? I then read for him 1 John 3:19: "By this we shall know that we are of the truth, and reassure our hearts before him whenever our hearts condemn us; for God is greater than our hearts, and he knows everything." I sent the man home to think about that for a week and to return with a written prayer in which he responded to the Scripture passage.

The prayer was labored and written without much real conviction. The client found it difficult to respond with a prayer when he had practiced so faithfully a response to his own feelings. But when he read the prayer out loud, he crossed a threshold. Looking back, I see that the growth process took place when God himself encountered him in the event of prayer. He was now ready to work more constructively on the process of clarifying and integrating his emotions. At the end of the counseling relationship, when we agreed that sufficient gain had been reached, he no longer needed a clinical supervisor. He had learned how to pray. We who seek to heal someone's private pain may well ask, along with Jesus' disciples, "Lord, teach us to pray."

Summary

These, then, are the spiritual dynamics that inspire and empower the therapy process:

- Through prayer that becomes a praxis of shared life with God, there is a resource for healing and a new historical life of faith;
- Through the use of Scripture that provides a creative discovery of God's truth, there is empowerment for change and a new freedom in the life of faith;
- Through the grace of God that touches the deepest core of the self with empowerment for growth, there is a new resource for the integration of personal and spiritual identity with gracious ego strength;
- Through the dynamic of the kingdom of God, the totality of the self as physical, social, and spiritual is grasped and upheld in its orientation toward a positive life on earth and a completed life eternally with God.

These are resources for integration and growth that attend the calling and ministry of Christians who counsel. In part 3 the person and role of the counselor will be defined more clearly as one who is a vital agent and mediator in the therapeutic process related to the life continuum of growth.

We began this book with the nature of the human person as the foundation for counseling, and we conclude the book with an emphasis on the person and role of the counselor.

Notes

1. Donald G. Bloesch, *The Struggle of Prayer* (Colorado Springs: Helmers and Howard, 1988), 63.

2. Ibid., 50.

3. Jacques Ellul, *Prayer and the Modern Man* (New York: Seabury, 1979), 60.

4. Ibid., 82.

5. Thomas F. Torrance, *God and Rationality* (Oxford University Press, 1971), 41.

6. Ellul, *Prayer and the Modern Man*, 81.

7. Ibid., 85–86.

8. Ibid., 71.

9. Ibid., 175–76.

10. Ibid., 177.

11. Dietrich Bonhoeffer, *Ethics* (New York: Macmillan, 1955), 141.

12. John and Paula Sandford, *The Transformation of the Inner Man* (South Plainfield, N.J.: Bridge Publishing, 1982).

13. Ibid., 11, 17.

14. Ibid., 20.

15. John Pedersen, *Israel: Its Life and Culture*, vol. 1 (London: Oxford University Press, 1973), 107.

16. John Macmurray, *Reason and Emotion* (London: Faber and Faber, 1935).

17. The implications for Rational-Emotive Therapy with regard to pastoral counseling have been developed in a dissertation written by the Rev. Dr. Jeffrey M. Dire, *Rational-Emotive Therapy: Implications for Pastoral Counseling* (D.Min. diss., Fuller Theological Seminary, 1984).

18. Pedersen, *Israel: Its Life and Culture*, 1:127.

PART THREE

COUNSELING IN A
CHRISTIAN MODE

8

Counseling as a
Christian Calling

My father lived and died as a farmer in South Dakota and, to
my knowledge, strayed no more than a hundred miles or so from
his birthplace. He was strongly attached to the soil from which
he came and in which he was finally laid to rest.

He did not talk about farming as a calling in life. He simply
made no distinction between what he did for a living and his life
as a person.

As a small boy I often brought lunch out to my father in the
field. One time I was sitting next to him on the soft black earth
that his horse-drawn plow had just turned over, when suddenly
he turned to me and asked me to stick my hand down into the
soil. "Son," he said, "this soil is part of your life—you take care
of it and it will take care of you."

Only in later years did I realize how powerful and formative
that action was. At first I thought it meant an attachment to the
soil, mistakenly thinking that he himself was bound to the earth
in some kind of fatalistic way. After serving in the army air force
during the Second World War, and after completing college with
a degree in agricultural science, I myself took up the life of
farming. For seven years I pursued that vocation, tracing out my
own destiny in the good earth.

How do we account for the shift of passion from one objective
to another? How do we explain the inner certainty with which
we change direction without doubting the correctness of the first
and without questioning the rightness of the next?

Did I unknowingly stumble into some kind of "agogic

157

moment" (chap. 3) in which I grasped for more than the soil could offer and so reach out for some personal goal and life fulfillment beyond the world that ended with the last row of corn?

I experienced my conversion over a period of some time, I remember. From a background of nominal Christian faith with occasional church attendance, I moved intentionally and passionately into a personally expressed faith in Christ marked by renewed life in the church and its ministry.

Triggering this conversion was an encounter with a fellow farmer, a young man who had a vital Christian faith and with whom I developed a friendship. His sense of immediacy with God and his directness and freedom of expressing his faith attracted me. When we discussed questions and issues related to life, our work, and Christian faith, my own responses were vague and noncommittal.

On one occasion my friend put the question directly to me. "Ray, are you saying that you are really a believer and not merely an observer?" My answer was yes, and we shook hands as though we had closed some real estate transaction. That, I believe, was my own entrance into an agogic, or growth, situation, which released in me a faith in God that not only integrated my life in a spiritual sense, but later led me, with my family, to leave the farm and pursue theological training and pastoral ministry.

In this chapter we want to look more closely at the concept of a calling of God. First we will discuss counseling as a Christian calling, then we will analyze the motives and intentions of the Christian counselor who seeks to understand this profession as a calling of God. Finally we will examine what it means to be "occupied" with this calling and what distinctives a Christian who counsels can experience and add to the therapeutic practice.

Counseling as a Christian Calling

After my agogic situation, people talked to me about a "call of God" in my life. I must confess that I did not experience it as some kind of divine voice or mandate that came suddenly out of thin air. Looking back, I can now recognize several factors that led to this radical change in my life.

Certainly the encounter with my friend was a transformative and authentic growth moment, for it released a motive power in me to profess personal faith in God. This friend's role in my life fulfilled all that we have discussed in chapter 3 about the agogical moment. He met me in what Jacob Firet called "equi-human" address, using his shared humanity as a basis for a trusting and meaningful relation between us. My friend was, in fact, an intermediary who did not assert the prerogative as mentor or the power as authority over me.

The relation summoned out of me some kind of counterpart to my friend's own person. This would not have happened if he had not himself been a believing person with an integrated life and faith. It was the vital, engaging, directly personal, and fully human presence that he brought into the relationship that invited me to meet him at the same level.

But it was also more than that. The experience of a new circle of Christian fellowship and support, coupled with the experience of teaching high school-age young people in the local church, continued this growth process. Over the period of a year or more there were released in me a motive and a desire to invest my life in the lives of others. I saw change and growth take place in the lives of others with whom I had significant relationships. I was initiating growth encounters with others and thereby enlarging and sustaining growth and change for me.

In making the decision to leave the farm and to sever the connection that my life had with the soil, I fully expected to suffer, not regret, but a kind of melancholy. It would be, I thought, a kind of death that would leave part of me unattached. In a sense, I felt that I was leaving my father as well as the soil behind. It was a pleasant shock to discover, even after only a few months, that my new "calling" to study for the Christian ministry had not left an empty space, nor did I long for what had been or what might have been. My career change was not, I think, a kind of denial, but rather a quiet and deeply rooted transplanting of my life from one soil to another.

My father had not attached my hand to the soil on that day long ago, although that was how I had interpreted it. Rather, he had attached my heart to my hand. My inner self had become bound to my outer life, so that whatever task I put my hand to was done with a sense of finality and completeness that brought joy, rather than a feeling of fatalism, which spelled melancholy and despair.

These reflections on my experience and sense of calling as a Christian counselor are not meant to suggest a pathway to follow, but an approach to the concept of a calling of God "from below," so to speak. In the first three chapters of this book I outlined an approach to counseling that began with the structure of personhood as a guide to therapeutic growth and the role of the counselor as growth partner. We can now look more closely at how a Christian would fulfill his or her calling in the role of a counselor. In this chapter we will focus on the special relation between the practice of counseling and God's calling in life. Every Christian is called into relationship with Christ, and each Christian's life constitutes a fulfillment of that calling. My thesis is that for Christians who counsel, counseling can be a means of fulfilling that divine calling.

How Do I Know My Calling?

When one's inner life becomes attached to one's outer life, it is the beginning of a concept of a calling of God. God does not simply issue a call that interrupts and intercepts life from without. Instead he enters into the sphere of life and encounters us in such a way that we are summoned to respond to him in "like kind." That is, he gives himself without regard to reward or "payoff" in order to make the giving valuable. God values love and self-giving. It would be naïve and unhelpful to think of God's calling coming to us "out of the blue." Some do speak of having a dramatic sense of God's intervention, which they interpret as a unique "calling" to some task. These special interventions, however, can also be authentic forms of discovering one's own calling.

As a rule, the calling of God should not be sought only in the dramatic and extraordinary. Nor should it be associated with some kind of "identity crisis" or used to solve a lack of identity and purpose in life. The people whom Jesus "called" to be disciples already seemed to have a well-established personal identity and purpose. Their "hearts were already attached to their hands," as the metaphor I have used puts it.

Jesus did not feel ambivalent about his own identity when he "found [himself] in human form" (Phil. 2:8). He did not need to be rewarded or to gain something from his act of leaving eternal glory to become human. He gloried in being human as the single task of his life and as the fulfillment of his divine sonship. His calling as the Messiah grew out of his sense of personal identity. He responded out of his own being to the God who continued to say from heaven, "This is my beloved Son, with whom I am well pleased" (Matt. 3:17). His response to the needs of those around him awakened his power of love and his instincts for righteousness and holiness.

I thought that the attachment of my hand to the soil determined my life; so I thought I depended on the soil to stimulate my heart and fulfill my life. But this was not correct. Actually, in further understanding the experience, I saw I had become "unattached" to the soil when I "attached" my heart to my hand. The soil and the task of farming the land were not an external "stimulus" that produced a sense of purpose and meaning within me as a "response." Otherwise, Christian calling could have become only a kind of "fate" or duty to which I was bound as a way of fulfilling my Christian life. The criterion for my "effective calling" would then have been bound up with the results or with my success in this calling. Maybe that is why farmers tend to speak of "crop failures" rather than "farming failures."

Once I saw that my heart had become attached to my hand, I sensed that my calling would be fulfilled wherever I put my hand. The soil became a metaphor, much like Jesus' use of the phrase, "No one who puts his hand to the plow and looks back is fit for the kingdom of God" (Luke 9:62). Jesus is speaking of the attachment of the hand to the plow, not the plow to the soil. This "singleness of heart" without ambivalence is the personal and integrative context in which one perceives a calling of God.

What Is a Christian Calling?

Seeing the call of God in life as located in the congruence between the inner and outer life helps us to understand what it means to take up life as a "Christian calling." This can also be a healthy corrective to concepts of Christian calling that tend to make us dependent on results for confirmation of the call or, even more serious and devastating, tend to shift the sense of calling from one's inner motivation to the demands of the "ministry" of one's life.

This is particularly an occupational hazard for parish ministers, though I suspect that it also can become a problem for Christian counselors and therapists. Some enter the profession of ministry because of a "call of God." The form of this call becomes identified with a particular "vocation," or calling, such as being a pastor of a church. The call of God is understood to have a priority over all of life, even over family and friends, and especially over the maintenance and fulfilling of the self. "God first, others second, and myself last" goes the Bible school warning to those who go into "full-time Christian service."

It would be hard to exaggerate the psychological, spiritual, and even physical devastation that this misunderstanding has caused many Christians who sincerely attempt to live out this "calling of God." First they assume that God "assigns" a person to a task, promising a reward to the faithful servant at the end. This task then becomes a "calling" when the demands of the ministry itself in terms of insatiable human needs take over. Now the calling itself in terms of the duty to serve others replaces God as the source of the call. At the same time, their identity so merges with the task that a "personage" replaces the "person," to use Paul Tournier's words. And because they expect a reward to compensate for the sacrifice, they concoct rewards out of success at any cost. Or, failing that or because of that, they are finally driven to reward themselves through surreptitious sensuality or some other delicious deviation.[1]

A calling becomes Christian when our life with Christ becomes identical with our hand and heart. Or, to put it another way, being Christian is a calling that is fulfilled in and through that which becomes one's destiny here on earth. Our destiny is related to that which consumes our life. Paul says, "I have been crucified with Christ; it is no longer I who live, but Christ who lives in me; and the life I now live in the flesh I live by faith in the Son of God, who loved me and gave himself for me" (Gal. 2:20). The Christian calling does not lead us away from our life and destiny here on this earth, but is a gracious calling to live with the knowledge that our life is a fulfillment of "Christ in us."

How Do I Fulfill My Calling?

Once a person is overly attached to the ministry situation, a fatal "cause and effect," or "stimulus-response" mechanism can develop. Theologically the concept of a calling by which one lives out life can be understood as a structure of freedom and response, not stimulus-response. The freedom and response relation can take place only within a relationship that is fully personal. That is, only a personal being can encounter another being in such a way that a response is elicited that is derived out of freedom and not out of necessity.

"The love of Christ controls us," Paul says (2 Cor. 5:14). The somewhat ambiguous genitive construction in the Greek leaves open the possibility that it is both Christ's love for us as well as our love for Christ that is the controlling, or compelling, force. A sense of calling is centered in the perception of the self as positively oriented toward others and God. Calling does not arise out of a need that the other fulfills, or out of a need that the other places on me as a demand.

If we continue to think of a sense of divine calling as a basis for undertaking the profession of counseling as a Christian therapist, we must not allow counseling itself to become the calling. We are not "called to counsel," but called to be Christian in our counseling. The calling remains a dynamic of freedom and response in our relationship to God. Above all, this calling is congruent with the growth and development of our personal identity as a process. Being Christian is thus "being called" to live one's life to the fullest, being open to change, and experiencing God's presence and blessing in the place, time, and work that occupy life.

The Motivation for a Christian Calling

We cannot examine the nature of calling as a perspective on counseling as a Christian vocation without looking more closely at the motivation underlying our sense of calling. We have learned to our dismay that our motives are not always consistent with our intentions. One source of ambivalence is surely due to the unreliability of our motives as expressed through our commitments.

Jacob Firet, discussing pastors, warns against confusing motivation and motives. Motivation as a source for behavior is not very clear, he says, citing Gordon Allport: "As for motivation . . . psychologists are in a state of turmoil and disagreement."[2] Firet also suggests that the concept of motivation is more inclusive than what we usually have in mind when we speak of "personal motives." A person's motives may be considered as the consciously held reasons for doing or not doing something. Motivation, by contrast, is the driving force behind a given behavior, a force that may at times be quite different from the motives expressed by the person.[3] In this way of looking at the issue, motives are the reasons we give to ourselves and others for our decisions and actions, while motivation is a deeper drive that may be hidden from us.

Candidates for pastoral ministry are usually asked to state their reasons, or motives, for seeking to enter pastoral ministry. The orthodox answer is some form of a testimony to a perceived sense of God's calling. What may be far more significant are the underlying motivations, which may, in fact, be hidden from a candidate's conscious mind. When these underlying motivations become evident, the character or quality of our actions may be called into question. My expressed motive may be to serve Christ through a form of professional pastoral ministry, and I may have a strongly held sense of divine calling. As it turns out, my actual motivation may be to find self-gratification in the honor and prestige attached to the ministry. When this real motivation becomes evident to others, they will view my ministry as self-serving and unworthy of Christ. Paul was charged with such unworthy motivation, and he defended himself strongly to the Christians at Thessalonica, appealing to their knowledge of his actions and intentions when he was laboring among them (cf. 1 Thess. 2:1–16).

It is obvious that candidates for counseling as a Christian ministry might run into the same problem with discerning their own motives and motivation. From a psychological perspective, motives and motivations are complex and, at best, only inferred out of certain styles and patterns of behavior.

John Macmurray makes what I believe is a more helpful distinction between motives and intentions. "Though every action must have a motive," he writes, "it is not determined by its motive. It is determined, as this specific action, by the operation of intentions."[4] In each action of a personal agent, he suggests, we must presuppose a "system of motives whose differentiations refer to the Other. . . . The agent can accordingly act either for or against the Other." In other words, persons in relation always have motives that are differentiated in terms of the others with whom one is in relation. These motives can be either positive or negative as viewed with respect to the other, but in and of themselves simply as motives, they do not determine the relation as personal. There must be an underlying *intention* that is rooted in the structure of personhood and the relation itself.[5]

For example, parents may have a complex system of motives (motivations) that enters into the intentional act of parenting. Likewise, children may respond out of a complex system that entails motivations, fear, needs, rewards, and stimulus-response dynamics, etc. But the intentionality that forms and sustains the structure of the relation itself can be grounded in the act of love, which is a deeper construct and dynamic in the relation than motives and motivations. A parent may discipline a child when the parent's motives are mixed and confused. The parent's anger, frustration, and feelings of powerlessness may be inappropriately expressed as rage against a child when the parent's intention is actually to discipline the child for its own good. Where intentions have become imbedded in consistent acts of love, security, and care between parent and child, these destructive and inappropriate motives may be healed. Object relations psychology would say that the parent must be "good enough" and not perfect. Being "good enough" is sustaining intentionality based on love with enough consistency that lapses do not destroy the objective identity of the child as good and loved.[6]

This is not to say that motivations or motives are only incidental to the dynamics of the relationship. Underlying motivations may be so powerful as to render the relationship virtually dysfunctional or even pathological despite the intentionality of love. I point out the distinction to show that a sense of calling may be grounded in something other than mere psychological motivations.

This level of intentionality cannot be ascertained from a strictly psychological approach. A projective type of psychological test may uncover, by inference, underlying motivations that aid in diagnostic evaluation. But the structure of intentionality by which one acts out of a sense of duty or "calling" is more related to the dynamics of growth we have described than a psychological, stimulus-response dynamic. What makes intentions different from motivations is that we can expect others to state clearly their intentions and to be held accountable to them.

Unwillingness to state our intentions would be itself a sign of a motivation that is less than open and honest. By saying that I am a Christian who counsels, I am stating an intention to counsel in a way that is Christian.

The love that moved Christ to "die for all" (2 Cor. 5:15) is what "constrained," or gripped, Paul. The apostle uses the Greek word *synechei* to express this sense of being grasped by the power of another's love and the source of one's own actions. Jesus uses the same verb in Luke 12:50 to describe his own "constraint" to complete his course of action by going to Jerusalem even though it meant suffering and certain death.

This sense of "being constrained" suggests to us a better concept than motivation for understanding the dynamics of a sense of calling. *Synechia,* or constraint, does not arise from within the person as a psychological or intrapersonal disposition. It is another power, the power of the One who has come over him, that constrains Jesus. The "sense" of this inner response to the compelling power of another's love can be recognized through motives and motivations as an inference. But more than that is not possible.[7] It is possible, however, to counsel under the "constraint" of serving the other with Christlike love and care.

We can be forgiven for failing to live up to this intention if such failure is acknowledged. Failure to fulfill such intentions does not constitute ambivalence when the failure is confessed and shared. Ambivalence results from failure to state intentions and, instead, to allow our calling to be driven by motivation alone.

"Constraint" calls us to live as Christians and devote ourselves to duty that unifies rather than divides the self. Duty is freely choosing to devote ourselves to others under the constraint of serving Christ. We never merely devote ourselves to duty, but to the "one who called me" and continues to uphold me in love. "The man of duty," wrote Dietrich Bonhoeffer, "will end up by having to fulfill his obligation even to the devil."[8]

On this basis there must be more than a sense of "duty" directed toward ultimate love, toward God. This devotion is single-minded and prepared to take up whatever duty "comes to hand" to give it expression. Because love of God is bound up with love of neighbor, and because all devotion (except what God experiences within his triune relation) is mediated through duty, the other person becomes the middle term in the relation of devotion to God. Knowing that our life and work satisfy God's calling us to be Christians is a kind of wisdom that actually gives us the strength to fulfill our calling.

This "wisdom" that comes from God and that God gives to all generously and without reproach comes to those who receive it in faith.

> But let him ask in faith, with no doubting, for he who doubts is like a wave of the sea that is driven and tossed by the wind. For that person must not suppose that a double-minded [*di-psychos*] man, unstable in all his ways, will receive anything from the Lord (James 1:6–8).

No finer exposition of this text has been done than that of Søren Kierkegaard in his classic work *Purity of Heart is to Will One Thing*. The double-minded person, says Kierkegaard, cannot will the good because that person cannot will one thing. We do not will the good for the sake of reward or to avoid punishment or even that the good should triumph in our lives. If we did so, Kierkegaard says, we would be "constrained" by the results of our actions rather than by the good itself.[9] Kierkegaard helps us to see that we must overcome our inner ambivalence before we can integrate the heart and the hand. Or we could say that the way to overcome this ambivalence is to unite the heart and the hand so that devotion attaches itself to duty to directing itself to God, who is the Good, and the source of one's devotion.[10] We must root out this inner ambivalence by pursuing the intention back to its roots, exposing the double-mindedness that lurks behind all ambivalence—or the "wish," as Kierkegaard puts it.[11]

We cannot help but remember the words of Jesus, who encouraged his disciples not to lay up treasures here on earth, but to lay up treasures in heaven, "for where your treasure is, there will your heart be also" (Matt. 6:19–21). "Let not your hearts be troubled; believe in God, believe also in me. Believe me that I am in the Father and the Father in me; or else believe me for the sake of the works themselves" (John 14:1, 11).

In encouraging his disciples thus, Jesus was reminding them of his own single-mindedness. He pointed them to devotion, and if they could not grasp that, to see his devotion in his work—in that which became his duty. His heart was attached to his hand, and his heart was one with the Father.

This single-mindedness gives us freedom to live and act in such a way that the calling of God becomes identical with the action itself, rather than with the results of the action. There is an inner freedom and certainty of life in action that liberates the self from even the ethical constraints of "duty." For, as we have said, duty itself can become demonic apart from its source in devotion to God.

The sense of fulfilling one's life as a divine calling is not an esoteric or mystical feeling. It is not limited to those who take up the "full-time ministry" of serving as an ordained pastor or missionary. This sense of calling is the single-mindedness with which Christians can take up the task of counseling or psychotherapy with a kind of "non-attachment" to the results, where devotion can be attached to duty, but duty not become the master of devotion.

Several things have now become clear in our discussion of the practice of counseling as a Christian calling:

- A sense of calling is related to the congruence between our inner life and our outer life, where the "heart is attached to the hand";
- God's specific calling is discovered through the vocation or task that fulfills and satisfies our heart and occupies our hand;
- Christian calling involves being under constraint to embody the love and reality of Christ through one's life and work;
- We fulfill our calling through the devotion that binds love for Christ to the task at hand, to make devotion our duty, in freedom and grace;
- In stating openly our intention of fulfilling our Christian calling through our ministry of counseling, we clarify our motivations and expose them to correction and healing.

The Occupation of Christian Counseling

What does it mean that a Christian takes up counseling or therapy as an "occupation"? Is there a distinctively Christian style of counseling? I would answer yes, but not as a distinctive model of therapy. Rather, the distinction lies in how we approach the task as a Christian calling. Or, we could say, the distinctiveness is the quality of the experience that the Christian brings to the task of healing the client.

This statement seems to claim that Christians might do "better therapy," or that Christian counselors have some kind of therapeutic advantage. This is not my intention. The person and presence of every counselor make a difference in the therapy session. The counselor is not a neutral figure or a nonentity. Many clients have more positive experiences with a female therapist then a male therapist, or vice versa. From the counselor's standpoint, I wish to speak of what this "style" or distinction can mean. The counseling style will also have implications for the client in therapy, though not necessarily in "doing better therapy."

When we counsel with the sense of fulfilling a Christian calling, we can be fully "occupied" with this task in a healthy and whole sense. This is what provides the style and makes the difference in counseling. With the assistance of four questions taken from Kierkegaard's essay *Purity of Heart is to Will One Thing*, I will explain this distinctive approach more fully.[12] These questions will provide an outline for further reflection on the occupation of Christian counseling.

1. What is your occupation in life? "Occupation" in this sense means our calling, not our profession. We may choose a profession to fulfill our occupation or calling. Every person has an occupation, though not everyone has a profession. I aim here to look at counseling as an occupation that a Christian chooses as a means to fulfill his or her Christian calling. This can be done at both the professional and nonprofessional levels. It can also be done part-time or full-time. The question "what is your occupation?" goes right to the heart of the matter with respect to how one's calling as a Christian is being fulfilled in the world.

There was a time when farming was my profession. It "occupied" me as a task in such a way that my heart and my hand were attached without regard to the results. I felt no less meaning in the task when the crops failed than when they were bountiful. A failure brought consequences that had both tangible and intangible effects, but it did not rob the task of its sense of fulfillment.

I changed my profession, but not my occupation, when I became a student and later a pastor and now a teacher. To be sure, we ordinarily describe our occupation in terms of a profession or task, and that is a perfectly reasonable way to do it. But as Christians we can have a profession that is also a "preoccupation," in which heart and hand are joined. I suppose all of us have times when we are not really happy with our present task and wish for something more. But we must be careful that the "wish" does not become a disease, as Kierkegaard reminds us. Nor should the task be attended with a sense of duty only, for that, too, can become self-destructive and even demonic, as Bonhoeffer reminds us.

The practice of counseling or psychotherapy can be the occupation of a Christian, and it can be considered as a Christian calling. But the question to one who is undertaking this as a profession is what his or her experience is as a Christian in this occupation. This leads to the second question.

2. In your occupation, what is your attitude of mind? Or, how do you carry out your occupation? Kierkegaard follows up this question by asking, "Have you made up your mind that your occupation is your real calling so that you do not have to make explanation hinge on the result, maintaining that it was not your real calling if the results are not favorable, if your efforts do not suceed?"[13]

I often find that graduating students suffer considerable anxiety about knowing the "right place" to begin. The risk of failing or of not achieving one's own goals (wishes?) can be paralyzing. Even more serious is the mental attitude with which such a person often takes his first job. "It doesn't really suit me and has no real future, but it is a beginning," he can be tempted to think.

When this happens, there is ambivalence and double-mindedness from the very beginning. The person is not able to devote himself or herself to the task because of a concern for results. Often the person wonders whether the profession is actually consistent with a Christian calling. The person may wonder whether psychotherapy can be "willed as the Good," to use Kierkegaard's phrase.

In this case there is a failure of integration at the very core of the venture, and the person launches out with a bad conscience. The person may give the excuse of having a problem with determining God's will, as though if one could determine the job as "God's will," this would make up for inner uncertainty. The will of God cannot be used as a criterion for the good in such a way that our own intention, decision, and actions are set aside. We find the will of God through our intending the good through actions that in the end are willed by God as good.

I have discussed this concept elsewhere, but I need to repeat here that God's will is the goal of a decision or action.[14] The will of God is really the "aim," which can be changed when the target moves. The will of God is not identified absolutely with a plan, a method, or even a vocation. These may change—and must be changed on occasion so that the will of God continues to be in view as the goal. To ask whether it is the will of God that I be a therapist, teacher, or pastor is not really the right way to phrase the question. I know it is God's will that what "occupies" my life and energies aims at producing a good measured in terms of God's love and desire for people, and for my own life given in devotion to him. I cannot resolve inner ambivalence to my task by resorting to a spiritual device that makes this God's decision rather than mine.

Many people may be concerned about counseling means and methods. Such people may compensate by looking for spiritually "valid" and "rewarding" results from counseling. They may seek to convert the non-Christians they counsel, rationalizing that the end justifies the means. This recalls our discussion about intentions as the clarification of motivations. We should always be capable of expressing our intentions openly at the outset of counseling. Christians who counsel do not need results to justify their calling to provide care.

This idea leads to the third question.

3. *What means do you use to carry out your occupation?* If the means are less legitimate than the end, then again there will be ambivalence and double-mindedness. From the standpoint of willing the Good as one thing, Kierkegaard suggests that the means and the end are the same thing. "There is only one end: the genuine Good; and only one means: This, to be willing only to use those means which genuinely are good—but the genuine Good is precisely the end."[15]

We may use the analogy of firing a rifle at a target. Reaching the goal is like hitting the target, but using means is like taking aim. In this case the aim is a more reliable indication of the marksman's goal than the spot that the bullet strikes. For instance, the shot may have hit in the right place by accident! The marksman may be blameless if the shell does not fire, but no irregularities of the aim are permitted. On this point, Kierkegaard comments, "Eternity is not curious and impatient as to what the outcome in this world of time will be. It is just because of this that the means are without exception as important as the end."[16]

Therefore we must examine the distinctive style of a Christian counselor according to the means, and not merely with regard to the end. If a counselor holds a Christian view of the person, the goal of therapy extends beyond the means of therapy. Therapy, of course, has its own specific goals, for which certain techniques or methods are appropriately used to produce therapeutic gain. But even the goals achieved by therapy are really means to the ultimate goal—the freedom of the self to love God and one's neighbor as oneself.

To make the point more clearly, we can remind ourselves of the growth process that should attend every genuine human encounter. I am insincere if I pursue a relationship without really making it my aim to enhance the other's life. If I have merely used friendship or a counseling relation as a means to manipulate the other to give me some advantage or to do what I want done, I have violated the integrity of the relationship. My motivation will undermine that integrity. It should be a stated intention that this will not be the case!

Some therapeutic means may achieve certain results, thus demonstrating the technical skill of the therapist, but these same means may fail to help the client reach the goal of integrative growth. That is, some goals achieved in therapy do not even aim at the larger, growth goal of integrating self with others and God. Here, too, the intentions of the counselor need to be expressed quite clearly. In certain cases the long-range growth goals may be identified but not made a specific outcome of the therapeutic gain sought. I can openly express to a person who seeks counseling that my intention is to provide orientation toward these long-range growth goals, which may include specific aspects of spiritual life and formation. This places specific therapeutic outcomes on a trajectory of growth without making therapy the means to this end.

At this point the question of means must be considered. For if

the means by which therapeutic aid is given do not relate at all
to the goal that lies beyond the specific therapeutic procedure,
the means become justified by results rather than by the
intention to provide growth toward these goals. Again, it may be
said, "The surgery was a success, but the patient died!" Yet, in
this concern for the experience of the client as a person who
seeks the Good, not merely good health, we are already moving
to the fourth question.

4. *What is your attitude toward others?* Do we actually love
our clients as ourselves and so fulfill the second great commandment? Kierkegaard focuses the question quite appropriately
when he asks, "Have you no special privilege, no special talent,
none of life's special favors . . . vanity has led you to take, so that
you could console yourself by means of it, and that makes you
dare not tell the uninitiated the source of your consolation?"[17]

Do we as counselors use therapy to conceal our own suffering? Do we console ourselves that we are not afflicted with such
pain and in need of such grace? "You help to set the simple
straight," says Kierkegaard, "but treacherously you have a
further consolation for yourself; your talent is so outstanding,
that it could never happen that when you awakened tomorrow
you were the stupidist person in all the land."[18]

The object of Kierkegaard's ridicule and acute questioning
was often the parsons, who represented to him the most
scandalous of people because they lived in state-supported
security but still charged fees for performing religious rituals.
But Kierkegaard was also questioning himself, for he doubted
that he yet had the singleness of heart to will the one thing.

"Blessed are the poor in spirit," Jesus said (Matt. 5:3). Jesus
most likely was not referring to the poor or the chaste, but to
those who have no need of adding to the wealth of their own
spirit by cleverly exploiting the spirit of others.

Counseling and the practice of psychotherapy usually are a
means of making one's livelihood by facilitating the mental
health of others on a fee basis. Here, too, the means become
identical with the end. Our attitude toward other persons will
determine what our *aim* is and how that aim is incorporated into
the means.

There *is* something distinctive about counseling as a Christian
calling. But that distinctiveness is not to be found in the method

or model of therapy. Rather, it is to be found in the aim of the therapist and how that aim informs the means of therapy. A therapist who is also a Christian aims at being as guileless in spirit as he or she is competent in therapeutic technique. When our occupation is being a Christian, counseling as either a professional or nonprofessional will be as good a soil as any other into which to thrust our hand, provided that it is attached to the heart.

Notes

1. For a further discussion of this problem, see my essay "Clergy Burnout as a Symptom of Theological Anemia," *Theological Student's Fellowship Bulletin* (March 1984).

2. Gordon Allport, "Psychological Models for Guidance," in R. L. Mosher, R. F. Carle, and C. D. Kehas, *Guidance*, 21ff: Cited in Jacob Firet, *Dynamics in Counseling* (Grand Rapids: Eerdmans, 1986), 240.

3. Ibid., 241.

4. John Macmurray, *Persons in Relation* (London: Faber and Faber, 1961), 110.

5. Ibid., 111–12.

6. The concept of "good-enough" was coined by Donald W. Winnicott to describe the infant's relation to its environment (*The Maturational Processes and the Facilitating Environment* [New York: International Universities Press, 1965]). Cameron Lee at the Fuller Seminary Graduate School of Psychology has extended this concept in his essay "The Good-Enough Family," *Journal of Psychology and Theology* 13, no. 3 (1985): 182–89.

7. Firet, *Dynamics in Pastoring*, 242.

8. Dietrich Bonhoeffer, *Ethics* (New York: Macmillan, 1955), 67.

9. Søren Kierkegaard, *Purity of Heart is to Will One Thing* (New York: Harper & Row, 1956), 55–56.

10. I want the readers to be aware of the fact that this essay on willing the good is written by Kierkegaard as an "edifying Discourse." This prayer is found in the essay: "Father in Heaven! What is a man without Thee! What is all that he knows, vast accumulation though it be, but a chipped fragment if he does not know Thee! What is all his striving, could it even encompass a world, but a half-finished work if he does not know Thee: Thee the One, who art one thing and who art all! So may Thou give to the intellect wisdom to comprehend that one thing; to the heart, sincerity to receive this understanding; to the will, purity that wills only one thing. In prosperity may Thou grant perseverance to will one thing; amid distractions, collectedness to will one thing; in suffering, patience to will one thing" (*Purity of Heart*, 31).

11. Kierkegaard describes the ambivalence of the self poetically and profoundly: "There are wishes that die in being born; there are wishes that are forgotten like our yesterdays; there are wishes that one outgrows, and later can scarcely recall; there are wishes that one learns to give up, and how good it was to have given them up; there are wishes from which one dies away, which one hides away, just as a departed one is hidden away in glorified memory. Those are the wishes to which an active person is exposed. They may be more or less dangerous diseases. Their cure may be accomplished by the extinction of the individual wish.

"Yet there is also a wish that dies slowly, a wish that remains with the real sufferer even in the pain of his loss, and that only dies when he dies. For wishes concern particular objects, and a great number of objects, but the wish applies essentially to the whole of life. . . .

"Oh, weary not your soul with that which is passing and with momentary relief. Grieve not your spirit with forms of comfort which this world affords. Do not in suicidal fashion murder the wish; but rather win the highest by hope, by faith, by love—as the mightiest of all are able to do: commit yourself to the Good!" (*Purity of Heart is to Will One Thing*, 150–51).

12. Ibid., 179–219.

13. Ibid., 199.

14. See Ray S. Anderson, *Minding God's Business* (Grand Rapids: Eerdmans, 1986), 87ff., 97ff.

15. Kierkegaard, *Purity of Heart is to Will One Thing*, 202.

16. Ibid., 203.

17. Ibid., 207.

18. Ibid.

9

Counseling as
Christian Ministry

"Pastor Ken, do you remember Martha, the woman I told you about who felt that she had received help in therapy from me that she could not receive in reading the Bible and praying? Well, she said something recently that really disturbed me. She said that she considers me to be more of a pastor to her than her own minister. I'm a psychologist, not a minister!"

"Sue," Ken Jones replied, "you are a Christian practicing therapy as a professional psychologist. You have a ministry to people that many pastors don't have, that of sharing Christ's own love and healing power."

"But I don't want to confuse psychology with Christian ministry. I have always thought of ministers as being ordained and on a church staff. You are the minister, I am the psychologist. Let's keep it straight!"

"I used to think that way myself," Ken replied, "but I think that we are both doing ministry and giving pastoral care, though we each have specialities. I would like to think that Christ ministers through each of us, so we are both ministers in that sense."

"Sounds strange to me, Ken. I wish I had a better grasp of what you are saying."

"God does not spend the major part of his time in church." The anonymous person who said that also stated, "His first and last acts are the creation and recapitulation of all things. Even in carrying out his purpose of salvation he works not only through his church but also through other agents."[1] I believe that Christians who counsel can be some of those agents. This

176

chapter is written for Sue and others like her who need a theological and practical foundation for counseling as a form of Christian ministry. If we regard Christ himself as indeed our model, we must recognize that he spent most of his time in forms of ministry that did not have religious certification!

All ministry is God's ministry.[2] Even Jesus did not come to introduce his own ministry. His ministry was to do the will of the Father and to live by every Word that proceeded out of the mouth of God. It was God's ministry to create this world out of the freedom of his own life and being. It was God's ministry to endow human creatures with his own image and likeness and to give them the freedom to be creative, to love, and to risk themselves in loving relationship with each other.

It was God's ministry to come to humanity in its failure and frustration and to bind himself in covenant faithfulness to that human history of misery and majesty. He did not turn his back on Adam and Eve when they broke off that relationship through thoughtless and presumptuous actions of self-determination. He did not leave them to their desperate attempts to make a way of life out of the jarring contradictions of erotic and erratic love that produced as much pain as pleasure, even though it did soothe their desperate loneliness.

No, God continued in his freedom to write himself into their history so that their fate was bound to his future—thereby giving them a new future and a renewed hope in the present. It was this ministry that Jesus took up as his own. He is himself the "paraclete," the advocate and comforter, the one who brought reconciliation "from below," so to speak.

Those who practice counseling and psychotherapy as a way of fulfilling a Christian calling are performing the ministry of Christ. In showing how this happens, we will look first of all at Christ's ministry as the foundation for all ministry; this ministry takes place through the members of his body, the church. We will then discuss the ministry of counseling as "incarnational" ministry, wherein Christ's ministry continues to be a presence and power through the human encounter between counselor and counselee. Finally, the counselor will be shown to be a "transactional minister," when the interactive and integrative process of spiritual growth is experienced and in some cases begun anew. The term "ministry" in this chapter will obviously be used in a nontechnical and yet profoundly Christian and biblical way.

Christ's Ministry and Our Ministry

It was the ministry of Jesus as an agent of healing and reconciliation that brought God "out of the temple" and put him on the streets. It was the ministry of Jesus that put divine love and grace on the side of those who were condemned by the law. It was the ministry of Jesus that united the divine heart with the human hand, that spilled the tears of divine compassion down the cheeks of a man; it was the ministry of Jesus that took the plight of the paralyzed and the brutality of deformity like a blow to the solar plexus.

Prior to Jesus, the word *comforter* had a hollow ring; human would-be paracletes, like Job's "comforters," meant well, but in the end they preferred to side with divine perfection rather than human degradation. Before Jesus came, the most skilled practitioner of healing and the most eloquent preacher of divine grace secretly felt that God had abandoned, if not punished, the diseased, the deformed, and the demonic. Most people were terrified of becoming too closely identified with the godforsaken.

But it was precisely this godforsakenness that Jesus took upon his own life and lips. His cry on the cross was more than the echo of the psalmist's lament—he actually had crossed to the side of the godforsaken, and from that "godawful" point of no return, he turned toward God as *his* Father, seeking the ministry of the Father in raising him, even from Sheol and the terror of that dark night of the soul (cf. Ps. 22; Matt. 27:46).

Jesus is the first paraclete (counselor), the one who invested his own person and life in the reconciliation of humanity. He promised and sent another paraclete, the Holy Spirit, who would continue his presence and ministry among them. This other "counselor" (paraclete) "the world cannot receive, because it neither sees him nor knows him; you know him, for he dwells with you, and will be in you. . . . I will not leave you desolate; I will come to you" (John 14:17–18).

The Spirit gave continuity between Christ's ministry and that of his followers, even as he testified to a continuity between his ministry and that of the Father. "My Father is working still, and

I am working" (John 5:17). In the same way that this work of the Father was manifest in him, and yet in a way that was not perceptible unless one had "his word" abiding in him (John 5:38), the Spirit would do his work in Jesus' followers who had his Spirit abiding in them.

Through his baptism Jesus was incorporated into the ministry of God, which led him to identify himself with those who were in need of reconciliation. True, Christ's specific actions of healing, casting out demons, and giving absolution from sin gave the appearance of "ministries." Yet his *total* life of identification with people, even to the point of death on a cross, was the enactment of his *ministry*. This is an important point. It reminds us that behind forms of ministry, or "ministries," lies a single ministry. This ministry is the power of divine love, invested from below, in reconciling persons to themselves and to God.

By this one Spirit, who is simultaneously the Spirit of God and the Spirit of Jesus Christ as the experienced reality of Holy Spirit, every Christian is "baptized into one body . . . and . . . made to drink of one Spirit" (1 Cor. 12:13). As each Christian has this "calling," so too each Christian has this "ministry" by virtue of being baptized into the one body of Christ.

Paul has labored hard to make his point. Despite the varieties of gifts, ministries, and "workings," it is the "same God who inspires them all in every one" (1 Cor. 12:6). There can be no mistaking his emphasis. Being Christian is being possessed by the Spirit of Christ and incorporated into his body. But his body is not an inert body. It is a functioning body, with many members, each of whom has a share in this one ministry and each of whom carries out this ministry both within the body and in the world.

This "baptism" into the ministry of Christ corresponds in some way to the water baptism of each Christian, so that one might say, "Baptism is the ordination into the apostolic, charismatic and sacrificial ministry of the church."[3] There is another special ordination that belongs to the ministry of the church. In this rite certain members of the church are set apart for full-time ministry in the church. We are tempted to see this as the only kind of ordination and the only kind of real ministry. But this would be to disenfranchise the members of the body of

Christ from Christ's own ministry and link ministry solely with a clerical office and role.

This kind of thinking led to the statement at the beginning of this chapter—"God does not spend the major part of his time in church." There are strong biblical and theological grounds for arguing that every Christian has a calling to the ministry of Christ by virtue of baptism. This ministry cannot be divided between the "ministry of the laity" and the clerical ministry of ordained persons. This distinction suggests that there are two levels or two kinds of ministry. But there is only one ministry, and that is the ministry of God embodied in the ministry of Christ and continued through the members of his body.

Jesus did not attempt to develop a "lay ministry" alongside that of the priestly ministry in the temple. While he supported and did not repudiate the authentic priestly ministry as the ministry of God, he himself offered this priestly ministry of forgiveness, atonement, and reconciliation to God "on the street," so to speak. Jesus did not spend the major part of his time in the temple!

I have developed this general basis for a theology of ministry to correct a common misconception of ministry as basically a clerical or "churchly" function. This misconception has forced an unwarranted distinction between lay ministry and the ministry of the ordained clergy and has left those who invest their Christian calling in nonclerical or nonchurch vocations without a valid concept of ministry.

I myself was once asked why I left farming to enter the "Christian ministry." And when I left the pastorate to teach in a seminary, I was asked again what prompted me to "leave the ministry"!

I understand quite well what lies behind these perceptions of ministry, and I do not expect that what is said here will change that perception to any great degree. But I want to stress that those who take up the task of counseling or psychotherapy as Christians *may*—dare I say *must?*—think of this work as a Christian ministry. I intend to show that the role of counselor can be a ministry in which Christ works just as fully and effectively as in a more clerical or ecclesiastical role. There will be different aspects to that ministry, but it will be the same ministry, because there is only one ministry, and that is the ministry of Christ through his members.[4]

Christ's Ministry Through His Body—The Church

The literature on the nature and form of the church and its ministry is so extensive that we cannot begin to cite or interact with it within the scope of this chapter. We can safely say, however, that the church is the expression of the form of Christ's presence and work in the world.

Without disparaging ecclesiastical distinctions that exist between "churches," my purpose here is to define church in its broadest and most concrete sense as the form that the body of Christ takes in the world through its members under the authority of and with the power of Christ. The church is the extension of the power and the reality of the "gospel of Christ" into the world. The church connects Scripture with the mission of the Spirit of Christ in the world. The church by whatever name or form must always self-critically assess whether it is faithful to the gospel and whether it is reaching the world through mission.

Because the church is people, not just an idea or concept, it always has a geographical center. It exists on earth, not in the air. And it exists somewhere before it does everywhere. It thus has a kind of demographic and geographical specificity that lends itself to the concept of being a parish, or parochial in its form. The apostle Paul wrote not only to Christians in Rome, but to the "gathered Christians"—that is, the church—in Rome. The parochial form of the church is a specific gathering of Christians in a localized setting.

But this does not exhaust the biblical concept of the church as the body of Christ. The church exists beyond its parochial boundaries in the form of the ministry of its members in what might be called "para-parochial" forms. In Paul's day local churches sent out individuals to extend the work and ministry of Christ in other areas and through other means. Paul himself organized special relief efforts for the poor in Jerusalem by creating an organization through which Christians could invest their time, energies, and resources. This is the kind of thing I have in mind in speaking of para-parochial kinds of ministry.[5]

Let us be more specific. Christians may serve as counselors and work full- or part-time on the staff of a local parish church as either "ordained" pastors or "nonordained" counselors. The status of being ordained or nonordained is a distinction that has to do with the role and ministry of being a pastor, in whatever way that role is defined in the polity of a particular church. The ministry of a counselor may include "pastoral care" offered as specialized counsel and therapy, even though one is not ordained to carry out other pastoral responsibilities within the church. To my mind, this is a matter of local church polity and does not constitute a division of the "one ministry" of Christ into the two levels of ministry.

Some hold that anyone who counsels on the staff of a church should also be trained and ordained as a pastor in order that the counsel and therapy given can legitimately be considered pastoral care. This tends, however, to suggest that pastoral care is a form of ministry that can only be channeled through a pastoral office. Arguably, however, it certainly would be an advantage for a counselor to function in pastoral responsibilities beyond that of counseling. What I question is the concept that pastoral care as a ministry of Christ can only be given by one ordained and set apart to a pastoral office. Pastoral care is first of all Christ's ministry, and it is given to the church to be exercised through its members. The Holy Spirit delivers paraclete ministries outside of the office of the clergy, as well as through it!

Christians may also serve in a variety of other ways as counselors and psychotherapists. Some Christians may be professionally accredited and state licensed therapists and counselors on a fee basis, working individually, in teams, or on the staff of clinics and counseling centers.

In short, Christians who fulfill their Christian calling through counseling beyond the structure of the local parish church are still working as members of the church of Jesus Christ, but in these cases in para-parochial settings. Where Christians organize a "Christian Counseling Center," a para-parochial form of the church has come into existence alongside the parish, but not outside of it. Such an organization, I believe, is not properly called a "para-church" organization, but a para-parochial organization as part of the church that is the body of Christ.

Again, I want to stress that the ministry of Christ is fully present in both the ecclesiastical form of the local, parish church as well as in the ministry of its members outside the church congregation. The specific problems this raises in terms of accountability, connectedness, and ecclesial order in relating the parochial and the para-parochial forms of the church need not concern us here. The New Testament clearly portrays both forms of the church, but sets forth no organizational structures as a model. The matter seems to have been left to the discernment of and accountability to the Holy Spirit.

Counseling as a Christian ministry, however, does have "limited liability."[6] Let me explain. The church in its parochial form has an "unlimited liability" with regard to its members. By "liability" I mean an implicit or explicit responsibility to attend to the larger spectrum of a person's needs.

All members of the congregation can expect that the other members will provide a presence and ministry of Christ along the entire spectrum of life, from birth to death. When in emergency situations they need food and lodging, they will look to the church for help. When they need the ministry of Christ in a time of tragedy, sickness, or death, they will look to the brothers and sisters in their church community. Often members of a church will be ministered to by those persons appointed to specific forms of ministry, including pastoral staff.

In a para-parochial form of the ministry of Christ such as a Christian counseling center, the team responds out of love and concern for a fellow Christian and extends the resources of that Christian community as far as possible with its own mission-specific task. But the organization is more of a mission-specific group than a community-specific group such as the parochial form of the gathered congregation. The ministry of the parochial organization will ordinarily be more of a Christian-to-Christian extension of Christ's ministry, not a function of the entire congregation itself. The assumption is that the Christian counselor or client has a Christian community (parish) to which he or she belongs. The para-parochial ministry then works in a symbiotic relation with this community, rather than attempting to replace it or duplicate it.

A Christian can expect that Christ will be fully present in the counseling as a form of Christian ministry. But the Christian counselor will have a "limited liability" with respect to providing the full spectrum of ministry expected of the parochial church. Sue Johnson can provide a form of pastoral care through her therapy as a Christian psychologist, but she can not become Martha's pastor.

In the technical sense of the term, psychology is a clinical skill that has a narrower focus than the total life situation of the client. This narrow focus does not exclude the total reality and values that belong to the client as a person, but, like a surgeon's narrow focus during an operation or medial procedure, it has a "limitation of attention" during a therapeutic procedure that focuses on specific therapeutic outcomes.

When this counseling or therapy is offered as a professional service, it is usually considered a contractual service rendered for a fee. A Christian psychologist or counselor who contracts his or her services to clients for therapeutic purposes will ordinarily specify the terms and expectations of the relationship from the beginning. Some therapists may wish to extend the "liability" of the contract beyond what is typical and include the realization of goals that are rooted in personal and religious values. This will often vary from client to client. The point is, the liability, or contractual expectations, will be defined more narrowly than the expectations associated with participation in the church in its parish form. This should not, however, mean that the Christian counselor is any less an extension of Christ's ministry through the church than if these services were offered through a full pastoral role on behalf of the congregation.

In the mission-specific ministry found in the para-parochial form, ministry focuses more on the life and person of the "agent" than does the parish church. This has special meaning for the role of the Christian counselor, who can present in a certain sense an "incarnational" form of ministry.

In summarizing what we have said thus far about counseling as a form of Christian ministry, we can say:

- Ministry is God's ministry to persons in the context of their own life and need;
- Christ came to fulfill God's ministry through his own ministry to persons, meeting them where they were and binding them to his life and source of healing and hope in God;
- Christ continues his ministry through each Christian, whose calling to ministry can be expressed in forms related to tasks and vocations in the everyday world;
- Christians who counsel can be agents of ministry by representing Christ in the counseling relation.

Counseling as Incarnational Ministry

The Christian counselor, of course, is not another "incarnation" of God! The incarnate One, Jesus Christ, continues to dwell in the Christian through the life and power of the Holy Spirit. This was the promise of Jesus (John 14:18–23) and the teaching of the apostle Paul (1 Cor. 6:19; Col. 1:27). This is true of all Christians, not merely some who are especially gifted. Christians do not merely have a Christian perspective or hold Christian beliefs and values; they are also present to others as the reality of Christ himself, veiled, of course, in our personalities and personages.

The counselor serves as an intermediary, not of ideas or concepts, but of the reality of Christ, who creates a growth process in which persons are given the motive power to respond from the depth of their being. This "growth process" is what I discussed as the "agogic moment" in chapter 3. The growth process has three components: motive power for change, an intermediary whose humanity is shared, and change and growth in the client.

The incarnation, as a historical occurrence of God present in the person of Jesus, has four stages, or levels, perceived in no particular chronological sequence.

- There was a *presence* that was equated with the presence of God himself;
- There was an *encounter* that brought the true knowledge of God and opened up the lives of those encountered to healing and hope;
- There was a *confession,* or affirmation, that Jesus was himself the Lord God, with a resulting confirmation that one had really received the gift of faith;
- There was a *profession,* a "vocation" of faith, by which one's life acquired meaning and direction.

For our discussion we will consider these four stages of the incarnation in pairs, with the first pair, presence and encounter, directly related to the counselor-client relation. The second pair, confession and profession, are less directly related, but nonetheless impinge on it.

Presence and Encounter

The first pair appear to be more implicit and indirect as far as a concept or talk of God is concerned. The second pair seem to be more explicit and direct with regard to one's expressed relation to God. After the New Testament period, theological reflection on the incarnate ministry of Christ led to truths and concepts based on the incarnate life of God in Jesus of Nazareth. But the reality of Jesus as personal being precedes and qualifies the truths and concepts as well as qualifying the process of conceptualizing as a way of proceeding toward truth. The contemporaries of Jesus experienced his presence and encountered him directly well before they were able to conceptualize or express their faith in him.

Therefore God's reality was as fully manifest through presence as it was through profession. That is to say, the incognito of the incarnation, to use a concept of Kierkegaard, concealed the full reality of God as a form of presence, but did not screen off God from the relation. Because we think of Christian ministry as verbally denouncing sin and announcing the good news, we tend to discount the fact that an "unannounced" presence of God is a "real presence." People encountered the presence of God whether or not they recognized and acknowledged this fact.

Somehow, the "John the Baptizer model" seems more prevalent in evangelical Christian witness than the Jesus model. Jesus went about largely incognito until people discovered, too late, that they were in the same boat as the Lord! It is interesting to note that, while many people got into the river with John to be baptized, nobody got into a boat with him to go fishing! It is also worth noting that when Jesus arrived on the scene as the "announced" one, the ministry of John had reached its goal; "he must increase, but I must decrease," John said of himself and his ministry (John 3:30). Yet the church continues to be more captivated by the ministry of denouncing and announcing as a verbal witness to God than by the incognito of presence and encounter.

This is to say that the "nonclerical" form of ministry as Christian counseling may be the very "incognito" that the incarnation seeks as a way of getting people "into the boat" where the growth process can begin. The encounter can only take place where there is a real *presence* of God in the situation, and the *real* presence must take place in the human encounter. This is what is meant by the incarnational form of Christ's ministry.

Kirk Farnsworth also speaks of incarnational integration, which is the "embodied" experience of persons who actually live out the concepts of wholeness defined by therapy. "Whole-hearted integration," he says, is

> incarnational. God's truth lives through us as we live as Jesus lived. The application stage is the process of following Jesus by living what we intellectually understand to be God's truths as his framework for interpreting our experience and guidelines for making responsible choices.[7]

Farnsworth's approach is somewhat different from mine. The concept of embodying truth is closer to a concept of "actualization" than it is incarnation. Jesus did not become incarnate by embodying truths of an abstract or intellectual form. Rather, his very being is the truth; he is the eternal Son of God who "became human." Nor do I emphasize theological or Christian "truths" of a purely intellectual nature that can be applied through a therapeutic process that produces integration. Effective integration comes through the growth and development of personal being itself as a somatic, psychical, and spiritual unity. The counselor does not merely conceptualize or verbalize truths that the client then "embodies" or "incarnates."

To a certain extent this can be an effective model, but by an incarnational approach to counseling I mean more than this. I do not deny that certain truths and concepts define the content of the reality of God and Christian faith. But we must also remember that, for God, truth is first of all concrete embodiment of being expressed through act, and not an abstract concept or proposition.

An incarnational ministry functions along the continuum of presence, encounter, confession, and profession. A counselor can be "Christian" in the therapeutic process at any one of the levels. One sign, at least, that the process of therapy is a growth process in which there is presence and encounter, if not yet confession and profession, is that the client "escapes" more rapidly the psychotherapeutic process, to use a concept of Viktor Frankl.[8]

Through the presence and encountering of Jesus Christ

through the Christian therapist, the client is moved to reach for meanings and goals that lie beyond specific stages of emotional or mental health. This is not a shortcut to mental or emotional health by taking another route. Rather, it is a way of penetrating through these symptoms and structures of disorder in order to address the person himself or herself at a deeply personal and, yes, spiritual level of being. This addressing of the person is the encounter of self with self, being with being, rather than the conceptual or abstract "telling" of something. This encounter breaks through the caricature of the self created by emotional and mental disturbances and brings the real "potential" of the self into the dynamic of the encounter. This "potential" is the reality of the self, not merely an abstract possibility.

We can see this reality as potential in virtually every encounter that Jesus had with other persons, particularly when his identity as the Son of God was as yet unrevealed. Many were humanized and socialized almost immediately from conditions that had relegated them to the margins of life. But his presence and encounter forced others deeper into the "caricature" of their real personhood, and they turned their spirituality into fanatical and murderous hostility. No one could remain neutral.

Confession and Profession

Through the presence and encounter of Christ, some people responded with confession and profession. Confessing him to be the Messiah, the woman who encountered Jesus at the well in Samaria professed that she had been transformed by this encounter. Hearing her testimony, her fellow villagers went out to see for themselves, and they too then followed her in making this confession (John 4). This woman encountered the real presence of God in Christ while he was still an anonymous Jewish rabbi. In probing deeper into her life, beyond her own rather superficial questions and comments, Jesus released in her a motive power to grow and acknowledge him as the Messiah. This was much more than an intellectual or rational apprehension of truth. She was transformed by this experience and subsequently confessed to others her faith in the Messiah. This is an example of what we discussed in chapter 3 as an "agogic situation" where change and growth occurs.

My point is this: Christian counseling is a ministry of Jesus Christ precisely because it can provide a growth process of presence and encounter with God as a context for the therapeutic process. This does not violate the therapeutic process through introducing conceptual or verbal forms of address that purport to speak of God or even of religious values. It is a "nonreligious" way of presenting ultimate truths of God and religion, to follow Dietrich Bonhoeffer's suggestion.[9]

A trajectory of faith is established that moves toward a recognition of Jesus Christ as the source of this presence and power that leads the self toward wholeness and relation to God. This "confession" may or may not occur in a given therapeutic process. And the "profession," by which the client takes up again or for the first time a life that is lived by faith and in faith, may or may not become visible during the therapeutic process. The Christian counselor serves as an intermediary for the incarnational presence and encounter with Christ. This ministry reflects Christ's "incognito" ministry, where he was in the same boat and on the same level as those to whom he ministered.

Because confession and profession are linked to presence and encounter by the reality of Christ in the situation, the counseling relation is the ministry of Christ even without explicit confession and profession. This is one important aspect of the incarnational aspect of Christian ministry that helps us to understand how it occurs outside of and beyond the more explicit and religious forms of confession and profession.

This is what Sue Johnson, the Christian psychologist, experienced in her counseling relation with Martha, though she did not have the theological concepts with which to understand and express it. And this model permits a distinction to be made between her ministry and the more ecclesial ministry of Ken Jones, her pastor. Both are ministering on the continuum of presence, encounter, confession, and profession, though at different stages at different times. Sue Johnson should also now understand that she has the freedom to move with Martha to the stages of confession and profession in her practice as a Christian psychologist, without becoming her "pastor." One hopes that Martha's pastor also understands this and can begin to relate more effectively as part of this growth process for her!

The Christian Counselor as Transactional Minister

With a nod toward Eric Berne, who offers a model of therapy based on transactional analysis and who, I believe, once said,

"Get well first, we can talk about it later," I suggest that the Christian counselor can be considered a kind of transactional minister.[10]

The perspective on counseling that I am attempting to develop in this book approaches the self as an integrative and growing person. This provides the basis for a therapeutic approach that sees the self as open to encountering others. These encounters in turn constitute the growth process (agogic moment) whereby motive power for change and growth is released. Here we need to distinguish more clearly between specific therapeutic gains that properly belong to the counseling situation, and the long-range growth goals that belong to the life continuum and integrative task of the counselor.

If therapeutic intervention is intended to address both therapeutic gains related to specific and diagnosable problems as well as growth goals, this needs to be made clear at the outset. For some psychologists, therapeutic intervention might be considered as a kind of personal encounter, such as the more existential and humanistic psychologies might seek. This is the kind of logotherapy advocated by Viktor Frankl, who urged his clients to discover and express a "will to meaning" for their lives.

But this already engages both the counselor and the counselee in the life continuum as a context for therapy, as discussed in chapter 2. When spiritual goals as well as psychotherapeutic gains are sought, the client is being led into a psycho-spiritual dimension of personhood. The purported scientific neutrality of the therapist as a neutral factor in the process has given way to direct involvement such that a form of "psycho-spiritual" therapy is taking place, like it or not. I am not suggesting that this is inappropriate, but that it be recognized and affirmed for what it is. I wish to provide a model for Christian counselors so that they may integrate therapeutic gains with growth goals in a way that has integrity both therapeutically and as a form of "transactional ministry."

Frankl himself argued that logotherapy did not attempt to persuade a client to accept any particular value or religious meaning for life, but he claimed that the "will to meaning" itself was sufficient to give a client reason to "escape" the therapeutic process. This enabled him to say that logotherapy worked as well for nonreligious as for religious persons. The concept of absolute neutrality with respect to meaning as related to values is debatable, however.

I suspect that this lies behind some of the current tension and conflict within the professional ranks of therapists, with some expressing concern that the more "value-oriented" therapeutic models are going beyond strict psychotherapeutic procedures. My own attempt has been to clearly differentiate therapeutic gains from the spectrum of goals and values that relate to the more existential and individual aspects of personhood. Both may be intended as a context for therapy. But attempts to approach personal and religious values through a therapeutic model alone seem to me to be confusing to both psychology and religion. For this same reason, I am not encouraged about attempts to integrate psychology and theology along these lines.

The attempt to place therapeutic gain and personal growth goals on a continuum of the psycho-spiritual dynamic of the human self cannot precisely state where therapy leaves off and personal and spiritual growth continues. I admit this. The distinction between the two, however, is meaningful and helpful as a construct that differentiates between therapy and personal wholeness while at the same time viewing both as essentially integrating in terms of the psycho-spiritual dynamics of the self.

The intention of a Christian counselor can hardly be limited to the narrower range of therapeutic gains, measured in terms of functions, behavior, and adaptation to a world culture. The culture of the kingdom of God, as we saw in chapter 4, intersects the culture of any given situation and seeks to modify it to include the dynamics of faith. By approaching therapy with a deliberate Christian orientation, Christian counselors are practicing a Christian ministry as well as giving therapeutic aid. We could deliberately separate counseling and therapeutic intervention from our Christian life and practice. But this book is not written in support of such a style. I am writing for those who desire intentionally to relate their Christian faith to counseling.

Counseling as growth therapy, therefore, lends itself to a transactional ministry in that an encounter takes place that both mediates the reality of God's grace and provides psychic relief and adjustment. This mediation of God's grace is not an "infusion," as though there is a kind of "sacramental" conveyance of religious life. Rather, grace is always connected to God's presence, his presence is connected with encounter, and his encounter is connected with action. The Christian counselor serves as this "transactional minister" who fills the gap between pastoral care and secular therapy. Helmut Thielicke suggests the need for this in a very pointed way:

> The nervous specialists to whom people are going in droves instead of to their pastors must also be *pastors*. They must be persons who are in solidarity with their patients regarding the question of meaning. Otherwise this exodus to secular counseling will have destructive effects.[11]

The implications of what Thielicke says are clear. If Christian counselors fail to act as transactional ministers and separate the therapeutic procedure from the encounter as a Christian, they might be performing transactional analysis, but not transactional ministry. Christian faith is always transactional, for a Christian who counsels interacts with others as a "child of God." The New Testament warns that failing to experience solidarity with others in a transactional kind of faith and action is to void one's faith (cf. James 2:14–17; 1 John 3:11–18).

Jesus' ministry to the woman at the well in Samaria (John 4) was transactional ministry in that, while she perceived him as a rabbi, he encountered her as the "Son of God" and Messiah. Thus, by transactional ministry we mean a relationship in which the Christian as "child of God" engages the other at this same level. "Unless you turn and become like children," Jesus said, "you will never enter the kingdom of heaven" (Matt. 18:3). Jesus also used the metaphor of "rebirth" to indicate the transformation that occurred when the Spirit of God touched the human spirit (John 3:3). This transformation can take place through presence and encounter even though it may not become explicit until the stages of confession and profession emerge in a person's life. The distinctive quality that a Christian who counsels brings to the counseling relation is this transactional reality of Christ's presence.

The implicit, indirect reality of presence and encounter points to the transactional experience of confession and profession. The growth process moves from encounter to confession or profession in such a way that the Christian faith experience becomes a shared one. Again, this does not necessarily need to take place during the "therapeutic hour." But the growth process creates the environment for establishing this trajectory of growth and faith in the process of therapy without violating the therapeutic procedure. Indeed, there is no reason to suppose that such an environment and transactional ministry will have anything but a positive and reinforcing effect on the therapeutic gains if it takes place in the solidarity and reciprocity of the humanity of both the counselor and client.

Therapy is not a "device" for evangelism, with therapy having only an instrumental means and value. We have already seen in the preceding chapter how this approach converts genuine ministry into a desperate desire for "results." However, a transactional ministry that takes the form of a genuine growth encounter can effectively bring the reality of Christ into the lives of both therapist and client. Here, too, the liturgical functions of the church can be linked with the therapeutic dynamics of the church through the ministry of Christian counselors.

Those like Sue Johnson who serve as professional Christian psychologists can become the bridge between the ministry of Christ where incarnational presence is practiced and the ministry of Christ where eucharistic and liturgical presence is celebrated.[12] The "profession" of counseling is not exemption from the practice of ministry. Nor do Christians who counsel need to shun the label "professional" in order to fulfill their Christian calling as ministers of Christ. But this professional role makes many Christian counselors uneasy. In the next chapter we explain why counselors can assume this role with good conscience, as long as they intend to serve as Christ's minister by extending healing and help to the child within each person.

Notes

1. "Christ's Ministry Through His Whole Church and Its Ministers," *Encounter* 25, no. 1 (Winter 1964): 105; reprinted in *Theological Foundations for Ministry*, ed. Ray S. Anderson (Grand Rapids: Eerdmans, 1979), 430–57. A contribution of the Department on the Laity to the Section on "The Redemptive Work of Christ and the Ministry of His Church," Fourth World Conference on Faith and Order held at Montreal in July 1963.

2. I have developed this theme further in "A Theology for Ministry," in *Theological Foundations for Ministry*, 6–21.

3. "Christ's Ministry Through His Whole Church," 434.

4. One of the finest discussions of the concept of each member of the church as a minister is found in the essay cited, "Christ's Ministry Through His Whole Church and Its Ministers." C. K. Barrett has also recently made this point through his analysis of the teaching of Paul in the New Testament, *Church, Ministry, and Sacraments in the New Testament* (Grand Rapids: Eerdmans, 1985), 31ff. A more recent book by Greg Ogden, *The New Reformation: Returning the Ministry to the People of God*, can also be highly recommended (Grand Rapids: Zondervan, 1990).

5. For a further discussion of the nature of the parochial and para-parochial forms of the church's ministry, see my book *Minding God's Business* (Grand Rapids: Eerdmans, 1986), 10ff.

6. Ibid., 38–39, 107, for a discussion of the concept of limited liability.

7. Kirk Farnsworth, *Wholehearted Integration* (Grand Rapids: Baker, 1985), 108.

8. The prevailing emphasis in Frankl's development of "logothera-py" was his attempt to move the client quickly through and past the psychotherapeutic stage and to "reintroduce the psyche into psychol-ogy." Psychotherapy has insufficient resources, he held, to deal with the total of psychic reality. See Viktor Frankl, *The Doctor and the Soul* (New York: Alfred A. Knopf, 1955), 15–16.

9. See Dietrich Bonhoeffer, *Letters and Papers from Prison*, enlarged ed. (New York: Macmillan, 1972), 328, 359.

10. Eric Berne, *Transactional Analysis in Psychotherapy* (New York: Grove Press, 1961).

11. Helmut Thielicke, *Being Human . . . Becoming Human* (Garden City, N.Y.: Doubleday, 1984), 447.

12. For a discussion of the role of liturgy in authenticating person-hood, see my essay "A Liturgical Paradigm for Authentic Personhood," in Ray S. Anderson, *On Being Human: Essays in Theological Anthro-pology* (Grand Rapids: Eerdmans, 1982), 179–93. See also Frank G. Dunn, *Building Faith in Families: Using the Sacraments in Pastoral Ministry* (Wilton, Conn.: Morehouse-Barlow, 1986).

10

Counseling as a
Professional Practice

The moment I stepped into his office the sweet odor of omniscience sedated my brain. The pool of knowledge that I had accumulated through almost a quarter-century of formal education plus an equal span of measured competence in my own professional shrank to insignificance.

It was nothing serious—no more than a routine physical examination. But I was now in the presence of a man who had mastered the intricacies of the human body, with technical names for all its parts and functions, and had a wall covered with diplomas to prove it. I had come to put the uniqueness of my body, with all its personal quirks known, into his hands for an hour or so. The intimate knowledge that I possessed would not appear on the final report, I knew. He was the expert. Though it was my body and my life, it was his knowledge and skill that had the authority to pronounce me well or sick.

I was in the hands of a professional practitioner of the science of medicine and surgery. He was the physician, I was the patient. The few, almost incidental, clues to our common humanity, such as the pictures of his wife and children on his desk, were not there to create a bond between us. It was his white jacket with the stethoscope casually draped around his neck that sent stronger signals. My Ph.D. was invisible, my family history only a source of interest for the sake of a medical workup. Even the tools of my trade didn't count in this arena. This was his turf, and he represented, in my mind at least, a kind of "godlike" personage who lived in a world forbidden to us mortals. The fact that it was my mortality that kept him in business and put food on his table didn't occur to me until I was safely back in my office!

This feeling, I suspect, is not unknown to the reader. We live in a society that reverences and fears the professional much as ancient peoples reverenced and feared the priest. The motorcycle officer who removes his leather gloves slowly without saying a word, the pinstripe-suited banker who smiles and shakes his head while glancing over the loan application, the robed judge who looks down from his stand at those whose fate lies in his hands—all these people and more remind us that we are basically "ordinary people." And without these professionals watching over us, our society would collapse like a straw house.

And let us not forget the professional therapist, ready to welcome us into the inner sanctum of psychic healing where our unruly feelings and irrational fears can be objectively examined and calmly dispersed.

For all our talk about Christian counselors who see their task as a Christian calling, for all our emphasis on counseling as a ministry, the greater share of Christians presently preparing for a counseling ministry have their eye on some form of professional practice. Many intend to serve on a pastoral staff or at least as a counselor on staff of a parish church. Some of these may also seek licensing by the state and enroll as members of a professional society.

Most counseling graduates, however, will provide therapy as a professional and/or clinical service under state license and as a certified member of a professional society. This chapter will focus on counseling as a professional service to aid practitioners in integrating the questions of Christian principles and practices with counseling. We will look first at the question of the role of Christians as professional practitioners and then define the professional more fully. We will also contrast the culture of professionalism to the culture of the kingdom of God, giving us a perspective from which to ask further questions about the practice of Christian counselors. We will look closely at the ethical question of professional practice in the context of kingdom ethics, and finally we will offer some suggestions for Christians who counsel as professionals.

Can Christians Also Be Professionals?

Can a Christian serve without compromise as a professional practitioner, offering therapeutic services on a fee basis, and have accountability to a professional society as well as state licensing standards? On the face of it, the question seems odd. Little concern appears to be raised over the private practice of physicians, attorneys, dentists, and other Christians who fulfill their Christian calling in these fields. What is so different in the case of a psychologist?

Alvin Dueck, director of pastoral counseling at the Mennonite Brethren Seminary in Fresno, California, says flatly, "As a member of the Christian community the individual healer is a representative of its story. Therapy then is not a private practice."[1] But he does not mean by this, as I take it, that no Christian ought to be a professional practitioner. It is the word *private* that receives his stress and criticism. He argues that individual therapists, regardless of how or where they provide therapeutic services to the public, function as an extension of the Christian community and are accountable to it for the ethical constraints on that practice. To his mind, the professional society cannot be the primary ethical community for the Christian therapist.

Granted, but why is this so different from any other Christian who has a "private practice"? Why is healing in the psychological sector of life so different from healing in the physical sector? I would suppose that the answer comes as a matter of degree. Some might feel that psychologists work closer to the ethical core of human life and thereby are under greater constraints to uphold the culture of the kingdom of God. That is debatable, I think. One could argue that the brokers of power in society—the bankers, real estate agents, and holders of political office— actually affect the social and ethical environment of life more than psychologists do.

The Old Testament appears to hold officials in the economic and political sector of society equally accountable to the ethic of the kingdom of God with the priests and counselors. No, I doubt that the case can be made that Christian counselors operate closer to the ethical core of life. Nor, I would argue, do they operate closer to the spiritual core. Spirituality is not lodged primarily in the mental or psychical sector of life. For the kingdom of God, spirituality is the love of God and neighbor and is invested in the physical and social well-being of persons as much as in the emotional and mental.

If there is a danger in "professionalizing" therapy from a Christian perspective, the risk is no greater than the professionalizing of any other sector of life in a way that dehumanizes and devalues the individual. There *are* differences, of course, between the effects of malpractice in dealing with human need. A careless surgical procedure that leaves a patient blinded in one eye is a painful loss, but the person can work around that disability and continue to live a rather full and meaningful life. An inept therapeutic procedure that leaves a client deep in a psychosis, destroying his delicate emotional network of personal relationships, is quite another kind of loss. And the devastation and loss resulting from spiritual seduction by a professional "minister of God" is incalculable.

"Let not many of you become teachers," James warns, "for you know that we who teach shall be judged with greater strictness. For we all make many mistakes" (James 3:1–2). This warning specifically addresses those who have the power and means to influence or even manipulate the development of the self in its mental, emotional, and personal life.

When I need help, I would rather go to the licensed professional than to an amateur who has the best of intentions but bungles the job. There is no biblical blessing on incompetence or inexperience as far as I can see. While his background was that of a simple carpenter from Galilee, Jesus was called "rabbi" by those around him. He was granted this title, not from being thought well-intentioned though naïve, but because he demonstrated a wisdom and competence beyond that of the other "professionals." He was fully professional, practicing a ministry of teaching and healing with expertise and authority. His conflict was not as a "nonprofessional" with professionals, but with the relationship of so-called professional teachers and religious authorities to the kingdom of God. This tension and conflict needs to be examined with respect to the way in which Christian counselors also serve as professional practitioners.

What Is a Professional?

The history and nature of professionalism, particularly as a phenomenon of Western society and culture, has been amply discussed.[2] William Goode suggests several factors common to the professional community:

1. Its members are bound by a sense of identity.
2. Once in it, few leave, so that it is a terminal or continuing status for the most part.
3. Its members share values in common.
4. Its role definitions *vis-à-vis* both members and non-members are agreed upon and are the same for all members.
5. Within the areas of communal action there is a common language which is understood only partially by others.
6. The community has power over its members.
7. Its limits are reasonably clear, though they are not physical and geographical, but social.
8. Though it does not produce the next generation biologically, it does so socially through its control over the selection of professional trainee; and through its training processes it sends these recruits through an adult socialization process.[3]

Professional associations are formed in part to establish the aims, practices, and procedures of a profession. Consequently these professional societies develop a particular self-image. These images suggest certain qualities inherent in the person who practices the profession, such as altruistic, tireless, competent, and accessible. These images also produce models for the development of specialized training and certification. The professional society assembles and develops a body of knowledge and shared skills that enhance the members. And finally, a professional society establishes the standards and criteria by which new members are trained and certified.

Clearly, a professional in this formal and technical sense is, as Goode says, a member of a "community within a community." As an attribute, a professional is one who models these characteristics in an exemplary way in a given situation. A fire captain, in response to comments praising the bravery or outstanding performance of one of his team, will usually say, "He is a professional—he was just doing his job."

Society looks to the professional societies as a source of quality control, though some tensions often exist between governmental bodies and professional societies that share similar concerns. There is, therefore, a "culture of professionalism" that creates the environment and context in which services are rendered, including that of therapy.

The Culture of Professionalism

When we see professionalism as a culture, we are closer to the conflict and tension existing between the culture of the kingdom of God and professionalism. The relation of the professions to society is symbiotic and complex. Professionals serve society in a variety of ways. They provide safeguards against opportunistic and incompetent individuals who prey on social needs. They provide the technicians who run the administrative units of social institutions like hospitals, mental health clinics, and legal-aid societies. Professionals provide models and images that enshrine the higher values of life such as integrity, altruism, excellence, courage, expanding knowledge, and progress. In a certain sense, professionals capture the ideals of society and model them in public view as an incentive to others.

By contrast, society allows professionals a privileged use of power, not only to define ethical reality, but to practice "social engineering." Society upholds the role of professionals by granting them courtesies often denied others. One only needs to examine the assignment of parking privileges around institutions managed by professionals to appreciate this. I myself was once assigned a first-class seat on a plane to Chicago because my ticket was typed with the academic degree title "Dr." in front of my name! The airline agent was paying obeisance to the mysterious but somehow supernatural power of the medical profession in granting this privilege. Somehow I did not feel that my Ph.D. would evoke the same courtesy, so I enjoyed my one-time-only privilege in grateful silence!

While societies depend on professionals for the technical skills and knowledge that contribute to progress, they also tend to shape the culture of professional communities. The *modus operandi* of professionals tends to be a reflection of the culture in which they practice their skill or trade. A society characterized as technological, market oriented, and developed around the concept of entrepreneurs will tend to produce professionals who worship technique, sacrifice service for fees, and idolize routinization and efficiency. I might also add, it is no surprise that professionalism has strong alliances with the business economy as a bellweather for the free enterprise system. While generalizations may seem unfair and extreme, we should remember that it is the nature of a society to shape its own institutions, and the services of a professional become institutionalized and regulated by the society in which they exist. This is as true of religious professionals as secular professionals.

The culture of professionalism tends also to create a primary community to which the individual practitioner is accountable. This community serves as the monitor of professional ethics and the provider of professional status. Because general society gives over to professional society the prerogatives for determining the public good in terms of the moral use of scientific knowledge, there is ordinarily little perceived conflict between the ethics of professional practice and the general ethics of society. The courts will usually defer to the "expert testimony" of professionals; families and individuals tend to be ethically powerless in the face of this legal-professional alliance.

When conflicts do arise, they usually take the form of governmental or politically motivated commissions that appeal more directly to the grass-roots than to professional expertise. The 1986 commission on pornography instituted by President Reagan is a case in point. Notably absent in the majority report were conclusions drawn from professionals in the social sciences, where the connection between pornography and violence does not have strong scientific support.

On the whole, however, professional societies wield enormous power under the cloak of objectivity and the prerogative of sophisticated knowledge. Power is no longer transmitted through consanguine relationships or contiguous social structures, such as family and community. Instead it is transmitted through a knowledge-based and technically closeted guild. Professionals at times may have great influence as power-wielders, but in a morally pluralistic culture they tend to become an autonomous ethical community.

Stanley Hauerwas has an insightful comment on this:

> Moral coherence, however, cannot be supplied even by the professions. For not only are their traditional commitments increasingly qualified by our moral pluralism, no one can live morally as a professional only. . . . The virtues and skills of the professions were not, nor can they ever be, sufficient to negotiate the moral demands of our lives inevitably placed upon us.[4]

The ethical culture of the professional community is thus in a double bind. It is a projection of the culture in which it exists and thus carries into its own conception of values and goals those of the general culture. At the same time, it creates its own ethical culture based on the perceived values of its unique bank of knowledge and technology. For this reason, the moral conscience of the professional community tends to be selective and "case-by-case" rather than integrative and wholistic. With no commonly agreed-on philosophy of personhood as the basis for the determination of the human good, the professional has to fall back on legal ethics rather than social ethics. Doing the least harm in order to promote the most good becomes a safeguard against irresponsible use of professional technique. But the "most good" is also tied to the growing edge of knowledge and technical skill. Professionals find it difficult to suspend the use of proven techniques. Because progress is the mandate that drives technique, ethical issues for professionals can become blurred.

As a result, the ethical culture of the professional community can suffer from a fundamental ambivalence. On the one hand, professionals self-consciously embody and attempt to model the higher ideals of the general society. Professionals want to be known for their altruistic service, concern for all persons regardless of economic or social status, and sacrifices made for the general good of society. On the other hand, the same professionals, as we have suggested, acquire their basic *modus operandi* from the culture in which they practice, which is basically pragmatic, opportunistic, and entrepreneurial.

This ethical ambivalence tends to pervade the ethical stance of the professional community as a whole, though individual professionals may resolve this through selecting a style that satisfies their own moral commitments. If the professional community is viewed as the primary context for professionals, however, this may constitute a serious problem for those who are Christians.

Survival in the marketplace for professional services drives many Christian professionals beyond their original idealistic and Christian value system. Because the culture at large is one that operates more or less on the free enterprise system, professional services that do not operate with the marketing strategy and economic pricing factors of the general culture may not survive. At this point, professional instincts merge with business instincts, and the professional entrepreneur is born.

One California bank has built its primary advertising strategy on appealing to the professional community by using testimonials of doctors, dentists, attorneys, and psychologists in their ads. They each testify to how that particular bank helped them establish a successful and profitable business through front-end financing. Professionals, apparently, are good investment risks!

Faculty members of schools for preparing men and women for the ministry of Christian counseling sometimes leave their academic positions to establish a private practice or a clinic. Having witnessed this migration, students can hardly be blamed for questioning the relation between psychotherapy as a ministry and as a profession. Psychologists are not the only professionals who live with the tension between the culture of the kingdom of God and the culture of professionalism. But Christians who seek to practice therapy as professional persons are looking for guidance and wisdom in relating the two.

Kingdom Ethics and Professional Priorities

To this point we have been speaking in quite general terms about the relationship between the culture of professionalism and the role of the Christian counselor. I have tried to put in perspective the concept of professionalism in general with respect to the culture in which it exists and its own professional culture. There is a complex symbiotic relation between the two, even though there are also some inherent tensions and even contradictions. Christians who enter the field of professional practice as therapists will discover this tension and struggle.

There is, however, another dimension to the problem. Christians are accountable to the culture of the kingdom of God. This is what lies behind the challenge of Alvin Dueck:

> To the extent that the Christian is called to be a member of God's kingdom community and is called to a covenant relationship with God's people, to that extent the profession as the primary ethical community must be seen as problematic.[5]

If we are bound primarily to the professional community with regard to professional status and credentials, then its culture will also determine to a significant degree the "professional code" for delivering therapy. If the *modus operandi* for the Christian therapist is also determined largely by the culture in general, then the "mode" as well as the "code" will stand in juxtaposition to the mode and code of the kingdom of God.

For the Christian, the kingdom of God constitutes the primary ethical community. This is clear with regard to the people of God in the Old Testament and is made explicit by Jesus in his "Sermon on the Mount." Moreover, the early Christian community as described in the New Testament existed within the particular culture and worldview of their time and place, yet the church, as the "community of the kingdom," constituted the primary community for the lives of the individual members. A kind of "dual citizenship" existed, as evidenced by the counsel of Jesus, "Render to Caesar the things that are Caesar's, and to God the things that are God's" (Mark 12:17). But when it came down to final authority, Jesus also said, "No one can serve two masters" (Matt. 6:24). There is no reason to think that this gave the early Christians permission to abandon the world to its own fate and concentrate on their own spiritual pilgrimage. There are ample warnings against ignoring the needs of those who are weak and in need of care and support. While the world apart from service to God may not acknowledge the values and goals of the kingdom of God, those concerned for the kingdom of God see the world clearly as belonging to its values and purpose.

Several implications of the kingdom of God can be delineated as they bear on the role of a Christian as a professional therapist.

1. There is a concern for the welfare and status of the marginal person in society. Woman and slaves, for example, were pushed aside by certain societies in which the church came into being. While it gave no ultimatum for the immediate and radical restructuring of the society itself, the Christian community received both women and slaves into full fellowship, along with others who were neglected by the world culture. Certain restrictions were placed on the role of women in specific situations, but the ethic of the kingdom of God required that no distinction be made between Jew and Greek, slave or free, male or female (Gal. 3:28).[6]

Provision was made for the widows who became Christian and were cut off from their non-Christian families (cf. Acts 6). Paul writes to Philemon concerning his Christian responsibility to his slave, Onesimus. He is to receive him back as a Christian brother, not as a slave. James discounts a religion that is in word only; he says, "Religion that is pure and undefiled before God and the Father is this: to visit orphans and widows in their affliction" (James 1:27). This is followed by the admonition, "Show no partiality as you hold the faith of our Lord Jesus Christ, the Lord of glory. . . . Has not God chosen those who are poor in the world to be rich in faith and heirs of the kingdom which he has promised to those who love him?" (2:1, 5).

Where the culture of professionalism tends to be elitist and selective and even discriminatory through its catering to the rich and privileged for the sake of success, it runs counter to the culture of the kingdom of God. This critical tension cuts across all the professions as a culture and is particularly a problem for the professional practice of therapy, which operates on a schedule of fees for services rendered.

2. *The kingdom of God bestows a distinctive character on its members.* In contrast, the professional-culture self attempts to image certain values and ideals to create models of humanitarian service without regard for personal gain, but the actual *modus operandi* tends to be pragmatic and self-serving. This is said about the culture of professionalism in general; it is obviously not true of every professional.

For the culture of the kingdom, however, the character of its members is manifest in its *modus operandi,* not merely in its "ethical code." The New Testament shows little concern for the ideal of altruism—it is much too realistic for that! What is of concern is the practice of love and aiming at "what is honorable not only in the Lord's sight but also in the sight of men" (2 Cor. 8:21). "Love does no wrong to a neighbor," wrote Paul (Rom. 13:10). It is the *practice* of love in providing for social need and social justice that characterizes the members of the kingdom. Christian "practice" determines the *modus operandi* of the professional practice.

Thus the character of the Christian professional is based on Christian practice, not on the professional culture itself. In this sense, Christians who are professionals can speak of themselves as professionals who are committed to the service of others as a form of service to Christ. To combine service with a commitment to the highest level of competence in practice is not merely a professional ideal; it is the normative standard of the kingdom of God.

3. *The quality of life distinguishes the people of God.* The professional culture tends to be individualistic and competitive, these characteristics being a projection of the culture in which professionalism is most pronounced. "We are driven!" cries the automobile ad. This play on words accurately portrays the spirit of the age and captures the prevailing ethos of the professional culture. The quality of life in the professional community is often notable for its lack of community and personal sharing at the human level. The peer relationships of professionals can become "tight" and "clubbish," but also guarded and superficial. Loneliness, depression, stress, and burnout tend to be facts of the professional's life. These are generalizations, to be sure, but they are unfortunately all too true even in Christian professional societies.

The culture of the kingdom, by contrast, depicts its members as having fullness of life, a "peace that passes understanding," and an affection and intimacy of personal fellowship that appears somewhat embarrassing to the modern Western individual. Without the Christian community acting as a context, the Christian could all too soon fall victim to the disintegrating and depressing character of professional culture. There is also an implication for the very context and kind of therapy offered by the Christian professional. If the professional is essentially a "private person," then "private practice" will indeed be problematical, as Alvin Dueck has warned.

4. *The kingdom's eschatological aspect provides a context for measuring immediate gains in terms of ultimate goals.* The culture of the kingdom does not make a virtue of suffering, nor does it emphasize an ethic of resignation. It critiques suffering even when no immediate relief is in sight.

Paul ends his great hymn of love with this eschatological perspective: "For now we see in a mirror dimly, but then face to face. Now I know in part; then I shall understand fully, even as I have been fully understood" (1 Cor. 13:12). Using the "editorial we" to speak of his own life perspective, Paul writes,

But we have this treasure in earthen vessels, to show that the transcendent power belongs to God and not to us. We are afflicted in every way, but not crushed; perplexed, but not driven to despair; persecuted, but not forsaken; struck down, but not destroyed; always carrying in the body the death of Jesus, so that the life of Jesus may also be manifested in our bodies. For while we live we are always being given up to death for Jesus' sake, so that the life of Jesus may be manifested in our mortal flesh. So death is at work in us, but life in you (2 Cor. 4:7–12).

"I worked harder than any of them," Paul said on another occasion (1 Cor. 15:10). Lest some should accuse him of not taking the present seriously, he says, "Do you not know that in a race all the runners compete, but only one receives the prize? So run that you may obtain it.... I pommel my body and subdue it, lest after preaching to others I myself should be disqualified" (1 Cor. 9:24, 27). And yet he can also write,

Rejoice in the Lord always; again I will say, Rejoice. Let all men know your forbearance. The Lord is at hand. Have no anxiety about anything, but in everything by prayer and supplication with thanksgiving let your requests be made known to God. And the peace of God, which passes all understanding, will keep your hearts and your minds in Christ Jesus (Phil. 4:4–7).

These are aspects of the culture of the kingdom of God. This is the culture that qualifies the culture of the world and the culture of professionalism. The issue is not whether one should serve Christ as a professional or nonprofessional. The issue is, how may Christians "practice" this culture of the kingdom as a context and resource for their lives and as a *modus operandi* for the practice of therapy as a professional.

Perspectives on Counseling as a Christian Professional

The discussion has come down to this: There is no biblical or theological basis for concluding that Christians should not be able to fulfill their Christian calling as counselors or therapists through a professional practice. Christians can and ought to serve society as professionals in all areas, including the therapeutic services.

Christians will find, however, that both the professional culture and the general culture of society need to be qualified by the ethical character and communal nature of the culture of the kingdom. Certainly the church itself should serve as the primary embodiment of the kingdom culture through its corporate life and the life of its individual members. But in the church, too, the culture of professionalism can be found. In our society, pastors are also professionals, for the most part, in their own eyes and as viewed by the members of the church. Christian therapists who are on church staffs, either as pastors or as full-time counselors, are not thereby free from the culture of professionalism.

In some ways it may even be more difficult to discern the spirit of professionalism when it becomes joined with a "calling" of God to full-time ministry. When the concept of profession largely defines the role of a Christian psychologist or counselor, the adjective *Christian* tends to shrink in its power to define. Christians who counsel in private, professional, or community clinical settings may be defined more in terms of professional status than of ministry practice. At times such a role identity is unavoidable. Jesus never denied the title "rabbi" when he was addressed that way. But he preferred to think of himself as a servant, as one who serves (Mark 10:42–45).

Indeed, the professional role, when fused with the concept of a Christian calling, can produce an unwarranted arrogance and authority. This tends to give an aura of omnipotence and omniscience to the person and renders the professional conduct of the "called of God" person untouchable. There will always be an uneasy alliance between the culture of professionalism and the culture of the kingdom of God as the ultimate reference point for the Christian professional. But this is no reason to avoid such a role. Each Christian who counsels can shape the role in such a way as to make it one's "calling," or occupation, as we saw in chapter 8.

There really is no single "model" for the Christian professional. There is only the *modus operandi* of the Christian who serves as a professional. And this will be defined and practiced by each Christian within the particular setting and circumstances of one's practice. The criteria for assessing the degree to which the kingdom culture is being practiced through professional therapeutic services have already been discussed and are found in the characteristics and ethics of the kingdom of God as contained in the gospel of Jesus Christ and presented in Scripture.

In drawing out the implications of what we have said so far, let me offer some suggestions for Christians who counsel:

1. *Christian counselors should have a strong link with a local church.* The church serves as a community of support, accountability, and empowerment for its members. For a full-time professional counselor, this community is especially important. We saw that in the case of Sue Johnson, her role as a Christian psychologist had become detached from any concept of ministry. No doubt she was a faithful church member and, as a Christian, served in some capacity within the church's life and ministry. But there did not appear to be any vital connection between her role as a Christian psychologist in the community and her context of Christian life and support.

The context in which church members fulfill their calling as Christians becomes the place where the kingdom of God intersects the world. The church thus invests in the life of its members so that the culture of the kingdom of God can serve as a redemptive force within the various cultures where this calling is fulfilled. Christians who serve as professional therapists can therefore help the church to interpret its mission to proclaim the kingdom of God. The issues facing the Christian therapist concern not only the state or the professional society, but also the church. The church must take responsibility for these issues. This cannot happen unless there is a vital connection between the Christian counselor and the church.

For example, the personal, mental, or emotional problems that cause a person to seek out a psychologist or therapist cannot be isolated from the client's network of other relationships. Clinical problems that emerge in the therapy session are related to a client's domestic, marital, family, and social structures. These networks of relationships contain moral, often religious, and occasionally legal issues that impinge on the therapist's role. The therapist's own values, convictions, religious beliefs, and commitments as a Christian also influence this role. Probably no people in our society other than pastors and priests provide access to the core of life in all these areas as much as professional counselors. Some would say that this is truer of counselors than of many pastors!

There is much wisdom in extending the pastoral care of the

church into the community through its members who serve as professional counselors.

2. *Counselors should have a support group of Christians who are not professional therapists.* The primary reference group for the Christian who counsels should be firmly based in a smaller network of other Christians who can provide perspective, spiritual support, and a representation of the culture of the kingdom of God.

The life of the Christian is a continuing hermeneutical task. We interpret the ethic of the kingdom of God through the lifestyle and kind of "practice" we choose. But this hermeneutical context is not a "private practice," for here, too, the community of other Christians interprets specific role functions and professional practices.

The church should not view this group as a substitute for other sources of clinical supervision or counsel. What takes place in the counseling room is to be held in confidence. Yet the Christian psychologist will encounter issues that require not clinical, but *Christian* perspective and interpretation. As we have suggested there is no single model for Christian counselors. Therefore each counselor will have to develop and sustain his or her own role through a process of experience and growth, shaped by convictions, confirmed through sharing, and sustained and affirmed by those who understand and accept its ambiguity.

The formation of this network will require an intentional commitment to keep oneself accountable and to maintain an integrative growth both personally and in relation to others. After all, if growth is the goal of therapy, it must also be the model by which the therapist lives.

3. *Christan counselors should have criteria for setting fees.* Christian counselors who set their income by charging fees may feel anxious and uncertain about this "professional practice." They should remember, however, that the paid professional pastor or counselor on the staff of a church is also receiving major income from those to whom the ministerial service is rendered. There is a difference in kind, but not in principle, with the Christian who serves as a professional on a fee basis.

The biblical principle is clearly stated: "The laborer deserves his wages," Jesus said. And he said this to his disciples who were to go out and bring the kingdom of God to people who would, in turn, provide for their necessities (Luke 10:7). Paul picks this up and repeats it in his pastoral counsel to Timothy, citing the Old Testament law, "You shall not muzzle an ox when it is treading out the grain" (1 Tim. 5:18).

As one whose monthly salary is derived largely from the tuition paid by students who sit in my classes, I too have suffered moments of doubt as to whether this is a "Christian" way to serve the best interests of the kingdom of God. I too feel uneasy when I read the open invitation issued as a mark of the kingdom of God: "Ho, every one who thirsts, come to the waters; and he who has no money, come, buy and eat! Come, buy wine and milk without money and without price" (Isa. 55:1). Even if I take this as an eschatological vision, part of the same scenario where the lion will lie down with the lamb, I suspect that it is meant to qualify to some degree the spirit of the world where "everything has its price."

Many Christians who counsel as professional therapists have shared with me their dilemma over the need to establish fee schedules for their therapy sessions. The common practice of charging an hourly fee for a therapy session no doubt is carried over from the psychiatric, medical model, where an hour of the "doctor's" time is considered to be a "professional prescription" for the cure, if not the cure itself.

As one outside this professional field, I can only make some general suggestions for consideration. Some have found it helpful to offer therapy on a professional basis using the principle of an hourly fee schedule, but accommodating those who desperately need the therapy but cannot pay the full fee. This "graduated fee schedule" is usually based on the "ability to pay" determined by a financial statement submitted by the client. Others have chosen to charge the full fee and allow the client to "run up a bill," with forgiveness of all or part of this bill at the end as a gesture of Christian grace.

Some Christian counseling clinics set up a special account that is supplied by gifts raised from Christians who wish to render assistance for those who need therapy but are unable to pay. This has the advantage of maintaining a standard fee schedule for all, but provides a special account on which the therapist can draw to supplement what the client pays. In this model, the ones who pay the regular fee are not subsidizing those who cannot pay, nor is the therapist required to subsidize the clinic by accepting less than the regular fee. For some, there is a real dilemma in wishing to extend their counseling on a need basis while also having to make a living through this ministry. The culture of the kingdom of God is never easy to integrate into the necessities of this world!

The critical issue here is not merely how we "sell" our services as professional counselors. The deeper issue makes all of us nervous who serve as professionals and Christians—what are the criteria by which we establish our rationale for living by the means of the comparatively wealthy while being committed to serving the needs of all, especially the poor? The formula statement, "the laborer deserves his wages," does not address the problem of those who need the "labor" but who cannot afford to pay the wages. Christians who counsel as professionals can exercise greater creativity in mediating this tension than most, because their work fulfills a Christian calling to serve Christ by meeting the needs of others, and it is a ministry where Christ is honored.

Summary

We have argued in this chapter that Christians can and often should function in the private and public sector by offering therapeutic services as a professional. There will be a tension between the culture of the professional, the standard of living chosen by the counselor for which the clients must pay, and the culture of the kingdom of God, in which the poor come first and the marginal are placed at the center. There is no avoiding this tension. But Christians who counsel are most aware of it and therefore most creative in finding a way to position themselves in the most strategic places to meet human need.

The calling and ministry of the Christian is to become an advocate for those who become marginalized and weak. Jesus said that he would send another paraclete (advocate) in the form of the Holy Spirit who would dwell in those who became his disciples. This Spirit enables the Christian who counsels to become a moral advocate as well as skilled caregiver. In the next chapter we will see what this means.

Notes

1. Alvin Dueck, "Ethical Contexts of Healing: Ecclesia and Praxis," *Pastoral Psychology* 36, no. 1 (Fall 1987): 53.

2. See for example: B. J. Bledstein, *The Culture of Professionalism: The Middle Class and Development of Higher Education in America* (New York: Simon and Schuster, 1973); E. Freidson, *The Professions and Their Prospects* (Beverly Hills, Calif.: Sage Publications, 1973); P. Good and D. Kraybill, *Perils of Professionalism* (Scottdale, Pa.: Herald Press, 1982); William J. Goode, "Community Within a Community: The Professions," *American Sociological Review* 22 (1957): 194–200; K. Lebacqz, Professional Ethics: Power and Paradox (Nashville: Abingdon, 1985); M. S. Larson, *The Rise of Professionalism: A Sociological Analysis* (Berkeley: University of California Press, 1977).

3. William J. Goode, "Community Within a Community: The Professions," *American Sociological Review* 22 (1957): 194.

4. Stanley Hauerwas, A *Community of Character: Toward a Constructive Christian Social Ethic* (Notre Dame, Ind.: University of Notre Dame Press, 1981), 126.

5. Dueck, "Ethical Contexts of Healing," 55.

6. For a discussion of the role of women in the church, see my essay "The Resurrection of Jesus as Hermeneutical Criterion: A Case for Sexual Parity in Pastoral Ministry," *Theological Student's Fellowship Bulletin* (March–April 1986): 9–15.

11

The Counselor as Moral Advocate

Therapeutic intervention will invariably be some kind of moral invasion. This is true, first, because professional caregivers are bound by a code of ethics that resides in the counseling standards of most professional societies. Second, professional caregivers enter into the moral structure of human life, because people are intrinsically moral beings. Lewis Smedes puts it as plainly as can be said:

> We have a deep primitive sense that morality is woven into the fabric of our humanness. Morality is not a con game that makes losers out of those who play it seriously. It is not a false rumor planted in an insecure society to help the weak keep the powerful in check by playing on their conscience. Nor is morality just an impressive name for the strong feelings we have about some things, a word we use to add some clout to our complaints. Morality is a basic component of any human sort of life, a reality we feel surely even if we cannot define it clearly. We do have choices, and they are sometimes between real moral options. The choice we make can put us in the wrong with God and our ideal selves—or leave us in the right. And being in the right means being in harmony with God's design for our humanity.[1]

The question of moral values and psychotherapy has provoked much discussion. While most professional caregivers will scrupulously avoid projecting personal values on the therapeutic process, many strongly feel that the therapeutic process cannot be entirely value free. Perry London, for example, says that "at some level of abstraction, it is probably correct to declare that

214

every aspect of psychotherapy presupposes some implicit moral doctrine."[2]

The very attempt to change the behavior of a client intrudes into the value system of the client. Moral issues arise because the resulting behavioral change will inevitably produce social consequences affecting other people's lives. There can be no "value-free" therapy, even though the caregiver must respect the value orientation of the client.

This produces a tension for the Christian who practices therapeutic intervention. This is especially true of the approach to counseling proposed in this book. Growth goals relate to the moral and spiritual horizon of human life. One cannot separate therapeutic gain from this horizon, even though therapeutic gains can be limited and relative. Because the therapeutic gains are actual changes and growth in the person, the larger, more comprehensive growth goals will also be involved.[3]

In discussing these issues and suggesting a strategy for counseling as a form of moral advocacy, I will develop two basic themes: the moral context for therapeutic intervention from a Christian perspective, and the role of the professional caregiver as moral advocate.

The Moral Context for Therapeutic Intervention

In Christian theology, ethical concern is grounded in the character of God, and therefore it is intrinsic to the nature and value of persons as created in the image of God. While the character of God is the basis for theological ethics, it also is the ground for a moral foundation for all human action and life. Karl Barth puts it this way:

> The morality or goodness of human conduct which ethics investi-
> gates has to do with the validity of what is valid for all human
> action, the origin of all constancies, the worth of everything
> universal, the rightness of all rules. With such concepts as validity,
> origin, worth, and rightness we denote provisionally and generally
> that which transcends the inquiries of psychology, cultural history,
> and jurisprudence—the transcendent factor which in contrast is
> the theme of ethical inquiry.[4]

Theological ethics thus grounds values, not in individual and personal values alone, but in the personal character and purpose of God as the transcendent content of all values. Moral criteria are not essentially religious, but are fundamentally human. Concepts of human nature will thus determine moral criteria. For Christians, the moral criteria of human life are personal and social, not abstract and impersonal. This is because humans are essentially social beings, created in the form of "fellow-humanity," or co-humanity. The command is to love God and the neighbor. One of the first ethical questions raised in the Bible is the question put to Cain after he had murdered his brother: "Where is Abel your brother?" (Gen. 4:9).

The command of God comes in the form of concern for fellow-humanity as well as for the character of the individual life. Christian moral criteria are therefore derived from God's revelation of the nature and purpose of life.

Of central concern to theological ethics in attempting to provide an answer to the questions of humanity, morality, and the commandment of God is the role of Scripture. Several alternatives present themselves, each of which has advocates in Christian moral theology:

1. The Bible is prescriptive, providing highly specific, binding moral instruction. In this view, the Bible is used as a manual for moral law in a case-by-case situation;
2. The Bible is instructive, providing an overarching set of values, ideals, and principles. In this view, the Bible is used as a textbook in establishing moral criteria, to be applied in specific cases;
3. The Bible is illustrative, providing a compendium of moral examples grounded in the life, teaching, and power of Christ as a moral guide for Christian ethics. In this view, the Bible becomes a compendium of moral wisdom.

While each of these alternatives contributes something of value to the formation of a Christian ethical value system, each also falls short of providing a methodology for making good moral decisions, especially in critical situations where there appear to be moral predicaments. James Gustafson, for example, writes,

The Bible is more important for helping the Christian community to interpret the God whom it knows in its existential faith than it is for giving a revealed morality that is to be translated and applied in the contemporary world. . . . The Christian moral life, then, is not a response to moral imperatives, but to a Person, the living God. . . . What the Bible makes known, then, is not a morality but a *reality*, a living presence to whom man responds.[5]

I agree with Gustafson that the use of the Bible as a methodological tool in determining the will of God falls short of its intended purpose. But I would argue that the Bible, as the revealed Word of God, provides the basis for establishing a theology of Christian moral life. This is an important distinction.

The inadequacy of the three alternatives cited is fundamentally methodological, not theological. That is, the Bible cannot be used as a method to arrive at ethical principles or moral criteria that can be abstracted from the participation of God himself in the moral situation of human life. Or, to put it another way, the Bible cannot substitute for moral freedom grounded in moral responsibility. While the Bible clearly has value in giving authoritative status to the will of God as a determining factor in theological ethics applied through pastoral care, the Bible cannot be seen primarily as an ethical textbook, neither perceptively, nor instructively, nor illustratively. There is a wrong use of the Bible as well as a right use in attempting to discern God's will in critical pastoral situations.

It is wrong to use selected proof texts to find biblical *strategies* or *solutions* to modern problems. The Pharisees had a "proof text" from the Old Testament Scriptures when they confronted the woman caught in adultery and presented her to Jesus for judgment. The correct use of the Bible in such cases is to take up the hermeneutical task of discerning the purpose of Scripture in guiding us to uphold the true nature of humanity through responsible decisions and actions. In this way Scripture serves the moral freedom of God to act redemptively and creatively. Scripture does not proof-text moral law but authoritatively upholds the moral will of God in restoring the moral and human quality of life. Jesus, for example, used the Old Testament Scriptures to validate God's purpose for the Sabbath and thus support his actions of healing on the Sabbath. He charged his adversaries with using the Scriptures wrongly in seeking to "catch" him in violation of a specific law.

It is also wrong to attempt to use the Bible to find parallels between our situation and that of the biblical writers. Where such parallels seem to exist (e.g., Rahab's "friendly welcome to the spies," Heb. 11:31), one cannot assume a direct correlation of ethical principle involved, because faith is the connecting reality, not moral principle. Besides, this would make the Bible largely irrelevant when such parallels cannot be found. The correct use of the Bible is to read such stories so as to find ourselves confronted by the same demand and command of God with the result that we act with faith, and not disbelief (cf. Rom. 14:22–23).

It is wrong, moreover, to attempt to extrapolate from the Bible one primary ethical principle or norm, be it love, the imitation of Christ, the kingdom of God, or the gospel as over and against law. The Bible itself, as the Word of God, would then be forced to surrender its authority to a principle or norm that stands independently of the Bible as an authoritative guide to faith and practice. This would be a return to the concept of autonomous morality, where one person, together with the Bible, possesses an absolute ethical criterion. The Bible shows, however, that all human actions and decisions can be inherently moral, and therefore we are accountable to the living God who will judge every decision and act based on his will and purpose for humanity (cf. 1 Cor. 4:1–5; 2 Cor. 10:18; Rom. 14:10–12).

The Bible itself forces us to see that there is an eschatological dimension to moral actions. No ethical system or moral principle can serve as an absolute criterion in the face of this eschatological claim on human moral life and actions. Theological ethics, therefore, must bring this eschatological perspective to bear in assisting pastoral care in deciding the critical moral issues of the present day.

God's moral will upholds created structures of human life and society, including the moral law by which human moral values and principles are determined. Human moral instincts are thus given by God and are to be used to uphold the quality of human life that God has created. Jesus validated the use of these moral instincts when he argued that the same human instincts that provided for the welfare of animals on the Sabbath ought to be considered as the basis for permitting him to heal a woman on the Sabbath (Luke 10:15–16; Matt. 12:9–13).

When Jesus stated that it is "lawful to do good on the sabbath" (Matt. 12:12), he pointed to God's purpose for people as an ultimate moral value. The determination of what is "good" cannot be made at the expense of the value of the person. So, too, in saying, "The sabbath was made for man, not man for the sabbath" (Mark 2:27), Jesus expressed the moral will of God as that which is for the good of the human person. In this case we see that the design of the Sabbath, which also was given to uphold a moral value, must be modified when necessary to accommodate the moral value of "doing good." God's moral law as expressed in the commandments is grounded in God's moral freedom. This means that forgiveness granted where the commandment condemns does not constitute a moral contradiction. The moral freedom of God to offer forgiveness is the antecedent for the commandment, in the same way that God's moral being is the source of all moral action.

Jesus' presence brought the eschatological goal into the already revealed design and purpose of God as institutionalized in the Jewish religion. At critical points of pastoral care, Jesus interpreted the moral will of God in terms of the goal toward which both design and purpose point. He did this in such a way that both the design and stated purpose of divine law were modified to allow for a moral decision that upheld as its goal the whole and healed person.

The relation of God's design, purpose, and goal can be illustrated in figure 4.

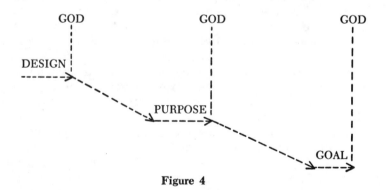

Figure 4

In this diagram the critical point of moral discernment is found where design, purpose, and goal are intersected by the vertical line representing God's contemporary presence. Making moral decisions entails having accurate moral instincts not only as to what constitutes the good, but also as to what constitutes God's will in terms of his purpose and goal. The ultimate source of moral wisdom is the moral freedom of God to move the events in history toward his good and glorious goal. There is, therefore, a purpose that must be interpreted in the process of making moral decisions.

Certain designs, such as the Sabbath as a literal seventh day of the week, have been created by God and invested with moral authority. The moral content of the Sabbath as commandment, however, is read in terms of its purpose and goal for people. Jesus correctly read this moral purpose and goal for the Sabbath in the act of healing. The Pharisees, who accused him of violating the moral law, abstracted the law of the Sabbath from the moral freedom of God and so failed to see the greater moral value in healing. Jesus thus made a moral intervention into the situation where human life had become tormented and deformed through disease. The law itself in the form of commandment could not produce this moral result. This intervention produced a "growth process" in which God's moral purpose was released through the actions of one who could act as an advocate of God's purpose and goal.

In figure 4, design first catches our attention as created or instituted by God. Some invest the concept of "God's design" with absolute and unchangeable moral character. But in reality, what God has "designed" may be the easiest for God to change for the sake of achieving his purpose and goal. Surely not every design created by God will be changed so long as "heaven and earth" continue as his created order. But we should be careful not to uphold a "design" for life with such moral passion that we forget or lose sight of the person who lives within that design. God's moral purpose and goal are attached to a process, not merely to a design.

Many have asked whether monogomous marriage might not be an example of a design that has an ideal or absolute moral character. My response is that it has a relative moral character as a design. This seems true for two reasons. First, marriage is one form of a created social order in which God's purpose and goal for persons can be realized. But it is not the only form; otherwise, those who do not marry would fail to realize God's purpose or would lack some moral quality that can be gained only by marriage. Second, God has demonstrated that he could realize his purpose and goal through forms of marriage other than the ideal of monogomous relationships. This is plainly the case in the Old Testament, for example, in the promise of Abraham coming into reality through Jacob and the four women through whom the twelve tribes of Israel were conceived.

At the same time, we could say that a monogamous relationship more closely approximates an order of marriage that fulfills the sexual, covenantal, and familial values implicit to the image of God than other forms such as polygamy. We can argue for the relative value of a moral order based on a certain design without attaching the absolute moral value to the design. This is important for counselors who are confronted with situations in which the formal design of the marriage meets the "ideal," but the life of the persons living in this form becomes inhuman and immoral as measured by God's purpose for humans living together. In the model that I present here, moral decisions are made where God's purpose and goal intersect with the actual life of the person involved. On this basis, we can support those whose only recourse is to separate from a marriage that has become abusive and immoral.

On the same basis, children may need to be removed from parents whose claim to "natural rights" and "moral authority" becomes nullified by their failure to create a moral structure of life as measured by God's will and purpose. God's "ideal" is always a living and creative life undergirded by promise and redemptive grace. All else is relative to that goal.

In making intervention into the life situation of persons for whom there is a personal dysfunction, there may also be a critical moral issue at stake. This moral issue may not be explicit in the therapeutic dynamic, but the larger, more comprehensive situation of the client may represent a clear moral dilemma. Even then, there is likely to be a "perceived" moral issue on the part of the client. Within the growth process by which the moral context of therapy can be understood, the therapist can also act as an intermediary of the divine moral will. This is a kind of moral advocacy by which the therapist fulfills a ministry of pastoral care as well.

The Role of the Professional Caregiver as Moral Advocate

We have said that the role of God as moral advocate occurs where an apparent moral dilemma makes a person vulnerable to the moral law itself. The moral will of God is invested in a goal for persons that often can be reached only through an intervention that takes the form of moral advocacy. The moral advocacy is for the will of God as the goal, not an advocacy for individuals as possessing absolute moral "rights" regardless of their conduct or actions toward other people.

By moral advocacy I mean extending divine grace to persons who are guilty of breaking the moral law or who are suffering a loss of personhood through the existence of a structure mandated by moral law. Moral advocacy reminds the marginal person of the moral right for personal dignity, freedom from abusive relationships, and full parity in social and communal life.

Moral advocacy can also be a form of pastoral care, not only in the sense of the broader responsibilities of clergy, but also in the narrower role of the professional caregiver. The pastor may offer pastoral care through the church, but may also be trained to provide counsel, therapy, and intervention through a variety of private and public agencies. Our focus here is on the caregiving provided at times of crisis, when life has become difficult if not impossible, where relationships have been distorted if not destructive, and where the tragic contravenes common sense and even faith fails.

We have in view here such situations as the physical and emotional abuse of a spouse in a lawful marriage; the abuse of children in families and social agencies; the breakdown of marriage and the trauma of divorce; the sudden death of a loved one; lingering illness or disease that destroys the dignity and value of life; addiction to substances or sex; and the loss of will, nerve, meaning, and purpose marked by midlife crisis.

Because these life crises strike at the very heart of what it is to be human, these situations constitute a moral dilemma and require moral advocacy. One way or another, a breakdown or failure of life constitutes a threat to the value of human life or to faith in God as an ultimate value.

The crisis situations of life are borderline situations with regard to the command of God and can appear ambiguous with

regard to what God's will might be. Here "normal life" cannot
provide the norms for making decisions or finding a direction
forward. Too often caregivers make the mistake of using the
normal as the paradigm for giving counsel and advice to those in
abnormal situations.

In theological ethics, as in medicine, we face the real
problems when normality and health are absent. Facing an
inhuman situation, the caregiver must become the advocate of
the marginal person. At this point the general principles of
health and moral order simply do not provide this kind of moral
advocacy. The "normal" cannot become the advocate for the
essential worth of the "abnormal" measured against the "normal." The "normal" is assumed to be "good," and what is not
normal by this definition can appear to be morally deficient as
well as abnormal, or not normal. That is what is meant by
"borderline" situations.

Many of the crises we have noted are borderline situations
where the command of God is ambiguous. This ambiguity exists
because the command and moral will of God are rooted in his
freedom, which demands that the person be free to discern and
do God's will. If God's moral will were absolutely embodied in
a commandment, such as "thou shalt not bear false witness,"
then we could conclude in every case that telling a lie is wrong.
Yet a moral dilemma occurs when a person is faced with a
situation in which telling the truth also means betraying a
person whose life depends on one's action. Ethicists have used
situations like this to argue that we must choose the higher
moral law—saving a life—over the lower moral law—telling
the truth. But this way of resolving ambiguity plays off one
moral law against another.

Often I am asked about a case in which one marriage partner
has had an affair that is unknown to the spouse. Through
confession, repentance, and therapeutic work the affair has
ended. But now the question remains, is there not a moral
obligation to inform the spouse of this infidelity and seek
forgiveness and restoration? Can this be kept a secret from the
spouse and the relationship still be built on mutual trust with
moral integrity?

My response is to view this as a situation in which a moral
decision has to be made. I ask the counselee to discern what the
purpose and goal of such a "moment of truth" are intended to

produce. Is this confession primarily for the moral value of the person making the confession? Having "told the truth" to a partner, has one now fulfilled the moral law of truth-telling, regardless of the consequences?

In my experience of pastoral counseling, the decision can go either way, depending on the situation. In cases where he or she decides not to inform the spouse of a past act of infidelity, the counselee has decided to bear the moral responsibility to uphold the good of the other, who may not be able to handle the burden if it were shifted. For facts can be told, as in the case of reporting an affair that has now ended. But the moral truth and character of that event have become deeply embedded in the fabric of the one who has confessed, repented, and experienced healing and forgiveness from God. For the spouse to be integrated into this process, the unfaithful person must not only disclose facts, but also share the moral basis for the facts.

My point is that moral responsibility is not merely to an abstract principle of truth-telling at all costs, but to the effect of truth on the structures of human relationships, which are already weak and fragile. It is sometimes easier to destroy a relationship with the truth than with a lie.[6] Of course these situations are fraught with peril and clouded with ambiguity! All the more reason, I would say, that we need to have an acquired sense of moral wisdom and not merely a "knee-jerk" moral reaction.

God's moral will is not a higher principle or higher moral law. Rather, it is directed toward the goal of human life; his moral laws are given so as to direct us toward that goal. If God himself were present in every case where moral laws collide, we would instinctively turn to him for assurance as to what would be the best moral decision. We would assume, then, that God's moral freedom is itself the greater moral principle.

This appears to be the way Jesus functioned when he was confronted with the collision between human values and the moral law as stated in the Old Testament Scriptures. He used the freedom of God's moral will to become the advocate for the person. This advocacy was clearly not to justify the situation or the immoral actions (as in the case of the woman caught in adultery), but to restore and liberate the person to realize God's moral will.

The Christian caregiver who provides pastoral care from the

perspective of theological ethics also acts as an advocate for God's moral will in a dual sense. First, the caregiver acts as an advocate of God's presence in the situation. This is possible because the risen Christ has sent his Spirit as the indwelling presence of God—"we are the temple of the living God" (2 Cor. 6:16; cf. John 14:18–23; 1 Cor. 6:19; Col. 1:27). The caregiver thus manifests the "real presence" of Christ in advocating to and on behalf of the one who is in a "borderline" situation.

Second, the caregiver acts as an advocate of the person's moral freedom to be a whole and functioning person. Here the caregiver does not merely stand in the counseling relationship as a moral authority, dispensing moral law or making moral decisions on behalf of the one who is caught in the moral dilemma. Rather, the caregiver advocates the client's moral authority in being a person who bears the divine image.

In counseling from a Christian perspective, we must assume parity on both sides of the situation. The moral authority is not lodged merely on the side of the intermediary. The encounter at the human level produces the moment in which the moral freedom and moral will of God are released as a motive power for change and growth. God's moral authority is demonstrated in healing and transforming, not only in judging and condemning.

For example, when a woman is suffering abuse in a marriage relationship, she will often feel morally powerless due to her supposed obligation toward her marriage partner. This may even be reinforced by a feeling that she is being rightly punished for real or imagined failings in her role. Her counselor will need to advocate God's moral authority in order to intercept the woman's relentless sense of duty toward a "law of marriage." The counselor must stand with the victim over and against the so-called legal right of a marriage partner to inflict pain. In this sense the caregiver is willing to place himself or herself where God's moral will is perceived to be.

At the same time, the caregiver will advocate the moral authority that properly belongs to the victim of the abuse, but who feels totally without that moral freedom and authority. In this case the caregiver does not possess moral authority by virtue of a role or professional skill. Rather, the moral authority resides in the nature of personhood itself as determined by God to be free for the other in a healthy relationship.

It should be understood that a Christian perspective on caregiving does not introduce moral criteria that are not already present in the human situation. There is no "Christian ethic" that substitutes Christian morality for human morality. What the Christian can provide through caregiving is the advocacy of God himself. God is the power that liberates the moral freedom belonging to persons, for he gave that freedom to us as a divine endowment.

Those who provide caregiving without such a theological ethic can offer therapeutic intervention and even moral wisdom in directing the client toward the good. Yet the caregiver may experience moral ambivalence about serving in an explicitly moral role without a specific theological orientation. The Christian is free of this moral ambivalence and can clarify the moral criteria involved in what is otherwise an ambiguous moral dilemma. What might be an "easy out" for the one who seeks a resolution of the moral dilemma on strictly self-centered terms will be intensified into a true moral issue by the one who brings theological ethics to bear.

Theological ethics do not solve problems, says Helmut Thielicke; instead they intensify problems by showing the point of any particular decision.

> Its task is that of clarification. It does not seek to spell out precisely what must be done. It simply lays bare the full implications of that "what," so that the underlying issue of the particular decision is heard as a claim. Ethics in effect complicates matters by analyzing the contents of the decision. But there is a counterbalancing simplification for the one who then decides: When it comes to the point of actually taking concrete action his decision is simplified by the gift of the Holy Spirit.[7]

The Holy Spirit is called the "paraclete" in the New Testament (John 14:16, 26; 15:26; 16:7). One translation of this word is "advocate," one called to the side of another. Jesus intimates that this has been his own role when he says, "I will pray the Father, and he will give you another Counselor [paraclete] . . . even the Spirit of truth. . . . he dwells with you, and will be in you" (John 14:16–17).

The gift of the Holy Spirit as the indwelling presence of God's moral will resolves the moral ambivalence otherwise present in the caregiver. This advocacy frees the situation from the moral autonomy that can provide the "easy out"—my pain gives me a right to get even with the one who hurt me. Or, the injustice that I have suffered gives me the right to rescind my commitment. Yet this advocacy that binds all persons, even victims of their own immoral acts or the acts of others, to the moral will of God also sets free those bound by the inhuman laws and practices of others. One is also thus set free to forgive, which is a moral action related to one's goal of healing.

It should not be supposed, however, that the Holy Spirit is a moral criterion that counters other moral criteria. There is a form of moral autonomy that would claim the Holy Spirit as the content of one's own conscience. But the Holy Spirit clarifies that the content of God's moral will is intrinsic to personhood as a gift and goal and convinces us of the moral authority by which we act in accordance with these moral criteria. The Holy Spirit is not a "simplicity" on this side of complexity, but the simplicity on the other side of complexity. Oliver Wendell Holmes is reported to have said, "I would not give a fig for the simplicity on this side of complexity; but for the simplicity on the other side of complexity, I would give my life."

Having surveyed the moral options in a given situation from the perspective of the moral law by which human persons live, and having calculated the moral implications of an action, we cannot ultimately defend on abstract moral criteria alone the decision that is finally made on the basis of theological ethics. If it were always possible to give this kind of justification, many of our actions would become incredible in the face of the moral ambivalence inherent in the complexity of life, where good and evil are mingled. The moral advocate seeks out the moral issue on the basis of what one reckons God declares to be good.

We have ample revelation of the criteria for this "good" based on biblical testimony to God's purpose and goal for humanity. Jesus became impatient with those who quibbled over these decisions. Yet there is no shortcut to these decisions, as the good lies on the other side of moral complexity, not on this side of it.

When Abraham finally decides to sacrifice his son because it is God's will, there is no way back to the moral criteria by which he made that decision (Gen. 22). That is, there are no universal moral principles that justify this action. Yet he is bound by the moral will of God to obey.

When Jesus decided that the cross and his own incredible

obedience "unto death" were the good, because it was the will of the Father for the good of humankind, the simplicity of his decision lay on the other side of moral reason alone. There is no other way to practice moral advocacy, for we are not merely betting that the decision is the best one and that others using the same criteria will always come out on the same side. The issues are ultimately those that link the divine moral will with the human moral decision, and the personal character of God with the character and quality of life advocated here on earth.

In the end, theological ethics insist that the moral outcome of therapeutic intervention bears the weight of God's own moral will. Jesus provided for this when he said, "Whatever you bind on earth shall be bound in heaven, and whatever you loose on earth shall be loosed in heaven" (Matt. 16:19; cf. John 20:22–23).

It should be remembered that this is a costly kind of advocacy. The caregiver must be prepared to suffer the judgment of those who feel it necessary to uphold the moral law as interpreted by legal and formal structures. The presence of the liberating moral will of God will often appear ambiguous and even wrong to those who find security in "being good" as defined by legal morality.

For this reason, Dietrich Bonhoeffer insisted that the task of Christian ethics is not to be good, but to do the will of God.

> What is of ultimate importance is now no longer that I should become good, or that the condition of the world should be made better by my action, but that the reality of God should show itself everywhere to be the ultimate reality. Where there is faith in God as the ultimate reality, all concern with ethics will have as its starting-point that God shows Himself to be good, even if this involves the risk that I myself and the world are not good but thoroughly bad.[8]

For Bonhoeffer, this meant that we must be prepared to be regarded as having become guilty in order to be the responsible advocate for those who are victims of the established order.[9] But this can only be the kind of guilt that Christ himself bore, as the advocate of God and the advocate of the sinner in the same movement.

It finally must be said that the role of the caregiver as moral advocate is an extension of the body of Christ, if it is to be considered in the way that we have set forth. The kind of pastoral care that provides this intervention and advocacy should be offered in such a way that the primary caregiver is not also the sole advocate. A model of caregiving thus would include these guidelines:

1. The caregiver should be related to a Christian community where his or her spiritual and personal life is nurtured and affirmed as belonging to Christ and indwelt by Christ's Spirit.
2. The Christian community that upholds the integrity and ministry of the caregiver must be a theologically informed community as to the nature of pastoral care as moral advocacy.
3. The Christian community makes explicit its complicity in the moral advocacy of the primary caregiver; this is done as a covenant between the community (or its representatives) and the caregiver made prior to specific actions of caregiving that involves moral advocacy.
4. The primary caregiver, while preserving the confidentiality of a counseling relationship, seeks the wisdom of the Spirit through the caregiving network in providing advocacy where moral criteria alone do not resolve the complexity; that is, where the "mind of Christ" is seen to be the determining factor and will be one's final appeal.
5. In making these guidelines operational, the caregiving network must be carefully selected and prepared to serve as a team that understands and provides moral advocacy for pastoral care.

Summary

We have sought in this chapter to establish the theoretical grounds for the role of the Christian counselor or caregiver as moral advocate. We have argued that the moral authority for this kind of advocacy is grounded in the moral freedom of God. This moral freedom is not arbitrary or capricious. God has revealed his nature and purpose to be consistent and creative in being and upholding that which is "good" and that which promotes the good. When persons are in need of counseling, they are often also in situations that are critical and even life threatening. Christians who counsel must also be prepared to act as moral agents of God's gracious purpose in making intervention in crisis situations. This places the ministry of counseling in the context of pastoral care. The mode of delivering pastoral care through crisis intervention will be discussed in the next chapter.

Notes

1. Lewis Smedes, *Mere Morality* (Grand Rapids: Eerdmans, 1983), vii. Other books by Smedes that deal with the moral issues in making decisions include *Caring and Commitment: Learning to Live the Love We Promised* (San Francisco: Harper & Row, 1988) and *Choices: Making Right Decisions in a Complex World* (San Francisco: Harper & Row, 1986).

2. Perry London, *Modes and Morals of Psychotherapy* (New York: Holt, Rinehart and Winston, 1964), 6. For other sources on the issue of moral values in therapy see: Charlotte Buhler, *Values in Psychotherapy* (New York: Free Press, 1962); Mary Ann Carroll et al., *Ethics in the Practice of Psychology* (Englewood Cliffs, N.J.: Prentice-Hall, 1985); Gerald Corey, "Ethical Issues in Counseling and Psychotherapy," in *Theory and Practice of Counseling and Psychotherapy* ed. Gerald Corey (Belmont, Calif.: Wadsworth. 1977); James C. Hansen, ed. (Luciano L'Abate, vol. ed.), *Ethics, Legalities and the Family Therapist* (Rockville, Md.: Aspen Publications, 1982); John Hoffman, *Ethical Confrontation in Counseling* (Chicago: University of Chicago Press, 1979); Marshall C. Lowe, *Value Orientation in Counseling and Psychotherapy*, 2d ed. (Cranston, R.I.: Carroll Press, 1976); J. Peterson, *Counseling and Values* (Scranton, Pa.: International Textbook, 1970); W. Yoell et al., "Marriage, Morals and Therapeutic Goals: A Discussion," *Journal of Behavioral Therapy and Experimental Psychiatry* 2 (1971): 127–32.

3. Gerald Corey suggests that therapy should not be synonymous with preaching or teaching. "This is not to say that therapists should maintain an indifferent, neutral, or passive role by simply silently listening to and accepting everything the client reports. Instead, I propose that therapists challenge the values of their clients, and, if they care, when they sense that certain behavior is destructive, they will confront their clients and invite them to examine the pay-offs and the consequences of their actions. A core issue in therapy is the degree to which the therapist's values should enter into a therapeutic relationship. A therapist cannot have goals for clients and yet be devoid of value judgments, for goals are based on our values" ("Ethical Issues in Counseling and Psychotherapy," 222).

4. Karl Barth, *Ethics* (New York: Seabury, 1981), 4.

5. James Gustafson, "Christian Ethics," in *Religion*, ed. Paul Ramsey (Englewood Cliffs, N.J.: Prentice-Hall, 1965), 317.

6. For further reading on this subject, I recommend the essay by Dietrich Bonhoeffer, "What Is Meant by 'Telling the Truth'?" in his book *Ethics*, ed. Eberhard Bethge (New York: Macmillan, 1955), 363–72. Bonhoeffer cites the case of a teacher who asks a student in front of the class whether it is true that his father often comes home drunk. It is true, but the child denies it. The family has its own secret and must preserve it. To this reality the child loyally responds, even in denying the fact of the question. The teacher, says Bonhoeffer, has asked an "untruthful" question and has placed the child in an untenable position.

7. Helmut Thielicke, *Theological Ethics: Foundations*, vol. 1 (Grand Rapids: Eerdmans, 1979), 621.

8. Bonhoeffer, *Ethics*, 188–89.

9. Ibid., 245.

12

Dynamics of Pastoral Care in Counseling Praxis

"John, I am not a pastor nor am I a theologian," Sue Johnson said softly. "I can help you work through your anger and panic now that you have tested positive for AIDS. But when you ask me if I think that God has brought this on you as a judgment because of your former lifestyle, I cannot deal with that. You are a Christian and a member of the church; have you talked with your pastor?

"I don't feel free to do that," John replied. "Several months ago he said in a sermon that AIDS might be God's way of bringing moral judgment on the homosexuals. As a Christian and a homosexual, I am prepared to acknowledge that my lifestyle is a sin against God's purpose for my life if that would help. But why would God do this to me? Other people sin and seem to live healthy lives. I know that you are a Christian counselor, Dr. Johnson. I have prayed and it doesn't seem to help. I still feel this awful sense of doom—that even God has abandoned me. Can't you help me?"

"Why didn't someone prepare me for this?" Sue Johnson said to herself as she wrote up her notes following the therapy session with John. "I can deal with sin in my own life, I think, though I am not sure how I would feel if I were John. But I don't feel capable of dealing with the question of sin and forgiveness in the lives of my clients. Even if I felt capable, I am not sure that I should. Who am I to hear his confession and grant him absolution? I am his counselor, not his priest."

And so we meet Dr. Johnson again, whom we met in chapter 1. And she still has an uneasy conscience! She is, after all, a Christian who counsels. She also has been taught the concept of the "priesthood of all believers." But she has never really connected it with her role as a therapist. Does the promise of Jesus actually apply to her as well as to her pastor: "Receive the Holy Spirit. If you forgive the sins of any, they are forgiven; if you retain the sins of any, they are retained" (John 20:22–23)?

Can Christians who counsel share in the ministry of pastoral care even when it touches upon the communication of forgiveness as part of emotional healing? The thesis of this chapter is that this indeed is the case. This chapter is intended to give understanding and encouragement to Sue Johnson and all her fellow counselors and caregivers who are Christians.

The form of pastoral care I have in mind here is the ministry of Christ continued through all the members of the church. It does not belong only to "ordained pastors," as though the larger body of Christ has no share in this ministry of care. Christ himself was not "ordained" in the technical sense of holding an office that entitled him to dispense God's grace and benevolence. Rather, he was a layperson in whom the presence and Spirit of God were manifest.

This was true as well for the disciples whom he called and to whom he gave his Spirit after the Resurrection. All who have the Spirit of Christ continue to have the commission and authority to do Christ's ministry—which is the basis for all forms of pastoral care. Pastoral care, therefore, can be one form of the ministry of Christians who practice therapy, whether as ordained ministers or as professional caregivers. The relation of theological ethics to pastoral care is, in effect, the relation of God's moral will as expressed through his redemptive grace to persons caught in the web of personal moral failure and general moral evil. The problems of sin and evil raise issues in pastoral care that a theological approach to therapy must address.[1]

Pastoral care generally provides three forms of helping ministry by which persons can realize God's moral will: (1) an extension of God's grace; (2) a transfer of spiritual power; and (3) the creation of a healing community.

Pastoral Care as an Extension of God's Grace

The mode: intervention
The goal: forgiveness
The theological dynamic: a kind of absolution

The concept of intervention has its roots in God's gracious interaction with persons so they may continue to bear his image and may share his eternal life. By nature, humans are both creaturely and personal. The personal dimension of human life is contingent on relation to God, who is the transcendent source of personal being.

Without intervention into the creaturely process, personhood would not have come into being. God enters into covenant relation with persons and as covenant partner aligns himself with them over and against nature. Sin is a moral and spiritual problem resulting from defection from the covenant relation. Sin, defined as defiance of God's gracious relation to those who bear his image, results in separating persons from the gracious life of God. The consequences of sin can be related to the moral and spiritual disorientation that afflicts the person in this state of estrangement and alienation.

God's judgment against sin, according to theological ethics, is itself a continued intervention of divine grace, for if the sinner were left to the consequences of moral and spiritual disorientation, personhood would disappear behind the sickness and turmoil of life. Sin is fatal to personhood because its consequences lead to a fatalistic conclusion of human life.

The consequences of sin are not identical with the judgment of God on sin, though they may sometimes be coincidental. God's judgment is itself an intervention between sin and its consequence, so that the sinner is now related once more to God rather than left to suffer the ultimate fate of sin's consequence— "in the day that you eat of it you will die" (Gen. 2:17). This death is not itself the divine judgment, but merely the deadly consequence of sin. Divine judgment called Adam and Eve out of their fateful situation and called them back again into relation with the living God. Death and disease cannot be a judgment of God merely as fate, for his judgment is rooted in his grace and offers empowerment for repentance and faith, leading to renewal of relation. We cannot tear God's judgment away from the living God himself and make of this an unrelievable fate.

The specific goal of divine grace as intervention is forgiveness—the renewal of a positive relation between people and God. Forgiveness means restored relation, not merely granting an exception to a moral law. Thus forgiveness restores an authentic moral history of being in relation. Forgiveness is the ultimate moral good, which transcends the moral law without breaking it.

The moral law does not contain the possibility of forgiveness. Forgiveness is located in the moral good, which is necessarily personal. The moral good, therefore, must have its source in the divine intention, which is the same source for the moral law. In this way forgiveness offers a moral good without contradicting the moral law, for both have their origin in the same moral reality and intention of God. This is the specific content of a theological ethic with regard to forgiveness. Pastoral care recognizes the moral law and its criteria for determining what is right, and it provides moral advocacy through intervention in order to sustain the moral good. But pastoral care also provides moral advocacy when one stands in the wrong through the consequences of sin, and it provides a moral basis for forgiveness through the extension of God's grace.

We must take note that the consequence of sin may be perceived at times as identical with a divine judgment, as in the case of a natural catastrophe, an act of aggression by another, or even a fatal disease. In certain cases in the Old Testament, the judgment of God was considered to take the form of a physical affliction, such as the leprosy that struck Miriam, the sister of Moses (Num. 12:1–16), or the plague that struck the people of Israel when they forsook God and worshiped the golden calf (Exod. 32:35).

These exceptional cases, however, do not provide a case for separating God's judgment from his grace. In each case God himself intervenes and stands between the people and the consequence of their sin, even when the consequence is considered a divine judgment! This, again, is why divine judgment cannot be shifted away from its source in God and located with an impersonal thing such as disease or death.

Pastoral care must, then, prepare to make the same kind of intervention without being intimidated by the thought that a person's affliction or situation is the result of God's judgment against sin. God manifests the moral good of divine grace by intervening to restore persons, even if the consequences of sin are seen as divine judgment. God's judgment may express the consequences of violating a moral law, but God's grace expresses his moral will, which has as its goal the moral good of forgiveness.[2]

Quite often caregivers will be confronted with a situation in which a person may be considered, or consider himself or herself, suffering the consequences of an immoral or sinful action. The caregiver may feel morally ambivalent if she feels that moral law and divine judgment exhaust God's moral will. She may instinctively want to offer release from this moral judgment, but she may be unsure that it is right to do so.

Consider, for example, the dilemma of someone who must provide care for a patient with AIDS. Some caregivers believe that this disease may be a punishment of God. They assume that AIDS is contracted in most cases through sexual contact, particularly through homosexual relations. If they view homosexuality as sinful, and if AIDS appears to be a disease contracted primarily by homosexuals, then they conclude that the one who has contracted the disease is experiencing God's judgment against sin.

Those who provide caregiving to persons with AIDS may have theological or moral convictions that prevent them from intervening in a situation where they believe God's judgment has fallen on the person. However, we have shown that there are no theological grounds for assuming that disease and sin are connected in this kind of "cause-and-effect" relation. God has shown himself to be the covenant partner of the person and is aligned *with* persons, not with nature (which includes the possibility of disease) *against* persons. In the few cases in the Old Testament where God appears to have brought divine judgment in the form of a plague or a disease, he always graciously intervenes, forgiving the people and freeing them from the consequences of sin.

In the New Testament there are *no* cases cited where God uses disease as a judgment against sin. On the contrary, Jesus acted to dispel the notion that sin causes disease, and in every case he intervened between the disease and the person. Jesus' response to his disciples' question—"Who sinned, this man or his parents, that he was born blind?"—illustrates this point (John 9). Like Job's friends, the disciples assumed that suffering was directly due to sin, and that if the man would only confess his sin, God would heal him. But Jesus denied any causality between sin and the man's blindness. This only becomes an occasion for the works of God to be manifest, Jesus replied— and he proceeded to heal the man.

A theological ethic that provides moral advocacy as an extension of God's grace and forgiveness provides intervention in every case, even if one believes that the disease is a consequence of sin. This position does not have to make the offer of grace dependent on determining whether or not the person is experiencing the consequences of sin. Grace is itself God's moral intervention between the person and the consequence of sin, *even if* that consequence is viewed as divine judgment.

If we think of intervention as an extension of God's grace so that forgiveness becomes the moral good, we will have the courage to offer forgiveness on God's own terms and not merely out of our human instincts of pity or compassion.

But, you say, we cannot offer forgiveness until the person who has wronged God has repented and made restitution. No, this kind of thinking is contrary to the moral quality of forgiveness itself. For if forgiveness were only offered on performance of a moral act of contrition, then God's grace would itself be contingent on a human moral act. In fact, divine forgiveness is itself the ultimate moral act that enables the human act of repentance and restitution to take place. Forgiveness as an extension of God's grace does not depend on some prior form of meeting the demands of the moral law, but is itself the source of the moral good that produces faith and repentance.

The judgment of God takes place in the context of his forgiveness. For his forgiveness is his intervention by which he risks his own moral good again for the sake of restoring persons to their own moral and spiritual good.

Why, then, do we say that this kind of pastoral care is a form of absolution? Because absolution certifies the moral good that forgiveness provides. The moral law cannot provide absolution, for it cannot provide forgiveness. Only God can provide absolution, for he provides forgiveness as the moral good that upholds persons in the very moment when they are without a moral good or moral freedom of their own. The caregiver then serves as a moral agent, binding the moral good of forgiveness to the life of the person through intervention.

Absolution offered without intervention is impotent and inoperative. Intervention that does not intend to grant absolution ultimately betrays the moral good that forgiveness is meant to create.

Counselors who act as advocates for God do not dispense forgiveness and grace. Rather, as children of God they authenticate forgiveness and grace through accepting and affirming their clients. Nor do counselors usurp the liturgical form of confession and absolution as part of the corporate worship of a congregation under pastoral leadership. Instead, they authenticate this liturgical word through the growth process, in which a motive power to receive forgiveness is released and experienced (chap. 3). Counselors do not suddenly become priests, but—as Jesus himself did—they offer and authenticate the grace that God gives through their own "real presence." In demonstrating this divine acceptance they offer a kind of absolution.

John, the man who has tested positive for AIDS, seeks more than therapeutic aid to reduce his anger and anxiety and to develop adequate coping mechanisms. He expects Dr. Johnson, a Christian counselor, to help him resolve a spiritual crisis brought on by his homosexual lifestyle, his sin, and his viewing AIDS as a judgment of God. He has prayed without finding relief. He is willing to acknowledge his sin, but has not found forgiveness, for he has been led to believe that his physical condition is a direct judgment of God. This vacates the reality of forgiveness and leaves him with a sense of doom and despair.

Dr. Johnson needs help in understanding her role as a Christian who counsels and how she can make a positive intervention in this case, leading her client to experience God's forgiveness in such a way that he will have God as his advocate and not his adversary. John is seeking absolution and restoration through his Christian therapist, though he does not express it in those terms. The purpose of this chapter is to help Sue Johnson and others like her to meet this need through an intervention that becomes a form of pastoral care.

Pastoral Care as a Transfer of Spiritual Power

The mode: advocacy
The goal: liberation
The theological dynamic: a kind of exorcism

As we turn now to the second way in which pastoral care can be viewed as a helping ministry, we must look more closely at how moral advocacy empowers the one who is morally powerless.

In suggesting that pastoral care is a transfer of spiritual power, we must immediately make a qualification. *Transfer* does not mean literally transferring power from the caregiver to the client. We have already said that, on the one hand, the caregiver does not possess moral authority or power by virtue of his or her role. On the other hand, the caregiver *is* connected to the source of spiritual and moral power that is the basis of all healing and personal empowerment. We can look at an incident in the life and ministry of Jesus as an example.

As Jesus was passing through the crowd, a woman who had an incurable physical ailment desperately reached out to touch him, thinking, "If I touch even his garments, I shall be made well" (Mark 5:28). She was healed immediately. Simultaneously Jesus felt that "power had gone forth from him"; he turned to seek her out of the crowd (v. 30). When the woman admitted that she had touched him, he said to her, "Daughter, your faith has made you well; go in peace, and be healed of your disease" (v. 34).

There was, in effect, a transfer of spiritual power. The woman was in a powerless position. Perhaps she had concluded that her inability to be healed by the physicians was a sign of God's judgment on her. Jesus' miracles of healing encouraged her to believe that there was an available source of power by which she could be healed. She saw Jesus as a contact with that power and felt that she had to make only the most tentative touch to have this power.

The transfer of power was a form of moral advocacy in that health is a moral good that issues from God, while disease is a threat to this moral good that renders one powerless. Yet Jesus did not credit his power with effecting her healing, but her faith! He exercised his power not merely to liberate her from her illness, but to empower her by summoning up within her the spiritual power of faith.

This woman would have to face other kinds of illness and other forms of evil before her life on earth was over. Liberation from disease or demons is not an end in itself. Rather, the true end of liberation is the empowerment of persons to stand against evil with the assurance that they are not cut off from God's moral and spiritual good.

How does this transfer of spiritual power actually take place through pastoral care? First, the caregiver brings into the desperate situation the moral and spiritual authority of God's person and presence. The caregiver herself enters the void left by the devastation of evil and fills it with a moral and spiritual presence that sends a signal to those who are powerless that there is a good which will prevail. The caregiver does this primarily through her presence, but also, as appropriate, with words and even touch.

Second, the transfer of spiritual power—which empowers the client to believe in the moral good that is available from God— occurs as the client shares the pain and agony that the devastation has left in its wake. In taking on himself human suffering, pain, and distress, Jesus empowered the powerless. There is a kind of inner logic that we must clearly understand: the suffering of God brings those who suffer into contact with his divine power and goodness. Through sharing in the sufferings of God, we receive the power of God and thus survive the onslaughts of evil.

The caregiver reveals the suffering God through identifying with the pain of human suffering, and she releases the power of God by bringing God into contact with human weakness and distress. This is an incarnational kind of caregiving in which the presence and power of God are displayed, not in religious words or symbols, but through human actions and advocacy. Yes, prayer, worship, and religious symbols also may express the presence of God. But the transfer of spiritual power ordinarily comes through the nonreligious means of intervention and liberation. This is what is meant by the incarnational dimension of moral advocacy.

I have suggested that this form of pastoral care is a kind of exorcism. Theological ethics provides pastoral care with a perspective on evil that takes mental illness seriously as a pathology, but it also becomes the moral advocate of the person suffering mental and emotional distress from the onslaughts of evil.

Behind the phenomenon of the New Testament and the ministry of Jesus that depicts the evil of demonic oppression and that depicts healing as exorcism lies the positive truth that moral goodness does not only heal—it liberates. God's grace sets up a shield against invading forces and powers seeking to destroy the moral and spiritual life of persons.

As the self develops, it is vulnerable to forces that have great power in affecting the personality. Without this vulnerability, the person would not be susceptible to the power of the good as a form of personal and spiritual empowerment. However, this vulnerability also means that we are subject to confusion and misdirection, which can lead us to yield to the "spirits" that promise to fulfill our needs, desires, and intentions. Exorcism thus becomes the transfer of spiritual power, enabling the self to "cast off" this alien power and open itself again to the formative powers of moral and spiritual goodness.

Without positive, continual reinforcement of the good that constitutes the spiritual environment for the life of the self, we would all become "deranged" and subject to the conflicting and competing forces present in our moral and spiritual environment.

What appears as an extraordinary event of exorcism, particularly in the presence of Jesus as the personal embodiment of the moral and spiritual goodness of God himself, points us toward the ordinary and more routine forms of exorcism as the means for effectively transferring spiritual power and for liberating persons from conflicting and competing forces. These forces by their very nature defy categorization as either "from without" or "from within." The borderline between mental illness and demonic possession is ambiguous and undefinable.

A perspective of pastoral care that reduces all emotional and mental distress to psycho-somatic disorder casts the person hopelessly back on himself as ultimately responsible for his own sickness and healing. By contrast, a perspective of pastoral care that interprets everything from a headache to psychotic behavior as demonic possession voids the person of moral and spiritual identity and leaves him or her in an absolutely powerless condition.

Theological ethics respects the ambiguity that conceals the borderline between sin and sickness, between mental illness and the powers of evil. Moral advocacy is quite prepared both to treat and to rebuke disease. Treatment comes under the category of intervention, which applies techniques of medicinal and therapeutic practices to bring healing.

Rebuke as a category of intervention shields the afflicted

person with divine grace, saying *no* to certain forces and powers and *yes* to the powers of health and moral goodness.[3]

We should note that Jesus apparently did not practice an overt form of exorcism with any of his immediate disciples. Yet he did confront the forces of evil that sought to torment and confuse them. This is one way of understanding his saying, "Whoever causes one of these little ones who believe in me to sin, it would be better for him to have a great millstone fastened around his neck and to be drowned in the depth of the sea" (Matt. 18:6). Many scholars feel that these "little ones" were Jesus' own disciples. Jesus practiced moral advocacy to care for his disciples. He rebuked those who would seek to destroy their relation to him and warned that there are appropriate uses for millstones for such evil powers! Perhaps counselors ought to hang a millstone on their office wall as a visible sign of this warning against the power of evil.

Jesus even rebuked his disciples when their ideas appeared off-base. "Get behind me, Satan!" Jesus said when Peter suggested that it was wrong for him to go up to Jerusalem, where he would meet almost certain death (Matt. 16:23). In a single moment Jesus exorcised himself from a thought contrary to God's moral will, and he also exorcised his disciples from allowing such a thought to find a place in their minds and hearts.

Those who undertake the ministry of pastoral care must have the discernment and the moral sense to create an environment that clearly defines the kind of power that is evil and destructive and a kind of power that is good and constructive. From the perspective of theological ethics, it is not necessary to draw this boundary at the point of demons as against illness. But an environment should be created in which evil from whatever source and by whatever name is placed outside the horizon of moral goodness that positively defines the person who is the object of God's care.

Once again, I am not suggesting that the Christian counselor assume some kind of role as an "exorcist." Rather, I suggest that the very presence of a Christian is the "real presence" of Jesus Christ by his Spirit. In this form of presence lie the authority and power to affirm a positive and "whole" relationship and environment for the client that goes beyond—but includes—therapeutic acceptance and congruence. If "evil" manifests itself, then the counselor will be prepared to deal with this "alien" force in straightforward and matter-of-fact affirmation without questioning the source of this apparent "evil."[4]

In the case of John, the counselor needs to create an environment of support and affirmation that will shield him from the tormenting insinuations that he has become a victim of his sin and is alienated from God. This raises serious problems for the Christian therapist when John's own church and pastor apparently are not helping and, in fact, may be contributing to the problem. But this may not be actually the case. Sue Johnson can at least talk with John's pastor and attempt to create a bridge for John to find a network of people who can provide this "shield" of God's grace and love around him. Christian counselors can often provide a theological praxis by which pastors can discover new dimensions of pastoral care as a function of the church as the body of Christ.

Pastoral Care as the Creation of a Healing Community

> The mode: affirmation
> The goal: peace/shalom
> The theological dynamic: a kind of eucharist

A third way in which pastoral care can be viewed as a form of moral advocacy is in the creation of a healing community. Here we move more directly into the extension of the grace of God in the form of the Christian community, which can be seen as the biblical form of the body of Christ.

Sin produces estrangement and alienation from the human community. The immediate consequence of Adam's sin was an estrangement between God and human personal life and a form of alienation between human beings. The differentiation that properly belongs to the structure of human life in the form of the I-Thou relation has now become division. No longer is the other affirmed as "bone of my bones and flesh of my flesh"; now it is "the woman whom thou gavest to be with me, she gave me fruit of the tree, and I ate" (Gen. 3:12). No longer will Adam provide moral advocacy for the woman as he would for his own life. Instead, when his own being is threatened, he betrays her by blaming her for his moral predicament. Even God is put on trial, so to speak, by the moral autonomy of Adam—it is the "woman whom thou gavest to be with me!"

The test of true moral advocacy as a dimension of pastoral care is the willingness to affirm the person who would otherwise be vulnerable to the demands of the moral law and powerless in the face of God's judgment on sin. In authentic intervention the caregiver is willing to stand with the one who lacks status and to affirm that person as necessary to one's own good. The goal of moral advocacy is to reunite the one who is estranged to the community of believers.

Moses, for example, acted as a moral advocate when the Isarelites rebelled against God and worshiped the golden calf. Aaron, Moses' brother, gave up his advocacy for the people when he claimed a kind of moral autonomy to justify himself: "I threw it [the gold] into the fire, and there came out this calf" (Exod. 32:24)!

In contrast, Moses ascended the mountain to intervene between the sin of the people and the dreadful consequences that had fallen upon them. When God threatened to abandon his people and start over with Moses, Moses argued as the moral advocate of the people: "Alas, this people have sinned a great sin; they have made for themselves gods of gold. But now, if thou wilt forgive their sin—and if not, blot me, I pray thee, out of thy book which thou hast written" (Exod. 32:31–32).

Moses saw that God's stated intention to abandon his people because of their sin was a test of his knowledge of God's moral advocacy, which is rooted in covenant election. In arguing against the stated intention of God to bring a final and fatal judgment on the people as a consequence of their sin, Moses knew that he was arguing out of the moral goodness of God, which has as its ultimate intention forgiveness and affirmation rather than judgment and reprobation.

The content of affirmation is threefold. First, affirmation intercepts the consequences of sin and lays claim to the person who would otherwise be alienated from all hope of moral goodness. This affirmation also intercepts the demand of the moral law. Thus the moral law does not destroy the image of God in human beings, but is directed away from the lawbreaker to the lawgiver—to God who is the creative source of moral goodness.

One who offers pastoral care thus stands as a moral agent of this creative redirecting of the moral law so that the consequences of sin are not fatal and final. In doing this, that person stands as an agent of God's own moral goodness expressed in affirming the person as having extreme value to God.

Second, affirmation is the creative ritual that brings the estranged back into community. When the plague fell on the people as a direct consequence of their sin and God stated that he would not reveal his presence to them as he had in the past, Moses entreated God, " 'Yet thou hast said, "I know you by name, and you have also found favor in my sight." . . . Consider too that this nation is thy people.' And he [God] said, 'My presence will go with you, and I will give you rest' " (Exod. 33:12–14). Moses then led the people in celebrating their affirmation of God in a renewal of the covenant and a liturgy of Sabbath rest (Exod. 35).

Third, affirmation renews life through the offering up of thanksgiving. In the expression of thanksgiving the circle of moral advocacy is completed. What began as a movement away from moral goodness as defined by the moral law is now completed as a movement of moral goodness itself expressed as thanksgiving to God as the source of healing and hope.

David often experienced God's moral advocacy. In his psalms we see affirmation in the repeated refrain of thanksgiving.

> Fill me with joy and gladness;
> let the bones which thou has broken rejoice.
>
> Create in me a clean heart, O God,
> and put a new and right spirit within me.
>
> Restore to me the joy of thy salvation,
> and uphold me with a willing spirit.
>
> O LORD, open thou my lips,
> and my mouth shall show forth thy praise.
> (Ps. 51:8, 10, 12, 15)

In thanksgiving the theological dynamic of pastoral care becomes a kind of eucharist. At his last supper with his disciples, Jesus added to his words of affirmation—"I have called you friends" (John 15:15)—the ritual of giving thanks.

At this point pastoral care breaks out of the narrow confines of the therapeutic and clinical dimension and enters into the creative and healing community, which has at its center the eucharistic celebration of peace, God's *shalom*.

Here we see that pastoral care not only is an extension of the healing community, which provides the spiritual and moral resources for the kind of moral advocacy required, but also leads back into the very center of the community, where there is a "new and right spirit" expressed in eucharistic celebration.[5]

This is not an attempt to design a particular form of ecclesiastical ritual, but it is an argument for the theological necessity of a eucharistic experience that affirms a person's value to God. No person can see directly the moral goodness of God, as Moses learned when he requested such an experience (Exod. 33:18). We can, however, as Moses did, indirectly experience God's moral goodness.

The final and, therefore, the continual act of pastoral care is to experience God's moral goodness as constituting one's personal value and one's share in God's glory. We are not like Moses, who had to veil his face so that the people would not see the fading away of the glory of God in it. Rather, we are ministers of the new covenant in the Spirit. "And we all, with unveiled face, beholding the glory of the Lord, are being changed into his likeness from one degree of glory to another; for this comes from the Lord who is the Spirit" (2 Cor. 3:18).

It is the privilege of us who give pastoral care to see indirectly the very glory of the moral goodness of God in the face and life of those for whom we are moral advocates.

It is time to take the veils off and walk straight into the places where death, disease, and defeat have twisted life out of shape—for in those places we will find the glory of God.

Notes

1. Donald Capps, professor of pastoral theology at Princeton Theological Seminary, provides a helpful overview of the various approaches to pastoral care, including an emphasis on the multiplicity of biblical approaches, in *Biblical Approaches to Pastoral Care* (Philadelphia: Westminster, 1981). See also his later book, *Life Cycle Theory and Pastoral Care* (Philadelphia: Fortress, 1983).

2. Roger Hurding suggests quite strongly that counseling from a Christian perspective includes a ministry of reconciliation, which entails what I have called advocacy. "However we understand the compass of God's restoring work in Christ, the perspective of *reconciliation* is a crucial one in clarifying the aims of counselling. First and foremost, the 'ministry of reconciliation' is one in which God takes the initiative, 'reconciling the world to himself in Christ, not counting men's sins against them' (2 Corinthians 5:17–21). . . . Again, at certain

points in counselling we may be privileged to see the wonder of this most radical of transferences dawn on the person we try to help" (*The Tree of Healing* [Grand Rapids: Zondervan, 1988], 396–97).

3. In her doctoral dissertation at the Fuller Seminary Graduate School of Psychology, Marguerite Schuster attempts to explain the phenomenon of demonic power with respect to mental illness and emotional problems; see *Power, Pathology, Paradox: The Dynamics of Evil and Good* (Grand Rapids: Zondervan/Academie, 1987). Her basic argument is that openness to the phenomenon of demonic possession is grounded in the very nature of the self and thus should be taken into account in dealing with emotional and spiritual problems. Unfortunately, in my judgment, she attempts to prove too much. She views the human self as basically without any spiritual or moral power of its own. The self either will be controlled from without by the good Spirit and purpose of God, or by the evil and malicious purpose of Satan. As a result, she comes very close to identifying all forms of suffering with some form of "possession" by an evil spirit or spirits. It is understandable, then, that she should take a quite negative view of psychotherapy in favor of a form of pastoral care that treats most psychological problems as a spiritual power conflict. The failure of the book is as much in the inadequate theological anthropology used as the basis, as it is in the rejection of appropriate psychotherapeutic strategies.

4. For a discussion of the place of exorcism in the context of therapy, see the helpful discussion of a case in Samuel Southard, *Theology and Therapy* (Dallas: Word, 1989), 248–54. Southard comments on the case of a woman freed from a demonic power through a psychiatrist working with an Episcopal priest as a member of the team. Following her release from this power, this woman found a place of belonging and acceptance in a church where she said, "I wanted to be in a place where I was accepted and I wanted to help others who were all bound up as I was" (253).

5. Wolfhart Pannenberg, in his book *Christian Spirituality and Sacramental Community* (London: Dartman, Longman and Todd, 1983), offers the concept of "eucharistic spirituality" as an alternative to a concept of spirituality based on a constant and pervasive sense of sin. From a Greek Orthodox perspective, John Zizioulas develops a model of personhood as grounded in the body of Christ as a community centered on eucharistic life (*Being as Communion: Studies in Personhood and the Church* [Crestwood, N.J.: St. Vladmir's Seminary Press, 1985]).

Bibliography

Adams, Jay E. *The Christian Counselor's Manual*. 1973. Reprint. Grand Rapids: Zondervan, 1986.

————. *Competent to Counsel*. 1970. Reprint. Grand Rapids: Zondervan, 1986.

————. *More Than Redemption: A Theology of Christian Counseling*. Grand Rapids: Baker, 1979.

Aden, Leroy, and David G. Benner, eds. *Counseling and the Human Predicament: A Study of Sin, Guilt and Forgiveness*. Grand Rapids: Baker, 1989.

Anderson, Ray S. "Christopraxis: Competence as a Criterion for Theological Education." *Theological Student's Fellowship Bulletin* (January–February 1984): 10–13.

————. "Clergy Burnout as a Symptom of Theological Anemia." *Theology, News and Notes* (March 1984): 11–14. Fuller Theological Seminary, Pasadena, California.

————. "Conversion: Essence of the Christian Story." *Theology, News and Notes* (June 1986): 8–12. Fuller Theological Seminary, Pasadena, California.

————. *Minding God's Business*. Grand Rapids: Eerdmans, 1986.

————. *On Being Human*. Grand Rapids: Eerdmans, 1982.

————. "The Resurrection of Jesus as Hermeneutical Criterion: A Case for Sexual Parity in Ministry." *Theological Student's Fellowship Bulletin* (March–April 1986): 9–15.

————. *Theological Foundations for Ministry*. Grand Rapids: Eerdmans, 1979.

Anderson, Ray S., and Dennis B. Guernsey. *On Being Family: A Social Theology of the Family*. Grand Rapids: Eerdmans, 1985.

Balint, Michael. *The Doctor, His Patient and the Illness*. Marshfield, Md.: Pitman, 1957.

Barrett, C. K. *Church, Ministry, and Sacraments in the New Testament*. Grand Rapids: Eerdmans, 1985.

Barth, Karl. *Church Dogmatics*, vol. 4, pt. 2. Edinburgh: T. & T. Clark, 1961.

————. *Ethics*. New York: Seabury, 1981.

Becker, Walter. "Healing and Spiritual Disciplines." *Journal of Christian Healing* 6, no. 2 (Fall 1984): 35–40.

Benner, David G. *Psychotherapy and the Spiritual Quest*. Grand Rapids: Baker, 1988.

————, ed. *Christian Counseling and Psychotherapy*. Grand Rapids: Baker, 1987.

————, ed. *Psychotherapy in Christian Perspective*. Grand Rapids: Baker, 1987.

Bergen, Allen. "Psychotherapy and Religious Values." In *Wholeness and Holiness: Readings in the Psychology/Theology of Mental Health*, edited by H. Newton Malony. Grand Rapids: Baker, 1983.

Berne, Eric. *Transactional Analysis in Psychotherapy*. New York: Grove Press, 1961.

Bledstein, B. J. *The Culture of Professionalism: The Middle Class and Development of Higher Education in America*. New York: Simon and Schuster, 1973.

Bloesch, Donald. *The Struggle of Prayer*. Colorado Springs: Helmers and Howard, 1988.

Bonhoeffer, Dietrich. *Ethics*. New York: Macmillan, 1955.

————. *Letters and Papers from Prison*, enlarged ed. New York: Macmillan, 1972.

Bradshaw, John. *Bradshaw On: Healing the Shame That Binds You*. Deerfield Beach, Fla.: Health Communications, 1988.

Bromiley, Geoffrey. *God and Marriage*. Grand Rapids: Eerdmans, 1980.

Brown, Colin, ed. *The New International Dictionary of New Testament Theology*. 4 vols. Grand Rapids: Zondervan, 1975–76.

Buhler, Charlotte. *Values in Psychotherapy*. New York: Free Press, 1962.

Capps, Donald. *Biblical Approaches to Pastoral Care*. Philadephia: Westminster, 1981.

————. *Life Cycle Theory and Pastoral Care*. Philadelphia: Fortress, 1983.

Carroll, Mary Ann, et al. *Ethics in the Practice of Psychology*. Englewood Cliffs, N.J.: Prentice-Hall, 1985.

Carter, John D., and Bruce Narramore. *The Integration of Psychology and Theology: An Introduction*. Grand Rapids: Zondervan, 1979.

Clebsch, William A., and Charles R. Kaekle. *Pastoral Care in Historical Perspective*. Englewood Cliffs, N.J.: Prentice-Hall, 1964.

Clinebell, Howard. *Basic Types of Pastoral Care and Counseling*. London: SCM Press, 1984.

Collins, Gary R. *Christian Counseling: A Comprehensive Guide*. Rev. ed. Dallas: Word, 1988.

_____. *Psychology and Theology: Prospects for Integration*. Nashville: Abingdon, 1981.

_____. *The Rebuilding of Psychology: An Integration of Psychology and Christianity*. Wheaton, Ill.: Tyndale House, 1977.

_____, ed. *Helping People Grow*. Ventura, Calif.: Vision House, 1980.

Corey, Gerald. "Ethical Issues in Counseling and Psychotherapy." In *Theory and Practice of Counseling and Psychotherapy*, edited by Gerald Corey. Belmont, Calif.: Wadsworth, 1977.

Dire, Jeffrey M. "Rational-Emotive Therapy: Implications for Pastoral Counseling." D.Min. diss., Fuller Theological Seminary, 1984.

Dueck, Alvin. "Ethical Contexts of Healing: Peoplehood and Righteousness." *Pastoral Psychology* 35, no. 4 (Summer 1987): 239–53.

_____. "Ethical Contexts of Healing: Ecclesia and Praxis." *Pastoral Psychology* 36, no. 1 (Fall 1987): 49–62.

Dunn, Frank G. *Building Faith in Families: Using the Sacraments in Pastoral Ministry*. Wilton, Conn.: Morehouse-Barlow, 1986.

Ebeling, Gerhard. *Word and Faith*. Philadelphia: Westminster, 1963.

Ellul, Jacques. *Prayer and the Modern Man*. New York: Seabury, 1979.

Evans, C. Stephen. *Wisdom and Humanness in Psychology: Prospects for a Christian Approach*. Grand Rapids: Baker, 1989.

Farnsworth, Kirk. *Wholehearted Integration: Harmonizing Psychology and Christianity Through Word and Deed*. Grand Rapids: Baker, 1985.

Finch, John G. *Intensive Therapy and the Three Ways*. Pasadena: Integration Press, 1989.

Firet, Jacob. *Dynamics in Pastoring (Het agogisch Moment in het pastoraal Optreden)*, translated by John Vriend. (Uitgeversmaatschappij J. H. Kok-Kampen, 1982); Grand Rapids: Eerdmans, 1986.

Fleck, J. R., and John D. Carter, eds. *Psychology and Christianity: Integration Readings*. Nashville: Abingdon, 1981.

Frankl, Viktor. *The Doctor and the Soul: From Psychotherapy to Logotherapy*. New York: Alfred A. Knopf, 1955.

_____. *Man's Search For Meaning: An Introduction to Logotherapy*. Boston: Beacon Press, 1959.

_____. *The Unconscious God: Psychotherapy and Theology*. London: Hodder and Stoughton, 1977.

Freidson, E. *The Professionals and Their Prospects*. Beverly Hills, Calif.: Sage, 1973.

Gerkin, Charles. *The Living Human Document: Re-Visioning Pastoral Counseling in a Hermeneutical Mode*. Nashville: Abingdon, 1984.

Gilbert, Marvin G., and Raymond T. Brock, eds. *The Holy Spirit and Counseling: Theology and Theory*. Peabody, Mass.: Hendrickson, 1985.

Good, P., and D. Kraybill. *Perils of Professionalism.* Scottdale, Pa.: Herald Press, 1982.

Goode, William J. "Community Within a Community: The Professions." *American Sociological Review* 22 (1957): 194–200.

Gustafson, James. "Christian Ethics." In *Religion,* edited by Paul Ramsey. Englewood Cliffs, N.J.: Prentice-Hall, 1965.

Halleck, S. L. *The Politics of Therapy.* New York: Harper & Row, 1971.

Hansen, James C., ed. *Ethics, Legalities and the Family Therapist.* Rockville, Md.: Aspen Publications, 1982.

Hauerwas, Stanley. *A Community of Character: Toward a Constructive Christian Social Ethic.* Notre Dame: University of Notre Dame Press, 1981.

Hiltner, Seward. "Salvation's Message About Health." In *Wholeness and Holiness: Readings in the Psychology/Theology of Mental Health,* edited by H. Newton Malony. Grand Rapids: Baker, 1983.

————. *Theological Dynamics.* Nashville: Abingdon, 1972.

Holifield, E. Brooks. *A History of Pastoral Care in America: From Salvation to Self-Realization.* Nashville: Abingdon, 1983.

Hoffman, John. *Ethical Confrontation in Counseling.* Chicago: University of Chicago Press, 1979.

Hurding, Roger F. *The Tree of Healing: Psychological and Biblical Foundations for Counseling and Pastoral Care.* Grand Rapids: Zondervan, 1988. Original ed., *Roots and Shoots: A Guide to Counseling and Psychotherapy.* London: Hodder and Stoughton, 1985.

Jones, Stanton L., ed. *Psychology and the Christian Faith: An Introductory Reader.* Grand Rapids: Baker, 1986.

Kierkegaard, Søren. *The Journals of Kierkegaard,* translated and edited by Alexander Dru. New York: Harper Torchbooks, 1958.

————. *Purity of Heart is to Will One Thing.* New York: Harper & Row, 1956.

Koteskey, Ronald L. *Psychology From a Christian Perspective.* Nashville: Abingdon, 1980.

Kraus, C. Norman. *Jesus Christ Our Lord: Christology from a Disciple's Perspective.* Scottdale, Pa.: Herald Press, 1987.

Lake, Frank. *Clinical Theology: A Theological and Psychological Basis to Clinical Pastoral Care.* New York: Crossroad, 1987.

Larson, M. S. *The Rise of Professionalism: A Sociological Analysis.* Berkeley: University of California Press, 1977.

Larzelere, R. E. "The Task Ahead: Six Levels of Integration of Christianity and Psychology." *Journal of Psychology and Theology* 8 (1980): 3–11.

Lebacqz, K. *Professional Ethics: Power and Paradox.* Nashville: Abingdon, 1985.

Lee, Cameron. "The Good-Enough Family." *Journal of Psychology and Theology* 13, no. 3 (1985): 182–89.

London, Perry. *Modes and Morals of Psychotherapy.* New York: Holt, Rinehart and Winston, 1964.

Lowe, Marshall C. *Value Orientation in Counseling and Psychotherapy.* 2d ed. Cranston, R.I.: Carroll Press, 1976.

Macmurray, John. *Persons in Relation.* London: Faber and Faber, 1961.

————. *Reason and Emotion.* London: Faber and Faber, 1935.

Malony, H. Newton, ed. *Wholeness and Holiness: Readings in the Psychology/Theology of Mental Health.* Grand Rapids: Baker, 1983.

Meissner, W. W. *Life and Faith: Psychological Perspectives on Religious Experience.* Washington, D.C.: Georgetown University Press, 1987.

Miskotte, Kornelis. *When the Gods Are Silent.* London: Collins, 1967.

Moltmann, Jürgen. *God in Creation: A New Theology of Creation and the Spirit of God.* San Francisco: Harper & Row, 1985.

————. *The Crucified God.* New York: Harper & Row, 1974.

Moore, Robert L., ed. *Carl Jung and Christian Spirituality.* Dallas: Word, 1988.

Mowrer, O. Hobart. *The Crisis of Psychiatry and Religion.* Princeton, N.J.: Van Nostrand, 1961.

Ogden, Greg. *The New Reformation: Returning the Ministry to the People of God.* Grand Rapids: Zondervan, 1990.

Osterhaus, James P. *Counseling Families: From Insight to Intervention.* Grand Rapids: Zondervan, 1989.

Pannenberg, Wolfhart. *Christian Spirituality and Sacramental Community.* London: Dartman, Longman and Todd, 1983.

Pedersen, John. *Israel: Its Life and Culture.* Vol. 1. London: Oxford University Press, 1973.

Perls, Frederick (Fritz), and Laura Perls. *The Gestalt Approach and Eye Witness to Therapy.* New York: Bantam, 1976.

Peterson, Eugene. *Five Smooth Stones for Pastoral Work.* Atlanta: John Knox, 1980.

Peterson, J. *Counseling and Values.* Scranton, Pa.: International Textbook, 1970.

Philipchalk, Ronald P. *Psychology and Christianity: An Introduction to Controversial Issues.* Rev. ed. Lanham, Md.: University Press of America, 1988.

Polanyi, Michael. *Personal Knowledge.* London: Routledge and Kegan Paul, 1958.

Pruyser, Paul. *The Minister as Diagnostician.* Philadelphia: Westminster, 1976.

Rodiger, Georgiana G. *The Miracle of Therapy: A Layperson's Guide to the Mysteries of Christian Psychology.* Dallas: Word, 1989.

Rogers, Carl. *Counseling and Psychotherapy*. Boston: Houghton Mifflin, 1942.

Roszak, Theodore. *Person/Planet*. Garden City, N.Y.: Doubleday/Anchor, 1979.

Sandford, John, and Paula Sandford. *The Transformation of the Inner Man*. South Plainfield, N.J.: Bridge Publishing, 1982.

Schaffer, Peter. *Equus*. New York: Avon, 1974.

Schuster, Marguerite. *Power, Pathology, Paradox: The Dynamics of Evil and Good*. Grand Rapids: Zondervan/Academie, 1987.

Simcox, Carroll E. "On Being Both Christian and Religious." *Christian Century* (18 April 1984): 398–400.

Smedes, Lewis. *Caring and Commitment: Learning to Live the Love We Promised*. San Francisco: Harper & Row, 1988.

————. *Choices: Making Right Decisions in a Complex World*. San Francisco: Harper & Row, 1986.

————. *Mere Morality*. Grand Rapids: Eerdmans, 1983.

Southard, Samuel. *Theology and Therapy: The Wisdom of God in a Context of Friendship*. Dallas: Word, 1989.

Thielicke, Helmut. *Being Human . . . Becoming Human*. New York: Doubleday, 1984.

————. *Theological Ethics: Foundations*. Vol. 1. Grand Rapids: Eerdmans, 1979.

Torrance, Thomas. *God and Rationality*. Oxford: Oxford University Press, 1971.

Tournier, Paul. *The Meaning of Persons*. London: SCM Press, 1957.

Tweedie, Donald F., Jr. *Logotherapy: An Evaluation of Frankl's Existential Approach to Psychotherapy*. Grand Rapids: Baker, 1961.

Van Leeuwen, Mary S. *The Sorcerer's Apprentice: A Christian Look at the Changing Face of Psychology*. Downers Grove, Ill.: Inter-Varsity, 1982.

Von Balthasar, Hans Urs. *A Theological Anthropology*. New York: Sheed and Ward, 1967.

Weber, Otto. *Foundations of Dogmatics*. Vol. 2. Grand Rapids: Eerdmans, 1983.

Wicker, Allen. *Introduction to Ecological Psychology*. Monterey, Calif.: Brooks-Cole, 1979.

Winnicott, Donald W. *The Maturational Processes and the Facilitating Environment*. New York: International Universities Press, 1965.

Yoell, W., et al. "Marriage, Morals and Therapeutic Goals: A Discussion." *Journal of Behavioral Therapy and Experimental Psychiatry* 2 (1971): 127–32.

Zizioulas, John. *Being as Communion: Studies in Personhood and the Church*. Crestwood, N.J.: St. Vladimir's Seminary Press, 1985.

Index

Absolution, 117–18, 237–38
Adam, 17–19, 21–22, 35–36, 74, 177, 234, 243–44
Adams, Jay, 28n, 52n
Adler, Alfred, 102n
Agogic Moment, 66–67, 130–31, 157–58, 185
AIDS, 30–31, 45, 50, 236, 238
Allport, Gordon, 102n, 163, 174, 194n
Anthropology, biblical, 25
Aristotle, 97
Atonement, 112–13, 119n
Balint, Michael, 75n
Baptism, 98, 179–80
Barrett, C. K., 194n
Barth, Karl, 116, 126, 215
Becker, Walter, 111
Benner, David, 9n
Bergen, Allen, 58
Berne, Eric, 189
Bible, 124, 128, 130–33, 216–17; used for counseling, 35, 122–33, 217–19
Biblical counseling, 36–37
Bledstein, B. J., 213n
Bloesch, Donald, 136–37
Bonhoeffer, Dietrich, 143, 166, 189, 228, 231n
Bradshaw, John, 55n
Brock, Raymond, 53n
Bromiley, Geoffrey, 125
Brown, Colin, 101n, 120n
Buhler, Charlotte, 230n
Calling of God, 160–68; and occupation, 169–73
Calvin, John, 128
Capps, Donald, 246n
Caregivers, 22, 229, 239–40
Caregiving, 22–23, 56, 222–23
Carroll, Mary Ann, 230n
Carter, John, 9n
Change, openness to, 63–64
Church, 23–24, 99, 181–84, 209
Clebsch, William A., 23
Clinebell, Howard, 59
Clinical theology, 54n
Codependency, 83
Co-humanity, 21, 34, 216
Collins, Gary, 9n, 52n
Community, 92–94, 96–100, 243–46
Competence, 17–18, 20–21, 23–24

Conscience, uneasy, 13–14, 27
Conversion, 45–46, 115–18, 158
Corey, Gerald, 230n
Counseling, 7–8, 14–15, 25–27, 47, 84, 208, 233; as calling, 157–74; as encounter, 186–88; incarnational, 185–93; as ministry, 25, 176–93; as occupation, 168–73; para-parochial, 181–83; as profession, 188–89; professional practice, 195–212
Counselors, 22, 93, 97–98, 117–18, 190–91; agents of redemption, 90, 94; agents in therapy, 69–72, 107, 159; and Christ, 242; growth promoters, 56–75; lay, 22, 25; moral advocates, 214–30; in private practice, 95–96, 125, 197; professional, 95, 162, 184; role of, 57, 62, 72, 197
Culture and therapy, 82–83
Cure of souls, 23
Covenant relations, 234–36
Death, 234
Demonic possession, 241–42
Devotion, 167–68
Dilthey, W., 102n
Dire, Jeffrey, 154n
Disease, 234–36, 239, 241
Divorce, 90
Dueck, Alvin, 82, 96, 101n, 197, 203, 206
Dunn, Frank, 194n
Duty, 166, 170
Dysfunction, 20n, 33, 104–5
Ebeling, Gerhard, 135n
Ecological matrix, 39–40, 62, 96–97
Ecology of self, 32–33, 38–42
Ego psychology, 109–10
Ellis, Albert, 149
Ellul, Jacques, 137–42
Emotions, 123, 148–49
Erickson, Erik, 108
Eschatology: of moral responsibility, 218; of self, 49–50
Ethics, theological, 215–16, 218, 226, 228, 233, 237, 241
Evangelism: and counseling, 193
Evans, C. Stephen, 9n, 101n
Eve, 18, 21, 177, 234
Evil, 240–42, 247n

Eysenck, H. J., 57
Exorcism, 241–43, 247n
Fairburn, W. Ronald, 54n
Faith, 27, 132, 189
Farnsworth, Kirk, 9n, 26, 28n, 95, 187
Firet, Jacob, 66–71, 104, 107–8, 126–28, 130, 134n, 159, 163
Fleck, J. R., 9n
Forgiveness, 47, 232, 234–35, 237
Frankl, Viktor, 64, 106, 187, 190, 194n
Freidson, E., 213n
Fromm, Erich, 102n
Gerkin, Charles, 39, 46, 49, 53n, 54n, 55n, 76n
Gestalt, 17–18, 20, 24, 27, 32, 43, 48; therapy, 28n
Gilbert, Marvin, 53n
Glasser, William, 96
God, 20, 147, 151, 159, 219, 223, 234, 240; judgment, 234–36; moral freedom, 219; moral will, 218, 223; righteousness of, 91–96; as therapist, 21–22; will of, 138, 141, 171, 228
God-talk, 24, 119n, 139
Goldstein, Kurt, 101n
Good, P., 213n
Goode, William, 199
Grace, 16–17, 44, 107, 108–9; and conversion, 115–116; and spiritual growth, 109, 191–92; as reconciliation, 111–14; as therapeutic intervention, 103–18, 234–35
Growth, 19, 21; goals, 172–73; integrative, 61–62; motive power for, 64–69; as sign of health, 58–64
Growth process, 67–69, 72, 104, 105–10, 172, 185
Growth therapy, 59
Guntrip, Harry, 54n
Gustafson, James, 216–17
Halleck, S. L., 81
Hansen, James C., 230n
Hauerwas, Stanley, 48, 91, 201
Healing, 15, 16, 21–22, 145–49
Health, 33, 42, 58, 60
Hermeneutical task, 44–47, 210
Hermeneutic moment, 66, 130–33
Hiltner, Seward, 53n, 126–27
Hoffman, John, 230n
Holifield, Brooks, 97–98
Holiness and wholeness, 52n, 78n
Holmes, Oliver W., 227
Holy Spirit, 89, 113–14, 116, 178–79, 212, 226–27
Homosexuality, 236, 238
Hope, 100

Horney, Karen, 102n
Humanity, 17, 18, 72
Hurding, Roger, 7, 23, 52n, 53n, 57, 102n, 246n
Identity, 161–62; core of, 64, 104–5; embodied in community, 97–99; spiritual, 108
Image of God, 18, 20, 24, 27, 32–35, 38, 73–74, 107, 244
Incarnation: as counseling approach, 187–88, 240; and prayer, 142
Inner healing, 145
Integration, 7–8, 19–20, 25–26, 28n, 111
Integrative core of personhood, 31–32, 38
Integrative counseling, 13–28
Integrative task, 23, 32
Intimacy, 63
Jaekle, Charles R., 23
Jesus Christ, 24, 26, 45–47, 50, 81–82, 126, 142, 192, 225; and kingdom of God, 85–86; ministry of, 178–79, 239–40; as moral advocate, 225, 242; as paraclete, 177–78
Jones, Stanton L., 9n
Keller, Helen, 110
Kierkegaard, Søren, 21, 28, 167, 169–73, 174n, 175n
Kingdom of God, 18, 81-100, 200, 203–7
Klein, Melanie, 54n, 73
Koteskey, Ronald L., 9n
Kraus, C. Norman, 47, 55n
Kraybill, D., 213n
Lake, Frank, 54n
Larson, M. S., 213n
Larzelere, R. E., 9n
Lebacqz, K., 213n
Lee, Cameron, 174n
Lewin, Kurt, 102n
Life continuum, 32, 43–44, 48, 190
Logotherapy, 106, 190
London, Perry, 214
Love, motive power of, 73–74, 110
Lowe, Marshall, C., 230n
Macmurray, John, 148, 164
Malony, H. Newton, 52n, 59–61, 119n, 120n
Marriage, 220–21, 223–225
Maslow, Abraham, 73
Maturity, 20, 88–89, 90–91
May, Rollo, 73
Meditation, 152
Meissner, William, 53n, 108–9
Mental illness, 240–42

Ministry, 25–26, 177–80
Miskotte, Kornelis, 129
Moltmann, Jürgen, 28n, 113
Moral: advocacy, 222–29; decisions, 220–21, 223–24; dilemmas, 222–23; freedom, 90, 217; good, 235; issues in therapy, 215–21
Moral theology, 216–21
Moral vision, 91–92, 95, 201–2
Moses, as moral advocate, 244–45
Motives, 163–66
Mowrer, O. Hobart, 109, 119n
Narramore, Bruce, 9n
Nurture, 67
Nouthetic counseling, 52n
Object relations therapy, 37, 46, 54n
Ogden, Greg, 194n
Pannenberg, Wolfhart, 98, 247n
Paolino, Thomas, 42
Pastoral care, 23–24, 129, 209, 222, 229, 233; in healing community, 243–46; dynamics of, 232–46; extension of grace, 233–38; and spiritual power, 238–43
Pathology, 21, 40, 48, 64, 240
Pedersen, John, 146, 149
Penitential piety, 98
Perls, Frederick and Laura, 28n
Personage, 70, 162
Persons, 27, 36
Peterson, Eugene, 7
Peterson, J., 230n
Philipchalk, Ronald P., 9n
Polanyi, Michael, 98
Prayer, 14, 16, 139–41; as deliverance, 142–43; healing praxis, 145–53; as making history, 141–42; role in therapy, 136–53; shared life, 137–39
Praxis, 87–88, 110, 137, 146
Professional associations, 199–203, 207–8
Pruyser, Paul, 7
Psychologists, Christian, 15, 24
Psychology: biblical, 65–66; Christian, 16, 32, 41, 52n
Psychotherapeutic techniques, 27
Psychotherapy, 35, 57, 64, 106, 214–17, 247n
Redemption, as therapeutic intervention, 36, 47
Rogers, Carl, 59, 102n
Roszak, Theodore, 51, 56–57, 74
Salvation, 44, 76n, 115–16
Sanctification, 114

Sandford, John and Paula, 145
Sargin, T. R., 59
Schuster, Marguerite, 247n
Scripture, 26
Self, 17, 19–20; ecology of, 38–42; identity, 34, 48; socialization, 48–49; spheres, 39–40; spiritual, 34–35; systemic, 33–34
Self deception, 111
Self esteem, 41–42, 140–141
Self formation, 44–45
Selfhood, gestalt of, 24
Shaffer, Peter, 43
Shalom, 245
Shame, 31, 47
Simcox, Carroll, 111
Sin, 16, 25, 33, 47, 98, 107, 109, 116, 119n, 147, 232, 234–36, 243–44
Skinner, B. F., 73
Smedes, Lewis, 214
Soul, 38–39, 65
Southard, Samuel, 86, 101n, 247n
Spirit, human, 65
Spirit of God, 24, 74
Spiritual power, 238–43
Spranger, Edward, 101n
Stern, W., 102n
Therapeutic bond, 21, 27
Therapeutic continuum, 22–25, 27
Therapeutic gain, 26, 31, 37, 59, 66, 82, 100, 104–5, 191
Therapeutic insight, 68
Therapeutic intervention, 57, 71–72, 81, 107–8, 215–21, 234–35
Therapeutic methods, 23–24, 41–42
Therapists, Christian, 17, 152, 210–12
Therapy, 7; and culture, 82; ethical core, 197; moral issues, 215–17; professional, 25, 197–98, 199–203; value-free, 215; values, 230n
Thielicke, Helmut, 65, 192, 226
Torrance, Thomas F., 138
Tournier, Paul, 70, 162
Tweedie, Donald, 76n
Urs von Balthasar, Hans, 76n
Van Leeuwen, Mary S., 10n
Weber, Otto, 110, 112–13, 119n
Wicker, Allen, 38
Winnicott, D. W., 46, 174n
Wisdom, 86–91
Word of God, as empowerment for change, 121–33
Yeomans, Martin, 54n
Yoell, W., 230n
Zizioulas, John, 247n